Dó
Gary

Gerry Kelly
Ath Mór
2013

The Escape

Gerry Kelly

I

First published in 2013 by M&G Publications

Copyright © Gerry Kelly

Dedication

I dedicate this book to all those Irish Republican prisoners who, over the generations died while trying to escape and to those who escaped but died on returning to active service.

It always seems impossible until it's done.
Nelson Mandela

Acknowledgements

First and foremost, this book would not have seen the light of day without my wife Margaret. She has typed and re-typed repeatedly; has read and re-read drafts. She has supported, cajoled and encouraged me throughout - so she will share the credit and criticism alongside me!

I also want to thank all those others connected to the escape who have helped me and most importantly, shared information. The small group of people who read various drafts and hopefully kept me right and guided me, have my gratitude also.

Mickey Liggett from North Belfast wrote an excellent book some years ago entitled 'From Fetters to Freedom'. In it he researched the many escapes by Irish Republican Political Prisoners going back centuries. I thank him for allowing me to reproduce the list of escapes - which is impressive.

I would also like to thank the Iris Magazine for material supplied including photographs and maps connected to the escape. A special thanks to Aidan and Denis for the huge effort they have put into the production of the book.

Last but not least I want to remember Derek Dunne who wrote a great book on the '83 escape some years ago and who has since passed away.

Prologue

This book is as close to the full truth of the mass escape from Long Kesh in 1983 as anyone is likely to get. It is the inside story but, even 30 years later, not every detail can be given. The names of escapees are true, as are the names of Republicans who have died since. Pseudonyms are used out of necessity for others but in the main the actions described are true to people's memories.

Sometimes there were small conflicts of detail related to events. In such cases I used my judgement and some licence to join up the dots as all conflicting accounts could not be accurate.

The book is written, as most escape stories are, from the point of view of the political prisoners. Prison guards may write their own versions of prison history during the long conflict in the North of Ireland. That is their narrative. This is mine.

There will be detractors - there always are - but my experience in writing this book and talking to those ex-POWs involved, is that they maintain a great pride in having been part of this historic escapade. I share that pride.

Foreword

History, particularly the history of conflict between the Irish people and the British Government has a number of different narratives. There is no agreed narrative. The version which is least published is the Irish Republican one. I am an Irish Republican therefore it influences this story.

Briefly, for the outsider, the story of British colonial rule in Ireland spans 800 years and is marked with a series of armed insurrections. Taking a quantum leap – Ireland was partitioned in 1921 after the 1916 uprising and years of war. Six counties in the North-East of Ireland remained under British rule. The pro-British Unionists set up the Orange State. Its first prime-minister described its parliament as *"A Protestant Parliament for a Protestant People"* and so it was. Catholics and Nationalists were discriminated against in every aspect of life.

There were insurrections in every generation since. However, a peaceful civil rights movement was established in the late 1960's to demand basic rights and equality. It was brutally suppressed, including in the infamous attack on a peaceful protest in Derry where British paratroopers opened fire, killing 14 innocent victims.

Many young people of my generation took up arms as they felt there was no alternative. The military conflict was brutal and brutalising. Combatants on all sides caused much suffering and death. Likewise people on all sides suffered terribly. By all sides I mean Nationalist, Republican, Unionist, Loyalist, the British Army, Royal Ulster Constabulary (RUC), Ulster Defence Regiment (UDR) and the general population.

Imprisonment is also part of conflict and many thousands of Republicans went through interrogations, in which brutality and torture was often used. From there many went to prison. New jails were built to house them. In 1972 a prolonged hunger-strike by Republicans achieved Political or "Special Category" status for prisoners in jail on conflict-related charges. This distinguished them from criminals.

In 1976 the British government built the H-Blocks section of the Maze/Long Kesh jail and announced that "Special Category" status would end on 1st March that year. Anyone sentenced after that date was to be classed as a 'criminal'. This arbitrary date signified the beginning of a criminalisation policy. In essence the British Government believed that the prisoners were the weakest link in the Republican movement. Because the H-Blocks were a complex of single cells they believed that they could break prisoners one at a time as they filtered into jail after sentencing.

Thus began years of a prison regime which involved systemic and daily brutality. After years of protesting for the return of political/special category status two hunger-strikes took place. In the second hunger strike in 1981, ten Irish Republican POWs died. The protest years were marked by deep and bitter conflict which had taken centre stage in the overall conflict which had been going on for well over a decade. Twenty four prison officers were also killed by the IRA outside the jail. No ground was given between captives and captors.

Into that atmosphere and context sits this story, just two years after the Hunger Strike and in the midst of a continuing conflict raging on the streets, fields and byways of the North of Ireland. There is more than one narrative on this historic event. Many inches of newsprint have been created by various journalists and writers as well as guards. I have written this as an escapee and ex-POW.

Gerry Kelly
September 25th 2013

1983 Early June

G erry Kelly had not slept well, which was unusual for him. The reason for his unrest lay under his pillow. He reached up and touched the long cigar-shaped package. It contained highly sensitive information including maps and diagrams. He had studied the contents over several hours after lock-up the previous night. It was an elaborate escape plan and it filled him with hope and dread in equal measure.

Kelly was lying in a narrow six foot bed, in a cell measuring eight feet by eight feet in the notorious Long Kesh Prison Camp in the North of Ireland. The British authorities had tried to re-brand it 'Her Majesty's Prison Maze' in a forlorn attempt to shake off its notoriety as an Internment Camp in the 1970s, but the prolonged protest and hunger strikes of Irish Republicans into the 1980s had made that impossible.

His main worry at that moment, however, was to return the package (or 'beart' as it was known in Irish) safely back to Bobby Storey who was in C-Wing of H Block 7, while Kelly was housed in B Wing on the other side of the Block. Storey wanted up-to-date feed-back that morning. Kelly had already enclosed the incriminating documents in toilet tissue and lots of cling-film. He got out of bed and made his way to the plastic chamber-pot which was used for night sanitation. It sat in the only blind spot in the small enclosed space. He gathered the fine polythene into tapered ends and then melted them onto the body of the 'beart' with the cigarette lighter he had palmed.

1

It was almost 'unlock' time. He could hear the morning shift of guards coming on duty. Kelly slid on his jeans and manoeuvred the 'beart' down the back of them until he was satisfied that it would not be seen. He finished dressing, washed and went into the food hall of B-Wing to eat his usual porridge followed by tea and toast. All appeared normal but he didn't feel like that inside.

After breakfast he checked which guard was on duty at the gate to the 'circle' area. Satisfied, he lifted a transparent plastic bag full of sugar and headed for the guard. *"I'm gonna throw this sugar over to C-Wing. They've run out of supplies and as you know we're sweet enough in B-Wing."* He smiled as the guard waved him through indifferently. It had become normal practice for the four wings in the block to swap and barter supplies.

Kelly repeated the routine twice more with guards before gaining access to Cell 25 in C-Wing which was Storey's humble abode in the summer of 1983.

"Pull up a pew, Kells," Storey greeted him as he swung his large frame into a sitting position, dangling his legs over the side of the top bunk. He pushed his 6ft 4in bulk easily off the bed, landing light-footed before checking the corridor for guards and pulling the heavy steel door over for privacy. The conversation continued in low tones. Kelly quickly removed the 'beart' and handed it to his comrade with some relief. *"Seo duit a fhir mhóir."* (*"There you go big man"*). Storey immediately slid it down the back of his trousers.

The two men stood near the distinctive long slats of the H Block window. *"Well, what's the verdict?"* Storey went straight to the point.

"Bear with me a minute," Kelly answered, not wanting to be rushed. It was an important moment in his life, especially since he had spent over a decade in jail and the plan was almost fully developed.

"Let me summarise," he began light-heartedly ignoring his friend's impatience. *"We're in H7 which is a self-contained prison within a self-contained phase of the overall prison camp, which is contained within a British Ministry of Defence perimeter, which also contains a large British Army Camp."* Storey wondered where this was going but Kelly rushed on leaving no room for interruption. *"So the plan is for us to arrest the two dozen screws on duty in the Block without any of them hitting any of the 20 odd alarm buttons, or any of the several intercoms, two-way radios or telephones. Then a number of us will don screws' uniforms, after liberating them from their owners and arrest the screw on duty at the main gate of H7.*

In the meantime all the other screws are being stripped of their uniforms so that more of us can kit ourselves out for the next phase of the 'éalú' (escape). I like the reversal of roles here by the way; poacher turned gamekeeper so to speak. We then wait on the food lorry; arrest the unsuspecting driver and his orderly; we don't eat the grub but we do fill the lorry with Republican prisoners, apart that is from those comrades in the Rearguard who will stay behind to hold the block while we exit. We persuade the driver of the lorry that it is in his best interests to transport us all to the front gate of the jail. Off we go passing through a number of manned gates, where, if there is even a hint of suspicion from the screw on duty, he will be whisked into the back of the lorry to enjoy our salubrious company. At the Tally Lodge at the Main Gate a number of our comrades dressed as screws will take over the Tally Lodge, arresting those on duty there. Once we control the Main Gate area our lads will open the gate and let the lorry out. While they hold the gate area the rest of us will move to the BMOD gate. If there is any difficulty there we will arrest the couple of screws on duty and the armed Brit soldier who does gate-duty with them. All being well our Tally Lodge team should be in a car following us out by this stage having tied up the half dozen screws in the Tally Lodge. We all head off to rendezvous with the South Armagh Brigade of The Irish Republican Army who will escort us to the South Armagh border area, I presume, where we will live happily ever after or return to the Struggle - or both!"

Kelly smiled broadly and took a deep breath. He had rushed through the monologue deliberately without a break. Storey had let it go, not knowing whether his comrade was being sarcastic or just winding him up for 'the craic'. Storey was known for having a good sense of humour but for the moment it was somewhere down in his boots. He had, however, been keen to hear Kelly's opinion.

Kelly knew he had stretched Storey's patience. *"It's beyond cheeky Bob. It's complex and audacious. I like it more and more and I actually think it can be pulled off. If anybody can do it the IRA can do it. I'm definitely in - if there's a place?"* he added, pretending not to be presumptuous.

Storey's face beamed as he stretched out his hand. *"I felt like digging you about three times during your 'summary' there ye bastard."*

"I know a chara but I couldn't help myself. It isn't too often I can put you under a bit of pressure." After a moment he continued, *"I do have some more points on detail though if that's OK?"*

"Absolutely, fire away a chara," said Storey.

"Well I've actually only two for now Bob as I don't want to be lingering in C-Wing too long. We can talk at more length in 'teachts' (small notes written on cigarette papers) *or at football. The first is: "Who all knows at the moment?"*

"Just you, me, Bik McFarlane and Seamus McDermott. Seamus will be in charge of the Rearguard, amongst other things. This operation is on a need to know basis, the stakes are too high."

4

Kelly nodded in agreement. *"The second one is: We obviously need guns to take the Circle area and the Main Gate area. Will the IRA agree to that?"* Storey hesitated and Kelly interjected: *"Just to explain Bob. It's just that I have known of previous schemes where POWs have asked for guns or explosives and the leadership has been very reluctant. I can understand why, but..."*

Storey had had enough time to weigh up his answer. *"We already have them Gerry,"* he answered definitively.

"I'm impressed," Kelly replied with honesty. *"Let's do it A Chara,"* he finished with a broad smile.

When Kelly left, Storey felt that bit more confident after hearing Kelly's opinion. He also felt a very small twinge of guilt about being economical with the truth on the two questions. There were only four people who knew the proposal for taking over H7, including Kelly, but he had a small tight group in another block who had been working on intelligence and various escape-related tasks. At that stage they had possession of one short-arm, thanks to Seamus McElwaine, a lifer from Co. Monaghan, who had smuggled it in. He had been planning to use it in an escape bid at his Appeal Court hearing. They still needed to get another six handguns in. But he knew Kelly would understand the necessity of the 'need to know basis' very well. He smiled, as he hoisted himself back up on to the top bunk. He was thinking, *"Kells has just talked himself into a job and he doesn't realise it."* As Kelly moved back into B-Wing he was thinking, *"Big mouth! You've just talked yourself into a job!"* He could only smile at his self-admonishment!

9pm
4th May, 1981

T he nine o'clock TV news was about to begin. In the cold corrugated steel nissen hut, there was expectation and trepidation in the air. Kelly could feel it as he stood at the back of the group of his comrades. The Hunger Strike by Republican Political Prisoners, taking place within the H-Blocks section of the camp, was in its 65th day.

The first item on the news was about the jail. As the newsreader spoke a camera was showing a wide-angled view of a high and very long grey concrete wall stretching into the distance. It then focused in on the huge main gates of the prison. As they opened, a nondescript white transit van was driven out. The camera followed its progress until it stopped close to the jostling crowd of journalists. A prison guard opened the back door of the van. There were a number of people in the dimness of its interior. A middle-aged man could be seen sitting on the bench inside, his head lowered. It was a woman, however, who climbed carefully out on to the tarmac to speak.

After composing herself for a moment she lifted her head to the waiting local and international press and said to the world *"My son is dying."* It was a simple but devastating statement of fact. It appeared to Kelly that as a mother, she did not want to show or share her grief with the world on camera. As a Republican and Bobby Sands' mother, she knew she had to share that information with the world. Even the journalists were uncharacteristically silent. There was no interview. Bobby Sands' mother then simply turned and climbed back into the prison van to return with her family to be with her son on his deathbed.

In the nissen hut in Cage 11, Kelly and his comrades also turned away from the TV and moved back to their prison cubicles without saying a word to each other. A deathly silence lay over Long Kesh Prison Camp.

Bobby Sands was not the first Irish Republican to die on Hunger Strike, nor would he be the last. Indeed Michael Gaughan who had been on Hunger Strike with Kelly and other comrades, had died in an English jail in June 1974, followed by Frank Stagg in February 1976. They were both proud County Mayo men. Another nine fellow political prisoners were to die in the months after Bobby Sands but it was his death, the first Hunger striker of the ten to die, which resounded world-wide. He was the MP for Fermanagh & South Tyrone as well as an Irish Republican political prisoner and IRA Volunteer.

All Irish Republicans could tell you exactly where they were when they first heard of his death which occurred at 1.17am the following morning, the 5th May 1981.

Gerry Kelly was in his cell writing his thoughts on Bobby Sands. It was a fairly long and disparate political meander of some twenty verses. He realised later that it was not so much about Bobby Sands but actually about the impression Bobby's mother made on him that night as he watched her on TV.

Bobby's Mother - May 1981

Rosaleen Sands
You do not know me
I saw you only
On a television screen.

So reluctantly you announced:
"My son is dying"
Standing with such dignified calm
In your well of grief.

I felt an intruder
To your private torment
Witness to a mother's
Naked mourning.

Thank you
For allowing us to share
Your precious final moments
With this great man.

Brendan McFarlane was the OC (Officer Commanding) of the Republican prisoners in the H-Blocks during the prolonged Hunger Strike. Bobby Sands had put McFarlane's name forward to take over from him as OC of the Blocks. They were close friends and comrades and had come through years of prison struggle together. He heard of his friend's death on the small, crystal-radio set which had been smuggled in by the political prisoners.

With hundreds of other POWs he had spent years naked, except for a rancid blanket in a bare cell, unfurnished, bar the two filthy sponge mattresses on the floor, on which he and his cell mate slept. They had lived in cells covered in their own body waste. It was only when the Hunger Strikes began that they were all moved to dry cells with dry bedding. He sat now on the black bitumen cell floor quietly but unashamedly sobbing.

In a house in Andersonstown, a strongly republican area of Belfast, Bobby Storey, Martin Quinn and Paddy McArdle listened to the newsflash in silence. It was not unexpected news but they sat staring at the radio on the table in the small kitchen with their individual thoughts. The silence was broken when Quinn cleared his throat and said, *"Let's do it."* They moved with stealth to three separate 'safe houses' where they knew IRA Volunteers were waiting with weapons at the ready, wanting to hit back.

By the time the 1981 Hunger Strikes began, individuals in cells had resisted (some of them for over five years) an onslaught of systematic brutality and a regime involving almost daily beatings, living on rationed food, naked in unfurnished cells and covered in body waste.

The Hunger Strikes ended in October 1981 with 10 Irish Republican Political prisoners dead. At that point the prison struggle changed in character. Republicans came out of their cells onto the wings making them much more difficult to control for the British authorities because there were dozens in each wing, together in solidarity, instead of naked individuals, isolated, in separate locked cells.

To understand Bobby Sands and the other Hunger Strikers' commitment and sacrifice you must understand the David and Goliath battle that is the history of Ireland's relationship with Colonial Britain. The prison struggle has its context within that. British Prime Minister Margaret Thatcher sought to break Irish resistance through crushing the imprisoned members of that resistance. She thought political prisoners were the weakest link. That was her mistake because political prisoners can be one of the strongest links in the chain of any insurgent force.

There was, however, a deep demoralisation inside and outside of the jail after the loss of 10 comrades. But the prisoners began to regroup and strategise. An upsurge in IRA activity in the wake of the prison deaths resulted in some key and leading activists being arrested. They were awaiting trial in Crumlin Road Jail in Belfast. If sentenced, they would be moved to the H Blocks.

Autumn 1982
H-Blocks

Those arriving in the H-Blocks from Crumlin Road jail by late 1982 included leading Belfast republicans Marty Quinn, Bobby Storey and Paddy McArdle. Already the prisoners under the leadership of the OC Seanna Walsh had formed a 'Task Force' in the protesting Blocks which were to filter volunteers from protesting wings to the mixed wings composed of Loyalist and Republicans mingling together and housed in adjacent cells. Well respected republicans like Larry Marley, Denis Cummings and Seamy Finucane were asked by the POW Camp leadership to reorganise republican structures in the mixed wings which had lapsed over time. They were joined by other leading figures from various urban and rural areas across the North. The fight back was underway. A new phase in prison struggle had begun.

The Republicans started agitating for 'Republican Only' wings and 'Loyalist Only' wings. The agitation gradually increased in militancy to an intolerable level for the prison administration. Groups who had been at war outside the jail couldn't be expected to live cheek by jowl in jail. The prison guards quickly realised that far from the Hunger Strike bringing the battle to an end they might face years of further protest. The guards were deeply demoralised and not in control. In the end the jail was ungovernable and the prison administration was forced, very quickly, to shift all the loyalists into separate segregated accomodation.

When Martin Quinn entered the H-Blocks in the first half of 1982 he was no stranger to the environment. He had already been on the blanket protest with Kieran Nugent who was the first Republican POW into the newly built H-Blocks. Nugent was also known for his now famous refrain to the prison guards when they told him to put on a prison uniform: *"The only way you'll get me to wear that convict uniform is to nail it to my back!"* Marty Quinn was one of the first blanket-men to be released. He returned immediately to the struggle with an undiluted enthusiasm.

Bobby Storey first entered jail during internment at the age of seventeen. He knew the routine as he got out of the van and entered the reception area of the jail. He chuckled to himself on seeing the sign 'Reception'- as if it was a hotel. At this stage he had been charged and in jail seven times between Britain and Ireland. Up to now a combination of tight republican security, silence during questioning and some luck had meant that his incarcerations had been relatively short lived. Between internment without trial and remands, he had spent almost seven years in jail.

As he sat waiting to be processed in the small cubicle, known as a 'horse box' because of the cramped and narrow space, he was thinking of his stint on remand in a London jail. He had been charged with attempting to break Brian Keenan out of jail. Keenan was a legendary figure in the IRA but not known for his diplomacy. A smile lightened Storey's face as he recalled their first encounter after arrest. This was in the aftermath of Storey and others entering Britain secretly, being arrested in the early hours of the morning by the heavily armed and less than subtle Anti-Terrorist Squad and then enduring several days of intense interrogation.

Storey spotted Keenan on the prison wing that first day of remand and had approached him, hand outstretched in greeting. He was genuinely glad to see his comrade whom he had known for many years. Keenan much smaller in frame clasped his hand, *"How are you Brian?"* said Storey. *"Never mind that shit!"* retorted

Keenan looking up at his face. *"Who fucked up?"* Storey burst out laughing and the older man's face cracked into a smile despite himself. *"It's not good to see you ye bastard,"* Keenan relented.

The horse box door had opened and the guard, who had noticed Storey smiling, looked at him quizzically but only said, *"Right Storey, home sweet home, you're for H-Block 6."* *"Aye and you should be a comedian,"* cracked Storey as he joined the other prisoners climbing into the jail van. Storey had been sentenced to 18 years imprisonment so as he moved through the jail he was alert to all pieces of useful information he could mentally store.

Paddy McArdle was about 5'9" with a medium frame. He continued the routine he had started on remand. He was doing the push-ups as part of his training in the cell. It was painful but he persisted. It was near Christmas 1982 and the cold was biting at the scar where he had been shot.

During the three-way discussions between Paddy McArdle, Bobby Storey and Marty Quinn, McArdle had been very keen to be left off the new staff which had been formed, to concentrate on escapes in his remaining 18 months or so. This worked for both Storey, who would have overall operational responsibility for such things, as well as for Quinn who would have the final say. As McArdle was soon to be released there was no need to worry about him hogging escape ideas for himself!

McArdle introduced himself to Larry Marley who had a reputation as a 'schemer' and was well liked by everyone who knew him. He told Marley about the escape committee. Marley was a veteran with years on the protest, so was known and respected by the camp OC and it was agreed that he should take the leadership role on escapes.

An escape committee under Marley was put together over a period which consisted of Paddy McArdle, Seany Bateson and Caoimhin

Blake. All escape plans had to be submitted to Marley. The team started with the basics and an inventory of all materials relevant to escaping was drawn up. Hacksaw blades, stone chisels, knives, pieces of guards' uniforms, buttons and badges were all accounted for. An order went out to dispose of irrelevant bits and pieces while all remaining material was gathered from all the Blocks.

They set about demystifying the jail. It was a huge complex, covering 360 acres which included the adjoining British Army base. But drawing up a plan was made easier with the uniformity of the 8 separate H-Blocks. Wire fencing and walls were set out in equidistant sections. Prisoners who went to the gym, workshops, or visits brought back information on guard positions, alarm points and any other relevant intelligence.

Photographs from the media were smuggled in later, as well as some ordinance survey maps. People out on parole or going to and from outside hospitals supplied more information. Prisoners were transported in blacked-out vans but there was always a patch of paint scraped off a blackened window or a crack at the door hinge or a conversation between guards in the front seat which added a small piece to the jigsaw.

Marley had always said *"Think big in escapes. Its great to get one person out but it would be massive to clear the camp."* He had the gift of the gab and he used it to good effect. He selected others to strike up conversations and relationships with the guards. He trained people to have innocent conversations with them from which information could be gleaned. He would talk about anything - football, holidays, cars, alcohol, entertainment, women and families. The first step was to have any discussion, to find out likes and dislikes; to talk mortgages and money, betting, debts etc. Through this charm offensive a profile was built up of the jail but just as importantly, of the guards who controlled it.

The way to their hearts was not political disaffection but ordinary everyday conversations. It was the relief of not being an enemy, of having almost normal relationships. Information gathering had to be discreet so at first a conversation could contain 20 innocuous questions to cover a key question.

Marley and McArdle were continually looking for other resources. They were working methodically through the H-Block to find out where people worked. A number of the republicans had drifted from the republican structures, Fearghal Heaney was one of them whom McArdle had known from outside. He was not sure that Heaney would come on board but he was absolutely confident that the matter would not go past him.

Heaney worked as an orderly and was able to move more easily than most. He was in a trusted position. He singled out guards who talked regularly about money and gambling. Heaney agreed to work them but McArdle told him to pass information through Marley as he was afraid his own high profile would compromise Heaney if the guards noticed too much contact between them.

There was another orderly called Declan McStravick. Marley, who had known McStravick separately, started the process of bringing him on board. He was another political prisoner who had drifted from the republican structures. But very quickly he was back in charracter and enthusiastically working with Marley. These men had only a few years of jail-time left and they knew the heavy risks they were taking. It started with just transferring communications or comms from Block to Block. In this way most of the information gleaned could be double checked or at times triple checked.

The information base was substantial now but without a real plan. This intelligence was not only able to discern what prison staff were supposed to do but also what they actually did as a matter of habit or complacency. Marley had information on the main gate and security Tally Lodge. He knew the routine and the times;

the rooms of the Tally Lodge; the security checks and lack of them; the alertness and complacency.

Storey had been getting regular reports from Marley. His emphasis was on big numbers but he was prepared to put small numbers or even single escape bids to Marty Quinn.

The food lorry in which the escapees concealed themselves

Easter 1983
H-Block 3

O n a Sunday, around Easter 1983, McArdle and Marley were strolling around the exercise yard, quiet in each others company, when the silence was accentuated with a squeal of brakes.

"Is that a van?" McArdle asked absently.

"I think it's the Happy Wagon," Marley answered referring to the food lorry. *"Aye, 'spot the beef'- it's a Sunday."* It was a standing joke amongst prisoners that the meat served up for Sunday dinner was so thin you could nearly see through it. Hence the term 'spot the beef.'

The conversation almost casually extended into their normal conversation around escapes.

"The food lorry is big isn't it?"

"Yeah"

"Wasn't there an idea in one of the schemes put forward to lie on top of it with a dirty white sheet covering someone?"

"Yeah, but it's an 'internal vehicle' and it doesn't leave the jail." *"Wait a minute. In the middle of a conversation with one of the lads in the kitchen he said something about the drivers shifting furniture for one of their mates. So it would have to leave the jail at times."*

"Can we fill it and drive out the main gates?"

In both their minds there emerged a focus for the intelligence they already had and the possibility of getting more. So contact was made with Storey. The bones of the escape were that the food lorry visited each Block three times every day. To get the lorry filled with political prisoners, a Block or Blocks had to be taken and there was good information on the Main Gate area of the prison.

Marley intensified the probing through the orderlies. What was security like at each gate? Was the lorry searched? Were there passwords? Did the lorry ever leave the jail? Where was it left overnight. Where between trips? How many drivers? Who were they? What differences where there on a Sunday and bank holidays? Could it go anywhere in the jail? Did it go into the adjacent British Army Camp?

Which Block or Blocks and who would be on the escape was down to Quinn. At this stage Storey was in H7 and Quinn was in H2. In fact they had not been in the same Block since they had arrived in Long Kesh. They were able to arrange meetings on visiting and gym days however. They went through the possibilities: Take the punishment unit on its own, take all the Blocks, take two or take one. What weapons are needed? Where is the best control of a block? Where is the best concentration of long termers? Where was the most developed relationship with guards?

Pat McGeown had been made Adjutant of the H-Blocks when the new staff took over. He was an ex-Hunger Striker. Quinn had briefed him at an early stage but as Adjutant it was agreed that he needed to deal with the day to day running of the Camp's prisoner community while Quinn oversaw the escape. McGeown had tried to escape from the Cages with Brendan McFarlane and Larry Marley. All three had been transferred to the Blocks because of it. He was no stranger to escape plans. More importantly his head was not cluttered with the history and minutiae of the plan as it

18

had developed and changed. Quinn wanted an opinion which was fresh and untainted by attachment to the scheme, an objective view. He listened to Pat McGeown's thoughts and opinions, and mulled them over in his mind overnight before making his final decision.

In the end Quinn called it. H7 was isolated. It had a reputation for having broken down controlled movement, having a more relaxed atmosphere and more casual relationship with the guards. Even though the front gates of H7 and H8 faced each other, H8 was empty of prisoners while refurbishment of the block was taking place. So the escape could not be detected from another block. H6 sat to the rear but any escape activity would be at the front of H7. There was a substantial cluster of long termers including life-sentence prisoners who would want to escape and would hopefully be prepared to take chances where necessary. Bobby Storey was deeply involved in the escape and had substantial recent operational experience. He was well known by the IRA leadership on the outside, who would need to be convinced that such a complicated operation was in good hands. There were a number of high profile prisoners in H7 which would have good political value if they escaped including Brendan 'Bik' McFarlane who had been Camp OC during the 1981 Hunger Strike, Seamus McElwaine from Fermanagh, Seamus Campbell from Tyrone and Sean McGlinchey from South Derry.

Also there was a high degree of control by the POWs in H7 as they had for some time been transforming the atmosphere in the Block from hostile to calmer relationships between guards and prisoners. The last question was of commitment. It was expected that anyone who escaped would return to the armed struggle. A general assessment was made of personnel. If they were prepared to go back to the struggle they would be prepared to do whatever it took on the day. The prisoners worked on the basis that *"to chop down a tree, spend most of the time sharpening the axe."*

Quinn knew that Storey could not suggest H7 because he would be proposing his own escape but he also knew that if they had a list for an operational OC on an escape bid, then Storey would be top of that list.

Storey moved into operational mode. Contact was intensified between him as Operational OC, Marley as Escape Officer and Quinn as final arbiter and conduit to the IRA leadership outside jail.

July 1983
H-Block 7

T he first priority was how to take over the entire H7 Block cleanly and how to hold it while the escapees made their way out in the food lorry. Next, how would the security or Tally Lodge at the main gate of the jail be taken. Finally how would the escapees get through the Brit Army camp cleanly and tie in with those on the outside. This complex plan had to be done on a need to know basis. Any security leak could be a disaster of massive proportions involving multiple deaths.

Storey approached and briefed Seamas McDermott first, followed by Brendan McFarlane. McDermott had only a couple of years left of his sentence to serve but he had operated with Storey in Belfast. They trusted each other absolutely. While Storey didn't know McFarlane well, his reputation preceded him especially as the Camp OC and negotiator during the Hunger Strikes. McDermott had been through years of protest alongside him.

They were all on one side of the H-Block. They would need to add to their group rapidly so that A and B-Wings were involved. In H7 there were 126 men. 24 were serving life sentences. 28 were serving 10 year sentences or more. Only 7 of the prisoners were over 35 years of age and 98 of the 126 were in their twenties. Most, though not all, had been active members in the IRA from different parts of Ireland, though concentrated in the North of Ireland.

Gerry Kelly in B-Wing had a reputation when it came to escapes. He had escaped from Mountjoy jail in Dublin as a teenager, followed by escape attempts from jails in England. After his hunger strike and transfer to Long Kesh in the 1970s he had been removed to the H-Blocks in early 1982. His latest escapade had been from the military wing of Musgrave Park Hospital in Belfast, where he had been transferred as a result of one of his lungs collapsing. Kelly was the longest serving political prisoner in the Republican Blocks having been in jail since March 1973. He was intent on escaping and the evidence was there to prove it. He was brought in to the small leadership team.

To take the whole block cleanly, the 'circle' or administrative area had to be taken first. Although it was called 'the circle,' it was actually the bar section of the H. It was a secure area which contained a governor's office, a principle officers' office, a medical room, a welfare room, a small guards' mess or canteen, and male and female toilets. It also contained a Control Room which was the nerve centre of the Block as well as the communications centre into the main control centre and administration block (known as the Emergency Control Room or ECR) for the overall prison and outside.

To seize control of the Block, first meant seizing control of the circle area and that needed guns. The wings had big numbers of Republicans who could overwhelm the small number of guards in each wing. The circle on the other hand was a sterile area and getting even a small number of prisoners into it at the same time was problematic. They needed to be handpicked and they needed to be armed for instant compliance and control especially because of the access to alarm bells, phones, radios and intercoms.

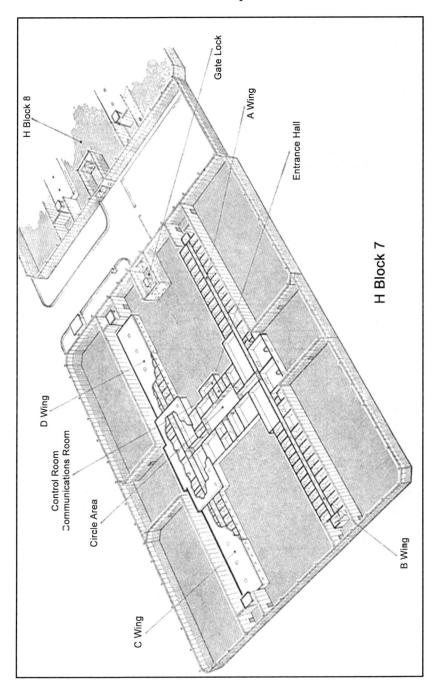

H Block 8

Gate Lock

A Wing

Entrance Hall

H Block 7

D Wing

Control Room
Communications Room

Circle Area

B Wing

C Wing

August 1983

Q uinn knew that it was time to put the escape to the IRA on the outside. He knew the structures as well as knowing some of the leadership personally. He was also very aware that such an ambitious escape plan would invoke political and military trepidation and enthusiasm in unquantifiable measures. He was relying on the respect for, and confidence in, the experience of McArdle and Storey as well as himself at both Northern Command level and more importantly at Army Council (AC) level. He didn't have any doubt the go-ahead for such an enterprise could only be given by the collective leadership of the seven person Army Council of the IRA.

A very secure line of communication was established through 'An Bhean'. The Northern Command OC was given the details of the escape from beginning to end with a request for six small calibre short-arms to take over the circle area and the main gate area. It was obvious from the questions being sent back to the jail from the Northern Command (NC) that it was being taken seriously and that the plan was being tested. The escape team answered all the questions. Some of the questions were helpful as they pointed out where arguments and actions had to be strengthened and after some weeks, Quinn was told that they could proceed to get the weaponry in.

It was known that Belfast had a number of small short-arms which would be ideal for their escape plan. They had been used in the escape of eight Volunteers from the Crumlin Road jail in 1980.

Marley had been given the job of getting those weapons smuggled in. There were a number of possible, though not necessarily probable, routes in. One was a person to person swap on the visits. Another was through one of the civilian staff who frequented the jail for education, welfare, legal or religious purposes. Another was convincing a guard to bring the weapons in. A further possibility was secreting the weapons inside materials such as blocks of wood for making handicrafts.

More intelligence was needed so Marley instructed Heaney to dig deeper. He knew that Heaney would use his own home-grown psychology to achieve the objective of getting the necessary additional information they needed from the guards.

Marley concentrated on details of the security portacabin, known as the Tally Lodge at the main gate of the prison. What exactly did a guard do on his way into work and on his way home from work? At the same time Marley was also working on Declan McStravick, another orderly. Heaney and McStravick knew each other but neither knew that Marley was working with the other. In this way facts were able to be checked and cross checked.

Robert Russell had been released briefly on parole because of a family bereavement. On his return he had been put into a small Tally Lodge outside the jail walls but just inside the overall camp perimeter which also contained a British Army encampment. It was just inside the encampment's main gate. When he returned from parole he was able to describe in detail the smaller Tally Lodge and all the tooing and froing of prison guards and British soldiers around it. Marley logged the information, noting the small problem of Russell being in H3 when the escape might be in another Block.

As the likelihood of the escape increased so the weight of failure started burdening the planners. They had all been involved in armed struggle and had all had lost friends and comrades. They knew that bad planning could cause a disaster and possible multiple deaths.

August 1983
Army Council Meeting

L iam Breathnach's eyes were well accustomed to the dim light in the back of the bone-shaking van. The floor had a series of old cushions on it and he had positioned himself with his back against the partition which separated them from the driver. The other three men had found somewhere to wedge themselves safely in case of any sudden jolts. This was the third vehicle they had been in or on, in as many hours.

Breathnach knew they were heading in the direction of the west coast of Ireland. The van had pulled off the tarmac road and was shuddering its way up a steep, rough lane so he hoped they had reached their destination. It had been a long three hours. A few moments later they came to a halt and the side door was opened for them. It was directly facing the back door of a modern bungalow. They were ushered into a spacious sitting room where five other people were waiting for them.

This was a meeting of the ruling Army Council of the IRA. The two other attendees were the Adjutant General and the Quarter Master General, who had a right to attend but without voting rights. The familiar greetings were exchanged.

Ciarán Dougan the veteran Republican was by far the oldest and amply filled the comfortable armchair at the side of the picture window

"You have surpassed yourself Lorcan" he said to the Secretary of the Council who had supplied the house.

"Glad you're impressed Ciarán. It's not long built and the owner is a well-respected local business man who is a quiet supporter."

"Aye. Well he would need to be a quiet one!" Dougan chuckled.

The view was panoramic. The house sat high on the side of a coastal hill. The Atlantic Ocean roared at its feet. Lorcan Brady liked the view but he was used to it as it was his native county. He was more interested in the fact that the only approach was up a long steep lane so they would have plenty of warning of any unwelcome visitors. They were also not overlooked from any angle so privacy was assured. The wood burner was lit for heat and in case any paperwork had to be destroyed urgently.

There were four city men. The other five were from various rural parts of Ireland, North and South. Apart from Ciarán Dougan, they ranged in age from 25 to 40.

After the necessary chairs were brought in from the dining room the AC Chairperson spoke. *"Ok lads. It's seven o'clock. We have a long agenda. I suggest we work until 11 o'clock and then hit the sack. I am going to ask the Chief of Staff (CS) for his report and then deal with matters arising from it and any issues from the last meeting before taking the agenda for the rest of the meeting. There is a pressing agenda item on a jail issue which I suggest we try to deal with tonight as the CS believes the Council should have a view on it."*

The first half hour was taken up with the Chief of Staff's report and outstanding issues from the previous meeting. Most issues raised with the CS were put down as agenda items.

The Chairman continued, *"The first item on the agenda is about a potential escape from the H-Blocks of Long Kesh and I'm going to ask the CS to cover it."* Everyone's attention was focused on the CS.

27

"Well, it is a mass escape. It will involve the possession and possible use of a small number of hand-guns in the jail. The 1981 Hunger Strike where we lost 10 good comrades is barely two years ago. If it goes well it will be a massive morale boost and an advance of the struggle. But if it fails it may well deepen an already existing demoralisation as a consequence of the Hunger Strike. If any more prisoners lose their lives as a result, then it will be a disaster. That's why I have asked for it to be brought to the Army Council as it will have widespread implications for the struggle either way."

"The bare bones are simple enough," the CS continued. *"There are a series of H-Blocks which house only Republican political prisoners. The idea is to take control of one of them, fill a lorry with long-term prisoners and drive out the front gate as quietly as possible. The lads have requested half a dozen small handguns. While the wings can be taken by force of numbers, the circle area or administrative centre of the Block never has more than a handful of prisoners in it. Without the numbers, they need weapons to secure it cleanly. They should only have to subdue a small number of screws in the circle but will have to repeat this at the main gate where about six screws handle entry and exit. The idea is then to rendezvous some miles away from the jail with the South Armagh Brigade who will transport them into hiding and safety. I know there's not a lot of information there but it has been planned to the last detail so I will take any questions. I'll hand back over to the Chair."*

The AC Chair nodded. *"Thank you CS."* They both knew that there would be understandable worries and different views within the Council. They used military titles instead of names to give the report a formal and serious aura.

There was silence for a moment and then a flurry of questions. The discussion went on for a number hours. The Chair wanted unanimity even though a majority of four to three could make it happen.

28

When the discussion moved towards the implications of such an escape he was fairly certain that the Council were up for it. He knew that everyone would be vicariously on the escape but especially ex-POWs in the room. The idea of smashing the H-Blocks in the wake of the Hunger Strike was tantalising. The fact that the Crumlin Road jail escape had been successful also helped. The biggest argument in his own mind was that he had faith in the plan and in their ability to pull it off, but the doubt was in the responsibility of it going wrong and the possible death toll. He was aware that a POW, Hugh Coney had been shot dead during an escape bid in 1974 at Long Kesh and another Tom Smith at Portlaoise Prison in 1975. The CS argued passionately but practically. Half way through the discussion darkness had fallen and they pulled the curtains and put on the lights. There was a ten minute break for tea but the discussion continued animatedly.

The Chair checked the clock on the mantelpiece. It was 11.30pm. He had done all he could. He didn't want to break for sleep without a decision. The atmosphere could be changed by the morning.

"Ok lads, I think we've thrashed it out high and low. Its decision time and I'm looking to make a proposal that the Council empowers the CS to decide whether and when such an escape is sanctioned." He didn't want to come back to the Council for another discussion. It was, in the end, an operational decision, albeit with huge political ramifications. So he wanted the responsibility left with the Chief of Staff but with the all-important blessing of the Army Council.

Ciarán Dougan raised his hand to speak and all eyes turned to him. *"There are undoubted risks here but let's remember: not only do Irish Republican POWs deserve to escape - we put a duty on them to escape! They deserve our backing."*

"Ciarán is right," interjected the Belfast Brigade OC

enthusiastically. *"I want to second the Chair's proposal. The CS should call it."*

The Chair of the Army Council surveyed the room. *"We have a proposal. All those in favour?"*

Every one in the room raised a hand including the Quarter Master General and the Adjutant General both of whom knew they had no vote. It was unanimous.

"Codladh sámh daoibh a Chairde." "Sleep well folks" the Council Chair finished with relief, yet knowing that every member of the Council would also be worried about the implications of their decision.

H-Blocks
Late August 1983
The Weapons

T he date had been set for the escape. It was for September 25th, a week after the All-Ireland Gaelic Football final, which gave them four weeks. The idea of doing it on an All-Ireland Final Day had been discussed but was rejected mainly because between 60,000 and 80,000 people would be travelling the roads of Ireland. The British thought that the IRA used the presence of so much road traffic to shift arms and military material across the border. So generally the British Army would be out in force on the roads in the North of Ireland that day.

Heaney and McStravick were approached separately. Neither knew about the other's involvement. They hadn't long to go to serve out the rest of their sentences, so suspicion of them was at a low level as well and the prison authorities knew that the two had moved away

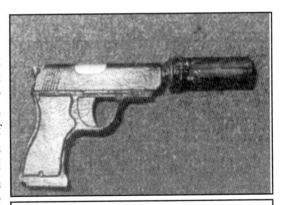

Replica gun used in the escape

from the Republican structures in the jail. They had in fact been very effective in gathering intelligence towards escapes and did not hesitate when it was put to them individually that they be part of moving weapons about the jail.

Doc Marten shoes and boots were popular with guards and prisoners alike. They were very comfortable and looked smart. More importantly, they had been used for smuggling by prisoners many times because the soles and heels were fairly thick and could be hollowed out to insert different objects. Using shoes to smuggle contraband was a well-known method of course. Through the years people had been caught, but the majority had not. There was always a risk but it was a calculated risk. Heaney and McStravick started wearing Doc Martens on a regular basis to get guards used to it.

There were no written communications about the guns. Heaney and McStravick were informed verbally as the consequences were potentially too grave. If the British knew there were guns in the jail, then they had used a 'shoot to kill' policy before. If they could produce weaponry at the scene, then the British believed they could stand over a 'shoot to kill' policy in public.

McArdle had gone to Dee Devenny, a comrade who had been a Quarter Master (QM) in the IRA outside. He had hands for anything practical. He was told there were guns coming in and 'hides' for weapons needed to be prepared. He was given Seany Bateson, as well as Finbarr McKenna to assist him. Marley had been on the blanket protest with them and he knew how reliable they were. Marley had been painstakingly making a banjo for months. It was a hobby of his and the banjo was in and out of cells all the time. Guards and prisoners alike were making cracks about it. *"Are you ever gonna play a tune on that?"* *"Hey you've no strings"* *"That banjo is banjoed! You may pack it in."* But it had become a fixture of the block.

However, there was always method in the madness when it came to Marley. When Devenny was given the word about weapons

32

coming in, he started to make compartments inside the sound box of the banjo. Marley introduced Devenny to the other comrades Seany Bateson and Finbarr McKenna and then went off the scene. He left Devenny to deal with them directly.

Heaney had been having doubts. He had the Doc Marten shoes shined a glossy black. When the guard searched him before he left the block he had asked him to remove his shoes and had checked them. However he had set his nervousness aside as it served no purpose.

Keeping one eye on the guards, it was straightforward enough to swap the shoes with one of his comrades. On his way back into the cell block he was only given a rub down search. He thought the shoes felt heavy but wondered was it just psychological.

Two of the weapons were smuggled inside in the one pair of shoes. They were small calibre weapons but still deadly. Heaney dandered in and changed shoes again in Marley's cell. When he left he felt exhilarated and then relieved. Proud that he had done his bit. McArdle and Marley checked the weapons releasing magazines, checking rounds, safeties, sleeves, muzzles and firing pins etc.

It was nearing lock-up and McArdle and Marley had the guns laid out under the pillow. They were on a high with everything coming together. Devenny had joined them and McArdle hopped onto the top bunk.

"Dee there's a couple of bars of chocolate under the pillow. Givus one up."

"Which one?" Devenny asked as he bent into the bottom bunk at the other wall.

"Gimme a Kit Kat," replied McArdle as he winked at Marley. Devenny was a bit peckish himself. He pulled the pillow back

33

and then his head jerked back hitting the edge of the top metal bunk.

"Ye wee fucker ye." Devenny was 6ft and built like a street fighter, *"Two wee fuckers,"* he corrected himself as he held his head and gazed at the short-arms, dark against the laundered white of the sheet.

They all burst out laughing. *"Where did you get them,"* he enquired as a reflex question which he immediately regretted as he didn't really want to know.

"Now, now!" smiled Marley *"You won't be eating them anyway. That's for sure."*

Almost immediately there was a commotion in the corridor. It sounded like lots of footsteps. Devenny automatically covered the guns. All their minds were racing. Was it a raid? Marley and McArdle were working it out. Only three people knew the guns were coming in that day, Heaney, Marley and McArdle. Could it be a set up? Had the changeover been seen?

McArdle jumped to the door to look out through the crack at the hinge. All he could see was uniforms and hear the rattle of keys. His heart was beating super fast. *"It's cops,"* he said to the others who were waiting on information. The tension rose dramatically. They seemed to be opening cell doors but only briefly, speaking and closing them again. They were working in pairs. *"They aren't armed,"* McArdle said quietly when he realised that there were no machine guns being carried and then that their side-holsters were empty.

McArdle moved slightly away from the door saying, *"They're coming. Let me do the talking."* At that the keys jangled in the lock and the door opened. Two cops filled the door. They were both at least 6'3" and one bent down to look in.

"What's up?" Asked McArdle deliberately cheeky.

"Sorry about this," replied the cop politely. *"But the prison officers are on a 24 hour industrial strike and we've taken over running the place for the duration. So bear with us OK?"*

"Ok I suppose," retorted McArdle grumpily, trying to hide his relief as the cop slammed the heavy metal door shut again.

After a few seconds of staring at each other, all three of them let their breath out in a long collective sigh. Just as they were gathering their thoughts for conversation the door was abruptly opened again and a number of hamburger baps and other bits and pieces of food and drink were handed in, all pre-wrapped in lots of stretch and seal plastic.

The RUC were obviously an unexpected and unknown factor. Would they do cell-searches or Wing or Block searches? The guns, if found, represented a possible 10 year sentence on top of the ones already being served and more if 'intent to endanger life' was added to a charge of 'possession.'

While one of them kept watch through the crack in the door the other two wrapped the pistols tightly in the stretch and seal to make them as waterproof as possible. They could have thrown the pistols out of the cell window or lowered them to the yard. That would have made it difficult for the police to charge them but the escape would have been jeopardised for months if not years due to the inevitable security clamp-down which would have followed.

There was an 'ablutions' (or washing) area at the top of the wing nearest the circle. It contained showers, toilets and a bath. In their wing the pipe under the bath had been slowly leaking for months. The bath was seldom used as most prisoners preferred the showers so the guards had been in no rush to get it repaired. The water was lying in a hollow in the black bitumen floor under the bath. It was decided to take a chance and deposit the weapons there while the abnormal and unpredictable regime continued under the RUC.

Devenny did the dry-run. He banged on the cell door and asked to use the toilet. As he walked up the corridor he realised that there was a far larger contingent of RUC men per Wing than was normal with prison guards. However, on his return he was able to report that he had not been searched or followed into the toilets. Marley and McArdle hid the weapons down their jeans and banged the door to get to the toilets.

As they walked down chatting about football they noticed that some of the cops recognised one or the other of them as they had been high profile republicans outside. Some of the RUC men passed remarks more to each other than to the prisoners – but they lined almost the whole way down the wing. There were no cops in the ablutions area so very quickly McArdle handed his pistol over to Marley who got down low in the bath cubicle and pushed both guns right to the back of the black pool of stagnant water trying hard not to cause ripples or to get his clothes wet. The two then walked back to their cell feeling a lot lighter having divested themselves, if only temporarily, of such a burden. The following 24 hours seemed like weeks as they worried about the weapons and the escape. They knew that only the prisoners cleaned the ablutions area and under the bath, but still they were nervous.

As it turned out the weapons remained in H3 for a fortnight while they worked out how to get them to H7. The other weapons came in a few days later using the same method but with McStravick this time. Marley decided to use the same system of shoe swapping through the workshops. He was at least two sizes smaller but he was wearing the larger size Doc Marten boots. He wasn't very tall and to McArdle and Devenny he looked a bit comical. He was a comedian in any case. He was practising walking in the larger shoes up and down the cell singing an old

Willie Nelson song from the 60s. *"It is Tougher than Leather, Should've known better"*

When Marley got to the end of the wing on his way out to the workshops, the guard opening the gate said, *"Where'd you get those shoes? They're crackers. You can see your face in them."* Larry had built up a good rapport with the guard over months,

"Oul Kate," laughed Marley whose wife was far from old, *"Got me them in McMurrays in North Street."*

"North Street? I might get the wife to get me a pair," said the guard as he relocked the wing gate after letting Marley and others through.

The swap in the workshop went smoothly and the weapons arrived safely to H7 but Marley was a bit uncomfortable with the exchange of the boots and the casual comments of the guard that day. Time was also running out for the deadline that had been set. However, the die was cast and the same method was used to get all the weapons to H7 over the following few days.

During lock-up McArdle and Marley both paced the floor worrying and listening for any untoward activity. They received a 'teacht' from H7. They were always awkward to open because they were so small and fidgety. That day McArdle fumbled more than usual. It was a single cigarette paper. *"Nice one Fig,"* it read. It was five days to kick off and the H3 team had done their bit.

Apart that is, for one last task: Robert Russell. He was the man with the information on the outer Tally Lodge.

Marley and McArdle were walking around the exercise yard. McArdle was convinced Russell was going to miss the big day. As they passed the gate into the wing Marley said to the guard

"Open the gate there, I need to see the governor." Not many would get away with that. Generally the governor only saw prisoners who put their names down on a list first thing in the morning when the guard opened the cell door with the question *"Any requests?"* But Marley was known by most of the prison staff. He had been in jail around 10 years and was liked and known as a bit of a character by most of the guards. So the guard opened the gate. He came back out to McArdle about 15 minutes later. As they walked away from the guard Marley was smiling broadly. He always referred to Russell as 'Big Fritz' because he was tall, square jawed and blonde. *"Big Fritz is off to H7 in the morning,"* he said.

McArdle looked at him incredulously. *"Are you messing?"* But Marley explained with some relish. *"It struck me about Big Fritz being a bit of a ladies' man, so I went out to the governor and told him I needed to talk to him alone. I said I knew a guard was normally present but the matter was too personal. So the governor told the guard to leave and shut the door. When we were alone I said, "We go back a long way and you're not the worst even if you are a governor so I'm telling you this because I don't want you to get into trouble and I don't want trouble on the block."*

"What are you talking about Marley?" Asked the governor.

"There's going to be murder in the block. There's a new guy just in called 'Yankee' - Jim Morgan. You know that big lad Robert Russell?" *"Yes,"* said the governor wondering where this was going. *"Well, Big Russell is going to kill Yankee cos he was shacked up with Russell's girl outside. This has been building for months since he found out. Nobody expected them to be in the same H-Block."* So the govenor says, *"Can't you do something to stop it?"*

Marley pressed on, *"Look at the size of the fekker! If you'll forgive my language, I knew him outside. When he gets something into his head there's no stopping him and he's nothing to lose cos he's doing 20 years." "You must have some control over him,"* entreated the governor, picturing the scene.

"Afraid not. Look I'm only telling you cos I have some respect for you but you can't break this confidence. I don't normally go to governors about comrades."

He knew this was true so I said, *"Listen, if you want a solution - send Russell up to his mate Marty McManus in H7. He'll be delighted and won't ask any questions and then just be careful to keep him and Morgan in different parts of the jail for a while til it cools down. But don't let anyone know I spoke to you about this."*

The governor thought for a moment then said: *"There is a Block shift due tomorrow, Russell will be on it and our conversation didn't happen."*

McArdle was looking at Marley with renewed respect. *"You are a bullshitter par excellence! I bow to your superior horseshit,"* McArdle said, slightly mixing his metaphors. They were delighted with themselves next morning when Russell bade them both a happy farewell. Their part was done. All that was left for them to do was to wait.

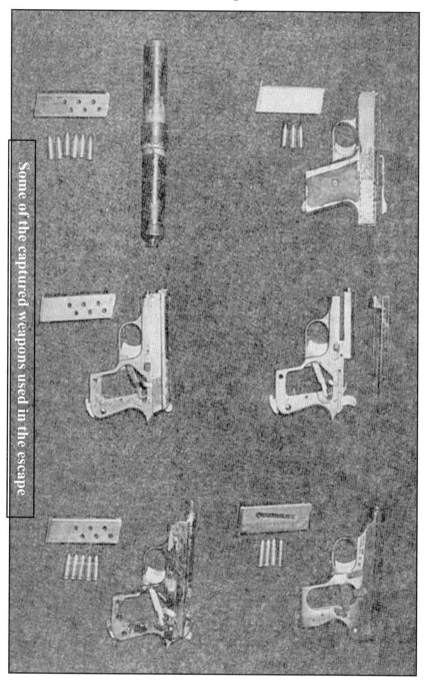

Some of the captured weapons used in the escape

Saturday, September 24th 1983 South Armagh

The old cottage kitchen looked packed with the 10 people who occupied the various seats. This was the inner sanctum of the South Armagh Brigade of the IRA. It was freezing outside but they had all shed their heavy outdoor coats in the heat from the Aga range. Some still wore their caps or woollen hats.

It was 10 o'clock and the meeting was about to break up. It had been three hours of sometimes heated discussion centred on tactics against the British Army with particular emphasis on weaponry. This was an experienced unit respected by friends and foe alike, which concentrated on intelligence gathering before executing an operation. Once in this inner circle there was a deep trust which allowed for very open and critical discussions. That's why it was so hard to get membership of such a group.

Unlike many other IRA units, this unit had, to a great extent, survived the attrition rate of death or jail. Their biggest problem was that the British had upgraded personal body armour to the point that light assault rifles, including the 7.62 calibre Kalashnikovs, and the .300 calibre Garand rifles were not penetrating it. Heavier weapons like the .50 calibre Barrett or the Russian made 12.7 calibre machine-gun were needed.

The Brigade OC brought the meeting to a close. As people started putting on their coats he spoke quietly to two of them who slowed their pace a little.

Brendan Moley and Brendan Burns sat down again. As their other comrades emptied into the darkness there was a quizzical glance or two back in their direction after the goodbyes. The silence was broken only by the crackle of radios and scanners which were always present, an early warning system from strategically placed scouts.

The farm house was situated in the North of Ireland. A few hundred yards away from the back window was the South of Ireland. It was ironically easier to do a meeting in the British jurisdiction because the British would only raid with caution and in numbers for fear of attack. In this part of the North the only transport used was helicopters, so it was hard for British troops to arrive with stealth. The fields closest were always well checked in the company of various dogs, before a meeting. Within the Southern Irish jurisdiction, however, the Irish authorities had no fear of attack as they knew it was forbidden within the IRA rules of engagement to open fire on Irish government authorities. So they would have no hesitation or fear in raiding and arresting people at gun point.

After a few minutes the scrape of a key announced the opening of the front door. The first to enter was a tall heavy set man in his mid-thirties. He removed the key from the Yale lock and made way for the two following him. All three were wearing water boots which were covered in muck. They had walked across the fields. They removed their headwear to reveal all three were at different stages of going bald. Brendan Burns couldn't help himself: *"Keep the caps on men it makes youse look 10 years younger!"* The first one in was the IRA's Northern Command OC. They all knew each other well. *"Your moustache is as good as it gets on your dome,"* he retorted always expecting some remark from Burns. Brendan Moley and the Brigade OC smiled from below bushy hairstyles. As they sat down to business, the Northern Command OC automatically took charge.

"Well youse know why we're here. The Army Council gave us clearance a while back to go with the escape from the H-Blocks. It's going ahead tomorrow and we need to be ready so I just want to make final checks. This is as tight an operation as any of us have done. The first part is up to the lads in jail. If they succeed the second part is down to us so let's do our bit well." He looked at Brendan Moley who was to take charge of the recovery operation.

"First of all," Moley began, *"the only people who know about this are here in this room. Too much can go wrong so I'm taking no chances. Myself and Burns,"* he nodded at Brendan Burns *"have scouted the route and done dry runs. I'll be driving the scout car and handling any other scouts and Burns will be handling the lorry itself. It's a 22ft Ford Box D850. We've steel in two layers of half inch and quarter inch with half inch space in between. It's well tested and will stop any assault rifle fire easily. It will certainly slow down any calibre above that like a .50 Browning. It has a .50 calibre heavy machine gun mounted in it with a back shutter which will lift to swing it into position on runners. It's mounted at the back and can take whatever might follow us whether vehicle or helicopter. Blue will be handling that and Belfast will have the M60 machine gun."*

Blue, whose given name was Micky Lynch, interjected briefly. *"We've tested the armour and as you know we checked and tested the Browning .50 heavy machine gun yesterday down in the pit - so it couldn't be heard. It's working well but in any case you saw it active recently against the Brit chopper in Crossmaglen."* He finished by referring to their attempts to take out a helicopter as it rose from the safety of the nearby Crossmaglen British Army Barracks.

Belfast whose name was Terry Magee was proud to be there as he knew the South Armagh squad didn't trust outsiders easily, but he was accepted as one of them even though they still called him 'Belfast'. He knew his weapons, having previously held positions as Quarter Master and TO (Training Officer) He had the added advantage of hopefully knowing a number of those who would be in on the escape. Even though he didn't know who, it was fair to guess that he would know some of them from Belfast. The OC continued *"Blue and Belfast will be in the back of the lorry. They will have a few rifles under their control but will only hand them out to selected escapees who they can stand over and only if it becomes necessary. We don't want all sorts of weapons floating about in a crowded yoke!"*

Magee spoke, *"Well we can't afford to risk too many weapons -- not to mention Volunteers - on this one, but we've managed to scrounge six extra weapons off the QMs. There are three AR 15s, an M14 and two M16s with plenty of ammo."*

"I have liberated the Egyptian AK with the folding butt to accompany me in the lorry cab - just in case we need extra punch at the front," Burns interjected beaming. They were starting to relish the challenge ahead.

"Try to bring our comrades back safely men," the Northern Command OC smiled back. *"Hospital might not be an option!"* His countenance returned to seriousness *"I know the lads requested spare weapons but I'm not sure it's a good idea. Hopefully this lorry will be packed with prisoners. How do you choose who gets a weapon. One accidental discharge from a weapon in such a confined space surrounded by steel will cause ricocheting all over the place and may wound a number of people or worse. Keep it simple. If you have to hand out arms you're already in deep shite!"*

"You have a fair point but we'll be careful," Lynch argued, *"The .50 and the M60 are both belt-fed so we'll need two of the escapees to assist in feeding ammo anyway."*

"We'll be careful," Magee repeated, *"We know the dangers but*

we could have a lorry load of volunteers and there are ones amongst them who aren't long in jail. They have the training and discipline and it will settle the lot of them if they see there's more than two weapons. Hopefully we won't actually need to use them. It could be more psychological than actual but if we're being chased or hit a problem with the enemy, it's good to have the extra firepower."

"OK" relented the Northern Command OC and then continued, *"We're obviously outside our comfort zone on this one. We've gathered a few other lads together who don't as yet know what's going on. They'll be gathering here tomorrow. The Checkers will do the surrounding area here with dogs in the early morning and then hold the area all day. If it's clear, we'll have radio points on all the surrounding hills. If the Checkers come across anything then we can shift the base over to Big John's area for kick off."*

Moley spoke, *"Since we're going as far down as Scarva I've arranged for radio men. I'll position them at every crossroads on the route between our base and Scarva. High points will be covered where they can let us know if there's anything odd on the roads. They think we need them for a landmine that's already laid but I'll talk to them tomorrow."*

"All cars and the lorry will have CB radios but as usual there will be no chat on the airways unless it's absolutely necessary. The lorry is rigged with about six different aerials, Blue and Belfast will be listening to the cops and Brit's radio traffic in the North. They will be able to pick up Gardai and Irish Army radio activity in the South. They'll also listen to the Customs' radio channels just in case. Again, our lads don't know that it's for a jail break. It's tight. I hope for the escapees' sake that their security is as water-tight."

The Northern Command OC interrupted casually, *"We're pretty sure it is. It was strictly on a 'need to know' basis but it's a*

45

complicated takeover. It's on tomorrow and the closer to the date the more prisoners needed to know. Anyway, all that's behind us, so there's no point worrying. By the way the escapees don't even know the pick-up. We have them rendezvousing with one of our lads at a garage on the A1 near Hillsborough. At that stage we'll know whether they are being followed or not."

"It's huge," Moley said to no-one in particular.

Burns finished the thought, *"Aye a huge blow to the Brits if we pull it off and a huge boot in the balls for the struggle if we fail!"*

"Every op has its own risks," the Northern Command OC intoned philosophically, closing down what could be a long discussion which he had already had with his comrades on the Army Council.

They went over the detail for the next day from A to Z and then got their outdoor gear on. They headed across the fields in the dark to their billets south of the border. There they climbed into various beds or sleeping- bags. They had already decided to stay away from their homes that night. All had been dropped off a half mile away from the cottage and then walked the fields to be sure they had not been followed. It would save them having to go through the necessary security ritual the next day, lessening the possibility of security problems, which might delay any one of them too close to the kick-off point

7am
H-Block 7
September 25th

Ironically jail had taught Gerry Kelly to appreciate time on his own. When he had been imprisoned in England he had always been housed in a single cell as a 'Category A' or 'maximum security' prisoner. He had also spent some long periods of incarceration in segregation units away from contact with other human beings. However the time he had spent in the nissen huts of the Long Kesh prison camp were years of very communal living.

He enjoyed the comaraderie of his fellow prisoners and friends but he also welcomed the lock-up at night in a single cell. He appreciated the quiet time to contemplate, or read, do a bit of yoga, write or simply daydream. Many of his comrades preferred to 'double-up' with others for the company and craic. He seldom had any trouble sleeping and usually woke in the mornings just moments before the shift of guards entered the wings.

Today was a little different. He had gone to bed around 10pm and had slept until about 5.30am. As he opened his eyes he knew it was early. Anticipation and excitement had his mind racing. He didn't get up but cupped his hands behind his head. Once more he went through the sequence of events he hoped would unfold that day–Sunday September 25th 1983. One way or the other the date would be indelibly marked on his memory.

He was surprised at how calm he felt despite the eagerness for the hours to pass quickly. He had gone to bed early for that reason. It was a bit like the adult version of waiting for Santa.

The previous night he had wandered into the food hall to watch the fortnightly video to pass some time. He hadn't bothered checking out what the title of the film was. As he left the cell Brendan McFarlane had just entered the wing so they walked in together and found a spot out of earshot of anyone, to chat.

McFarlane was just doing the rounds of the wings in case there might be anything outstanding. *"How is everything Bik?"* Kelly enquired quietly.

"No problems Kells. This is the last stop of the night. How are you feeling?"

"Sound as a pound a chara. Ready as I'll ever be. I checked all the lads in the Wing earlier and they're up for it. To tell you the truth and I can't explain this, but my confidence has just grown steadily as we get closer to the event!" Just then Kelly's gaze fell on the TV.

He gripped McFarlane's arm. *"Look Bik,"* he whispered nodding his head in its direction. 'I ESCAPED FROM DEVIL'S ISLAND' was emblazoned across the screen. *"Is that a good omen or what?"*

"I certainly hope so," McFarlane answered without changing tone in case he might draw any attention to them.

That was the first thing that came into Kelly's head as he opened his eyes. He smiled to himself but was in no hurry to step on to the bitumen floor which he knew would be icy. He still didn't budge as he heard the morning jangle of keys in gates as H Block 7 came slowly to life.

He listened to the heavy butterfly locks clacking open and the guard's footfall as he moved methodically from cell to cell opening doors. A few moments after the guard opened his door a tall, well-built, balding man in his mid-thirties, filled the doorway. *"How's it going Neil?"* Kelly greeted his comrade as he moved further into the cell. Neil White was one of the key members of the Rearguard, crucial to holding the Block while the escapees made their way out of the jail.

White came straight to the point. *"I've been thinking about this overnight Gerry. There's too much that could go wrong. Someone could be shot or killed. I haven't long left of my sentence to do and it isn't worth the risk for me. It's all right for you and the others, with due respect. You are doing two life sentences with little to lose. It's not as if getting another sentence will make any difference to you. I'm sorry comrade."*

It came out of him in a long rush without him breaking breath. He was embarrassed but not nervous. There was relief on his face now that he had articulated his decision. Kelly instinctively knew that there was no point in arguing with him, though he felt like screaming *"This is the morning of the escape for fucks sake!"*

Instead he said, *"OK Neil, I appreciate your honesty,"* with much more calmness that he felt. White left immediately but Kelly lay on for a few moments with his mind in turmoil. He settled himself after a few moments, got up and went about his usual routine of getting showered, dressed, making his bed and brushing out the cell. No one else in the Block knew and he couldn't talk to any of the other escapees in the Wing anyway. He thought that it might demoralise them-on the basis that it had demoralised him a bit.

Mass would be called in the food hall in D-Wing at about 10am so he would get a chance to talk to Storey and McFarlane then. In the meantime he needed to find a replacement for Neil White rather than present a problem to the team at Mass time.

He went into breakfast even though he wasn't feeling very hungry.

49

After collecting his porridge and milk he sat down at an empty table in the food hall of B Wing to think things out. There was some breakfast banter going on, light-hearted or grumpy, depending on the characters involved. Kelly thought it a bit more subdued than usual but that was no surprise in the circumstances.

As he was about to go for a mug of tea and toast, two comrades sat down at his table. They were close friends and from the same rough area of Belfast. They were both a few years younger than Kelly, in their mid-twenties and had been in Na Fianna Éireann, a militant Republican youth organisation when he was a Volunteer in the IRA in the early 70s. He knew they were solid and also that they had relatively short periods of their sentences to complete, so they would not be going on the escape or know anything about it.

"Maidin mhaith a chairde. (morning lads) Hows it hanging?," Kelly nodded in familiar greeting.

"Dead on Geraldo," answered Ruarai Carberry brightly. *"Sound Gerry. How's it going?"* Padraig Reagan spoke shyly as always.

"Won't be long now lads. Have youse got gate-fever yet?" Kelly continued, referring to the short time they had left until their release. It was often the final period of imprisonment that was hardest to do. Both smiled not wanting to retort anything too snappy or funny on the basis that they knew the comrade sitting across the table was serving two life sentences and 20 years. *"Anybody want tea and toast?"* Kelly asked cheerfully as he rose to get his own, genuinely happier because he had formed an idea.

He returned, after checking there was no one near enough to hear. *"A chairde, I have a wee problem,"* he understated with a smile. *"I need your oath that you won't repeat anything I'm gonna tell you."* Both nodded, interested but a bit worried.

Without naming Neil White, he went on to explain the dilemma of the let-down. He needed them in the end cell of B-Wing closest to the yard gate after the lunch time lock-up. They would be well camouflaged but had to protect the emergency alarm button at that end of the Wing. Under no circumstances could they allow anyone to set it off.

Neither hesitated in agreeing to do whatever was necessary despite the fact that they still didn't know what operation they were a part of. As far as they were concerned the IRA had asked them to be part of something and that was part of struggle. Kelly left them, pleased and proud of the two young comrades. Relief had replaced his earlier anxiety.

Around 9.45am Rab Kerr heard the guard shouting down into D-Wing, *"Kerr for the outside hospital."* He felt the hair on the back of his neck rising. The guard came down the wing looking for him.

"What's it for?" He had been suffering an abscess in his mouth for weeks.

"Operation on an abscess," the guard said.

"That hasn't bothered me in weeks," Kerr said.

"Are you going or not?" The guard asked impatiently.

"No. I am not going as I don't need it anymore."

"Right, then you have to sign a form that you refused medical assistance!"

"Whatever," Kerr replied *"Where's the form?"* He was trying to sound indifferent.

After signing the form he sent word to Storey in C-wing. Storey dispatched McFarlane, after a short discussion, to instruct any escapees that if anyone else was called for the outside hospital or dentist that they would have to go. They could take one refusal but could not risk another, in case it would raise suspicions. It was not easy to get an appointment to an outside hospital so two refusals would be very suspicious.

September 25th
H-Block Lunchtime Unlock

The lunchtime lock-up was always 1 hour 30 minutes, but today it was interminable. A number of the Republican prisoners had only eaten half of their dinner, forcing it down, with nerves tingling with expectation. It ended at about five minutes past two, slightly later than normal, with a shout of, *"unlock"* from the guards and the rattle of keys going into doors up and down the wings. People slid off beds and got up off chairs. Gerry Kelly stood up when the door was unlocked and walked out with a deliberate casualness which belied his state of alertness. Guards were getting on with the day's routine. Everyone was behaving normally it seemed.

Bobby Storey, Bik McFarlane, Gerry Kelly, Brendy Mead and Tony McAllister were the team for the circle area. Rab Kerr and Seán McGlinchey were to take the corridors in between Wings A and B, and C and D. A man was posted in the hobbies room of each of the four wings to ensure that no prisoner, ignorant of the escape, innocently complained to the guards about the obvious shortage of tools, as various handicraft tools had been taken out of the hobbies room to be used as weapons. Since the six handguns had arrived in H7, McFarlane had stored them under the noses of the guards. There were tall, heavy, cupboards sitting against the wall of the corridor which led to the store room of the circle area. They were never moved, but McFarlane had managed to prise a board loose which gave him access to the space underneath. There was a gap about three inches deep to the floor.

That morning he had retrieved them and passed them over one at a time to the Circle Team. They knew they were one gun short and Sean McGlinchey was chosen to do without. Everyone, including McGlinchey knew that he would floor the guard without difficulty.

It was now or never. The moment had arrived with all the ordinariness of a ticking clock. Those who knew about the escape on the Wing glanced furtively at each other but no conversation took place. The time for discussions had passed. Brendan McFarlane was the first to move out to the circle, followed at short intervals by Brendy Mead, Tony McAllister and then Gerry Kelly. All four, armed with pistols, went into the storeroom as if to get Wing supplies, a practice that had been established over a period of time. Large plastic storage bins were moved from the storeroom into the passage way so that any guard who might have wanted to relax or have a quiet smoke in the stores would have to go to the guards' canteen instead. That would make it easier to round them up once the plan was triggered properly.

Brendy Mead had some chewing gum so he broke a couple of pellets in half and handed them out to his comrades in the storeroom. It was up to McFarlane, when he had assessed that the circle had settled into a normal Sunday routine, to call down the wings and ask for the bumper to be brought to the circle. The 'bumper' was an electric floor polishing machine. That call would bring the Escape OC, Bobby Storey, to the circle area and would also alert all those prisoners who had parts to play in the escape that the venture was about to start.

Most of the guards were where they were supposed to be. There should have been three of them on each Wing. On this day, in A-Wing and B-Wing there were two down the Wings. In C-Wing there were two and in D-Wing there were three. So that meant there were three extra prison guards out in the circle area, or in rooms running off the circle.

Four guards were in the canteen. The Senior Prison Officer (S.O.) normally arrived at 2.30pm to relieve the Principle Prison Officer (P.O.) who would leave immediately after being replaced.

Cormac MacArt was one of the regular circle orderlies. But today he had deliberately stayed in C-Wing. He would assist in the Rearguard as he had only a short sentence left to complete. Storey had told him not to be in the circle for its takeover. MacArt was a tough Short Strand man who had a reputation for fighting with the guards over the years. When McFarlane had asked him weeks earlier to start offering to make the guards their tea and coffee, his first reaction was disbelief and annoyance. When he was told it was the IRA asking him, he had relented – very reluctantly. There had been criticism from other comrades that he had 'gone soft' and was 'a changed man'. Now, waiting to play his role, he had told Storey that morning that it was one of the proudest days of his life, no matter how it might end up.

Coming up to 2.30pm Brendan McFarlane was waiting anxiously. He knew everybody was straining at the leash. He had to give the signal soon. In each Wing people were ready. Guards had been shadowed by prisoners having conversations either with the guards themselves or with other prisoners in close proximity to guards. There were three alarm buttons in each of the Wings, one in the food hall, one at the yard gate and one at the top of the Wing close to the corridor between the Wings. All these alarm buttons were being observed and covered by prisoners as casually as possible.

In different Wings there were different methods used to keep an eye on whichever guard the prisoners were designated to watch. In C-Wing Joe Simpson had begun to iron clothes. He had the ironing-board out to block the guard's path to the alarm button on the wall. Paul Kane stood there talking with Joe about football. A couple of minutes later however, the guard left his post and went to the circle area for a tea-break.

At the top of C-Wing Gerry McDonnell and Robert Russell were tidying a pile of newspapers about five feet away from the guard that they were shadowing. Dermot Finucane's role was to cover the alarm button nearest the exit to the circle area from any guard trying to get near it. He was also going to lead the takeover of C-Wing. For that purpose he was standing talking to Seamus Clarke who was across the way in D-Wing. His job was the same as Dermot Finucane's. Seamus Clarke was discreetly guarding the alarm button in D-Wing and ready to alert people into taking over his Wing. Dermot McNally was washing a shirt in the sink, sizing up the guard. The guy looked pretty big and physically fit. It played on his mind for a while but there was no way this guard was going to get between him and freedom.

Terry Kirby was also at an ironing board in D-Wing on duty. Gary Roberts and Peter Hamilton had been primed by Rab Kerr and were armed with a hammer and a chisel. When Hamilton had been told to arm himself with a hammer, he had typically raised his fists like a prize-fighter, saying *"I don't need any hammer!"* But he was given it anyway.

Peter, 'Skeet' Hamilton was a character. A week earlier, he had been playing heavy metal music and digging away at the wall in his cell with a chipping-hammer. The OC had only caught on when he passed him and gave him a friendly slap in the stomach. He had hurt his hand on the chipping-hammer hidden under Hamilton's football top. He spoke to McFarlane and Kelly as both were his friends. When they in turn spoke to Hamilton and explained the complexity of the upcoming mass escape he relented with the words *"for fucks sake Big Nose"* (an endearment he used for all comrades), *"why do all your escape plans have to be at university level? What's wrong with us putting a ladder up against the wall?"* After both men stopped laughing he finished with, *"Youse have two weeks or I'm going back to stone breaking."*

Roberts smiled to himself as he entered the food hall. His position was to watch the guard in the food hall. He picked up a snooker cue and starting hitting balls on the table. Ciaran Jones came in and joined him in the game. Jones was a decent snooker talent, at least by jail standards, but neither of them could pot a ball that day. Roberts didn't know but began to suspect that Jones was also part of the escape plan. At this stage he had settled himself with the thought that a glorious try and failure was much better than not trying at all.

Kerr had quietly passed around a 'teacht' to the potential escapees before the lock-up the previous night. It was from Storey, *"A Chairde, we've broken the prison security. We have infiltrated the ranks of screws. We can escape and we will escape. Keep discipline. Do the part assigned to you and we will succeed. Beirígí Bua (We will grasp victory)."* It was a short and simple communication but a great morale boost which instilled confidence in Roberts. It had lifted his spirits –but he still couldn't sleep.

The alarm buttons at the bottom of each wing were at the furthest points from the circle. Two of the Rearguard, well covered up to prevent identification, were standing in each of the cells right beside the alarm, but out of sight from the rest of the Wing. Their job in each of these wings was to make sure that no guard got to that point. If however a guard moved in that direction, someone, a potential escapee, would have shadowed them as they moved.

The Rearguard was back-up, –it was needed to help. These were men who were not escaping so they were the people who were taking the biggest risks on the day.

Bobby Storey was also standing at a sink in C-wing washing a shirt. Time had slipped beyond 2.25pm, and he was starting to get worried, wondering why the shout had not been made. The shout for 'the bumper' was the essential ticket to get into the circle and start the operation proper. But he continued washing the shirt in nervous silence. He whispered to McCann that he was concerned. The shout had to come in the next couple of minutes. He knew that timing was of the essence and that the kitchen lorry could arrive at any time from 3pm onward. They had to have control of H-Block 7 before it arrived. Time was slipping away and most importantly they had to be at the security TallyLodge at the front gate of the jail in good time before the changeover of shifts at 4pm.

September 25th
South Armagh

T he two Brendans awoke to the sound of a cock crowing. Burns swore and moved deeper into his sleeping bag on the carpeted bedroom floor. Moley on the other hand swore but put his arms outside the bag and stretched his lean frame. His breath clouded in the cold September air. He shivered as he climbed out in his jersey, socks and boxers.

He knew it wasn't a pretty sight but he wanted to feel the benefit of his jeans and outer clothes when he braved the outdoors. He searched around and dressed quickly heading for the bathroom. By the time he got to the kitchen, Magee had the eggs boiling and the bread toasting. The others were in the kitchen or at the table eating. *"Go to work on an egg,"* Magee said, repeating the famous TV ad of the 60s and handing Moley an egg in the cardboard cup of the egg box. The numbers had expanded with a couple of radio men who had been on guard all night. It wasn't long until the 'checkers' landed in with their Jack Russell dogs barking and frolicking away in the yard. They were to check the surrounding fields for British army 'lying patrols' and once checked they would be secured and held for the remainder of the day.

They were all part of the preparation of a military operation but still oblivious to the purpose and target – and no-one asked. They knew it was important, as patrolling all night was a rare occurrence and they had seen the large red box-lorry in the hay shed which was normally used for heavy weaponry operations. It was armoured and its tyres were solid rubber so that they could not be punctured.

When breakfast was finished Magee, Lynch and the two Brendans made off on foot across the fields. They walked about half a mile before Lynch indicated a thick dry stone wall near a stream which he proceeded to carefully dismantle.

He lifted and set the stones down in order, like an archaeologist, with the wet and mossy side up. After going down about a foot he removed a 12 inch heavy plastic pipe capped and sealed at both ends. As Magee emptied its contents Lynch started dismantling another ditch in the same way to reveal another pipe. This was a temporary, moveable, arms-dump which had been prepared the previous week. They took two short arms, a fifty calibre Browning machine gun and saddle, the M60 and seven assorted rifles along with plenty of ammunition, and headed back to base.

They had also taken combat fatigues and had 'gloved up' with surgical gloves inside woollen ones. On arrival at the hayshed they got dressed in combat gear and checked all the weaponry to make sure it was clean and the moving parts were working smoothly, including the rounds in their belts and magazines. As always they spent a lot of time at this so they were confident that firing jams would be minimized. The Browning machine gun was attached to its bespoke mount and Lynch got comfortable with its weight and flexibility of swing and orbit. All the rounds, belts and magazines had been cleaned and wiped in the previous days so the present work was lessened.

At about noon they sat down to a light lunch of tea and various sandwiches. Everyone was in character. The anticipation and adrenalin was building. The mood was serious but with an occasional ice-breaker. Jokes were uneasy as all were locked into the job ahead.

At about 1pm the Brigade OC spoke quietly and clearly, *"It's now or never lads. Everybody knows what they have to do. As usual you may get a surprise or two. Moley is Operational OC so he decides on whatever is necessary. This isn't the hardest or most dangerous op youse have been on but it might well be the most important to date. On this one we can deliver a huge political blow to the Brits without firing a single shot if we're lucky. So - Good Luck!"*

With that they all got up and left. The Brigade OC and Northern Command OC took up positions near the Base radio to wait. The route had already been scouted and the driver had just returned to say that all looked normal for a Sunday. Moley led off in a green Audi 80. He had the engine well-tuned and with a great pick-up of speed if necessary but he wasn't for breaking any speed limits that day.

The escape from H7 couldn't start until after the lunch time lock-up finished at 2pm. But he didn't want to chance being late either and he knew that the lorry would be camouflaged by trees and be off the road once in position.

Just before 2pm Moley indicated off the main road and drove up a narrower side road. The lorry followed. As Moley glanced into his rear-view mirror he thought the lorry was huge, lumbering and conspicuously red against the Autumn green and browns. He was about to swing up the lane to the derelict farm which they had previously selected when he spotted a man walking towards them.

He drove on past and could see the man stop and stare at the lorry which had followed. The man continued to watch as they crested the hill. It was a narrow enough road and Moley didn't want to meet any traffic or be forced to reverse. The derelict farm had been picked for its isolation. He had to drive at least a half mile before a cross roads allowed both vehicles to manoeuvre to go back in the direction they had come.

The road looked clear as the Audi swung up the lane. Burns passed the entrance and then reversed skilfully through the narrow gateway. Just as the cab was moving through the gate Burns thought he glimpsed someone walking on the road but he was committed and swung into the farm yard and behind the row of trees that would hide them from the road. As the back end pushed gently against a fence he stopped and cut the engine. They weren't visible to passing traffic but both realised that the vehicles could be seen by anyone walking. They were a little outside the town, however, and so hoped they would draw no attention.

2.30pm
September 25th
H-Block 7
The Bumper

Brendan McFarlane was surveying the circle. It was 2.30pm. Warder John Adams sat quietly in the control room reading his newspaper, oblivious to all that was going on around him. Two guards passed across the circle, one going to the toilet, the other going to the canteen. In the Principal Prison Officer's office the S.O. and the P.O. were lost in conversation and the circle was empty of personnel apart from the circle guard who had the keys to all gates in the circle area. McFarlane had been waiting patiently for the P.O. to leave the block as he normally did when relieved by his S.O. Today he had not yet left. It was time to move.

"A and B Wing is the bumper down there?" shouted McFarlane. Every potential escapee who heard it felt a surge of adrenalin.

"It's not here Bik," McGlinchey shouted back, as arranged. McFarlane knew of course that the bumper was in C-Wing. In A and B Wings the teams started to move into position and McGlinchey mentally counted down his two minutes wait before he was to move towards the circle with dirty dinner trays. That was his excuse to get into the corridor between A and B Wings. He needed to be in a position to take the guard who sat between those wings and who was also close to an alarm bell. McFarlane took the few steps over to the gate into the C and D side of the H-

Block. *"Sammy,"* he shouted down to the guard, *"Is the bumper down there?"* Knowing that everyone would hear him. Sammy repeated the question down the wings.

"It's here," Storey replied after a very short but deliberate delay. *"I'll bring it out,"* he continued with a mixture of relief and anticipation. Once again the word bumper alerted teams into position. Rab Kerr began his 90 seconds countdown; he was in the other wing. He had to get out with his set of dirty trays so that he could take the guard between C and D-Wing.

Storey let the shirt slide into the sink; and took a deep breath. The shirt had been well washed! He whispered to McCann, *"Can you see the gun?"* McCann assured him that it couldn't be seen in his waistband. Storey collected the bumper from the food hall and made his way through three gates to the circle without incident. He then moved into the storeroom where the rest of the team that would take the circle were gathered. *"How are we all doing lads?"* Storey asked.

"Shiting ourselves," Kelly replied, disarming his comment with a broad smile.

"Likewise." Laughed Storey raising his eyebrows.

After the delay was briefly explained to Storey, Mead said that the S.O. Geordie Smilie was standing in the circle. The first part of the operation was to take over the guards' canteen and it would be very difficult to do this undetected if the P.O. or S.O. were wandering about the circle area. There was a brief discussion and it was decided that Mead should go out and tell Smilie that he needed to speak to him on a private matter. It was imperative that Mead got him back inside the P.O.'s office and kept him there. Storey finished by telling Mead not to produce the gun he had unless he had no choice, at least until the canteen guards were arrested.

Brendy Mead went out to S.O. Smilie making up a hopefully believable story as he walked. Smilie was coming to look right into the storeroom corridor anyway. *"Geordie,"* said Mead, his voice quivering a bit, *"I have to see you about a personal problem. It's sort of wrecking me. Do you think you could give me a few minutes?"* S.O. Smilie sensed Mead was in some kind of trouble. *"What is it? What's wrong kid?"* He asked.

"I've got to move out of this Block, the IRA is going to do me!"

"Why?" enquired Geordie Smilie, intrigued. Mead continued, *"Look I need to talk to you privately. Can we go into the office and talk about this please?"*

Smilie couldn't resist the plea in Mead's voice, so he said *"OK kid, come on."* Off they went into the office. Mead closing the door behind them.

McFarlane moved over with his mop and bucket to cut off the welfare office, because there was both an alarm and a phone in it, but a guard had moved in just in front of him. *"I've to clean the office, what are you doing?"* McFarlane said sharply deliberately showing annoyance.

"It will be a while Bik," the guard replied with a bit of a laugh. *"It's 13 digits!"*

McFarlane's heart sank. *"13 digits where the hell are you phoning?"* He almost barked back but at the last instant forced a laugh he didn't feel. *"Canada,"* said the guard laughing again, *"You don't expect me to run up a bill in my own house! I have to do it while I'm in work so that the government pays."* McFarlane watched him lift the phone as he started to dial a number.

The other four in the circle squad were quietly psyching themselves up in the storeroom when McFarlane rushed back to

64

the store and hurriedly explained the dilemma to them. It was a delay they couldn't afford. There was no option. McFarlane would have to go over and urge the guard out of the office. If that didn't work he would have to be arrested and the operation kick-started immediately. McAllister followed McFarlane out so he could report back on what happened. Bik was thinking as he was coming through the grille ready to have some sort of small argument with the guard over having to clean the Welfare office. Just as he came out through the grille into the circle, the guard came out of the office smiling broadly. *"By the way Bik I was just phoning my mate in H-1 to swap over some evening duty with him. Fooled you!"* McFarlane, greatly relieved, laughed out loud and went in to the Welfare office. He poured copious amounts of liquid polish on the floor. He put the mop and bucket across the door as if he was still working at it, to prevent anybody else from going in. He quickly returned to the store to report events to the others.

When he had finished he asked the circle-guard to let him out through the grille to clean the entrance hall to the Block. This positioned him beside the guard he was to arrest. Meanwhile Rab Kerr and Sean McGlinchey had left the empty food containers out at the grilles of the circle area. They talked football and cracked jokes across the circle at each other from behind the grilles that led to the wings, allowing them an excuse to linger for a while. They were working in tandem, trying to get their timing right. They were too far away from their allotted guards, however, as they sat at the far end of the corridor where the wings met.

In between A and B Wings and between C and D-Wings there was an observation hatch into the Wing food-halls, situated much closer to the alarm bells and guards. Kerr was between C and D-Wings, McGlinchey was between A and B. They were looking through these hatches as if they were trying to draw the attention of someone in the canteen. This was a common practice that the guards paid no attention to. Both were waiting on the signal from the circle that would let them know that they should take the guard between the wings which in turn would simultaneously set off the operation to take each wing.

There was a guard on duty at all times in the enclosed circle area whose job was to open and close all the gates leading off the circle area. Nobody could get into or out of the circle without him opening the gates. McAllister moved out of the store as planned and asked the guard in the circle if he wanted a cup of tea. As expected he indicated that he did. McAllister then moved into the guards' canteen as if to make the tea. Storey and Kelly were listening to all of this intently. Moments later, it seemed to them too quickly, McAllister came out and told the guard in the circle that his tea was ready. The guard then moved into the canteen. At this point Kelly and Storey moved into the circle area. The grille gate to the store room area was the only gate that was left routinely open during the day for ease of access. Storey left Kelly outside the door and moved into the canteen behind the guard – this was the prison officers' mess. Kelly stood at the Welfare office between the front hall grille and the guards' canteen. He was alone now in the circle area, waiting for Storey to re-emerge.

Storey closed the door of the canteen and he and McAllister pulled out guns from their waistbands. The guns were small .22 and .25 calibre weapons. They appeared especially small for someone the size of Storey who fitted the gun in the palm of his hand without any problem. They chose two guards of the four now in the canteen and pointed their weapons at them in dramatic firing stance. *"Get on the floor and do it quietly,"* ordered Storey, in no more than a loud whisper. He was trying to balance an authoritative voice while containing this part of the operation solely between the four walls of the room. There was a shocked silence. The guards were looking at the firearms in disbelief.

Storey cocked the weapon throwing a round up the breach for effect. He was keenly aware that the weapons were not impressive in size. Immediately all the guards except one got down on the floor. McAllister had a weapon with a homemade silencer fitted. If there had to be any shooting this early in the operation it would have to be done by him using the silencer, so as not to compromise the escape. McAllister's job was to cover the guards and only shoot if the operation was in jeopardy.

Harry Reynolds was the guard still standing, he was rotund and in his forties. At about 5ft 7in he must have been twice the weight he should have been. Generally there was little harm in him. He was best known for falling asleep on duty. Storey looked at him; there was no point demanding the impracticable. He pulled a chair over. *"Sit on that and don't move or he'll shoot you,"* Storey said matter of factly pointing at McAllister.

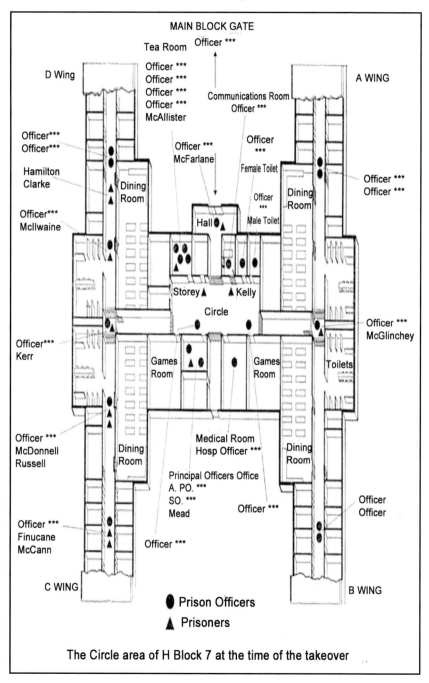

The Circle area of H Block 7 at the time of the takeover

The Circle
Pebble in the Pool

Kelly stood with his back against the wall. At that precise moment he felt extraordinarily alone in the administration 'circle' of H-Block 7 in the centre of the most notorious prison in Western Europe. It was 2.40pm. He touched the small calibre pistol hidden in the waistband of his jeans.

Kelly was listening intently and heard the muffled sound of Storey cocking his handgun and giving commands. Chairs and tables were scraping the floor as he and McAllister took control. He still didn't remove his own gun in case anyone emerged from any of the other side rooms off the circle area. Minutes later (it seemed much longer) Storey emerged, leaving McAllister to guard the guards. He looked at Kelly with a half smile twitching the corner of his mouth. There was no need for talk. Kelly had been psyching himself up for the next move.

This was the crucial point where the operation proper began. The whole of H-Block 7 had to be taken over with synchronized actions within the space of a few minutes.

As soon as Storey started walking away from the guards' canteen he started a ripple effect. It was like dropping a pebble into the centre of the pool that was H7. The concentric ripples were to go evenly through all the wings. Within moments the Irish Republican Prisoners expected to have arrested 24 prison guards;

have covered 20 emergency alarm points; seven phones and two intercoms and two-way radios; have secured the Emergency Control Room and every other nook and cranny of H7.

Simultaneously Kelly and Storey moved off in different directions. Kelly moved sideways past the metal grille that led to McFarlane in the entrance hall. That was the only sign needed. As Kelly went out of sight reaching the Emergency Control Room, McFarlane pulled his gun. As McFarlane was making his move, so was Kelly. He slid his right hand under his tee shirt as he came into sight of prison guard John Adams who was on control-room duty that day. In Kelly's hand was a small calibre pistol. He had practised this moment many times in the quiet of his cell.

They had discussed the psychology of the operation, knowing that no love was lost between guards and prisoners – especially those who had suffered through the protest years. Discipline was crucial to stop any deterioration into vengeful activity. The instruction to all Volunteers was simply *"use verbal aggression so that physical aggression is not necessary."* He moved into an aggressive firing stance in front of the grille gate between the guard and himself. The weapon was already cocked and ready to fire. Holding it rigidly in both hands with his arms at full length he moved swiftly forward until the gun sat unobstructed between two of the gate's bars. The guard was sitting as expected, at the table. Within reach he had two intercoms, a two-way radio, a phone and crucially a red alarm button. Looking over the sights of the weapon straight at his face Kelly very deliberately, very sharply said, *"Do not fucking move or I will shoot you. Now, do exactly what I tell you!"* He was concentrating on Adams' face watching for the slightest wrong move. He needed the guard's immediate and singular focus. Kelly needed him to believe that he had no choices, that the gun was real and that he would use it if necessary.

There was a split second while the guard made up his mind whether the Republican prisoner would fire. The guard did not move. Kelly continued speaking with deliberation. *"Do exactly as I tell you and you will not be harmed. Put both hands on your head."* The guard moved slowly to put both his hands on his head, Kelly assessed that Adams had made his decision, so he continued with the momentum. *"Do not touch anything. I want you to get down on your knees, nice and slowly."* The guard did as he was instructed. *"I want you to listen to me very carefully. Put one hand down on the floor. Now the other."* At this stage the guard was on his hands and knees. *"Now lie on your stomach. Put your hands back over your head."* Adams did everything that he was told.

Kelly put one hand in through the bars and pulled back the large bolt on the gate and swung the gate open. He now had an uninterrupted view and contact with the guard. He said, consciously using his Christian name to ease the tension a little, *"John, we have taken over the Block and we are well-armed. If you do what you are told there will be no problem. If you do not do what you are told then you will not make it through today, do you understand?"* The guard made no reply. Kelly let it pass. He continued, *"If anybody phones or comes through on the intercom or on the radio to see if there is anything wrong, ask them what the problem is. When you are told, tell them that you'll check. Go back after 30 seconds and tell them everything is OK no matter what they indicate the problem is."*

The guard looked up from his prone position with some difficulty. Kelly could guess he was calculating what he might or might not be able to do. He said, *"What if they don't believe me?"* Kelly moved down onto one knee in front of him without breaking eye contact and still pointing the gun with practised coldness said, *"John make them believe you."*

The control room was the nerve centre of the H-Block and getting the guard on the floor without incident was important, Kelly felt relieved it had gone so smoothly.

When Kelly had passed the double grille on his way to the control room, McFarlane knew it indicated that the operation proper had started. Unfortunately the guard that McFarlane was supposed to cover had stepped outside for a smoke. Forty yards away was a second guard. He was at the front gate of the compound enclosing H7. McFarlane had a silencer on the weapon. He knew that his was the most vulnerable position if a shot had to be fired as he was within earshot of the guard at the gate of H7 who could not be arrested just yet. He needed to keep things quiet.

He tucked the weapon behind his back, opened the door and said to the guard, *"The P.O. wants you in the circle for a minute."* The guard took a final draw from his half-smoked cigarette and squashed it underfoot and moved back inside. As he came through the door McFarlane had a last glance down towards the Block gate. The guard was in his hut and had not moved. McFarlane closed the door after the hall-guard. He produced a pistol which looked more formidable than the others as attached silencer added to its bulk. He wanted the guard to believe that the weapon was real. He pushed it into his ribs and spoke tersely, *"You are under arrest. Get onto the floor,"* and pushed him down with his other hand. The guard went down in some shock and lay with his forehead on the floor. McFarlane covered the guard's head with a pillowcase, as was planned, so that he did not know what was going on from moment to moment and that he could not identify any other prisoner except for McFarlane. At this point he searched around the guard's waist and relieved him of his keys which were needed to unlock the entrance hall area of H7.

Storey's next task in the circle, after taking the initial steps in the guards' canteen along with McAllister, was to create the pebble effect by walking across the sight lines of the corridors leading to A and B Wing on one side of the H and C and D-Wings on the other. He also had to sweep around the circle to make sure that all the rooms were searched and empty. This included the medical room, the toilets, the governor's room and the Welfare room. Storey was to check and clear any room that was in the circle area which had not already been cleared.

He reached the medical office door and tried to open it but it was locked. The hair on the back of his neck rose in an uncomfortable tingle. He rapped the door and a voice shouted, *"What do you want?"*

Storey answered, *"I have cut myself, I need to see you. Open the door I'm bleeding."* The medic was taking his time. Storey's imagination was in overdrive at what might be happening.

"I'll be out in a minute" the guard called out.

"Please Mister. The blood's flying out of the cut on my hand!" Storey emphasised fear in his voice to convey urgency. He also used 'Mister' as the guards liked the term even though republicans would seldom use it. In the couple of seconds it was taking the guard to get to the door, Storey was worried about the alarm-bell in the room or the guard being on the phone. Had he heard anything? The M.O. was taking too long to open the door.

Storey decided to kick the door in. As he stepped back for a forceful kick, he heard the key in the lock. The M.O. was opening the door. Storey was on him in a second, gun at chest level. *"Were you on the phone? What were you doing? What took you so long?"* The medic was in some panic. He was focused on the gun Storey was holding.

He said, *"I didn't do anything, I was sleeping."* At this point Storey lowered his voice and his heart rate.

"You are under arrest, get on the floor!" He put him on the floor

in preparation to move him across to the canteen. In the circle, the guards were to be moved from one point to another on their hands and knees, because there were alarm buttons at chest level that they could dive at too easily. The precaution was n e c e s s a r y because in the circle the ratio of prisoners to guards favoured the guards.

The Control Room H7

Storey herded the M.O. across the floor from the medical room towards the canteen. As they moved across the circle the door of the male toilets opened and Raymond Doherty, a tall guard of over six feet came out. He was looking down adjusting his trousers and had moved two or three steps out before he realised what was going on in the circle. Kelly, who was concentrating on the guard on the floor of the control room, heard the door opening and saw him out of the corner of his eye. He thought there was no-one else now in the circle to arrest this guard. He swung the gun round at shoulder height and arms length and shouted at Doherty, *"Don't move or I'll blow your head off."*

The guard raised his hands with incredulity. He started to stagger backwards towards the toilet door. Kelly didn't want him back in the toilets, as he knew there were windows facing onto the yard and front gate of the block which could be broken to warn the guard on the main gate of H7. So he looked directly into the guard's eyes above the gun-sight. He moved towards him and said, *"If you go any further I will shoot you!"* The guard stopped. Kelly told him to lie down on the ground with his hands over his head. He started to get down on the floor.

The control room guard saw this as his opportunity to move. He was lying face down, his head out towards a door which opened inwards. It was lying open against the inside wall of the control room. While the metal grille gate had been opened outwards by Kelly earlier, the inside door was opaque. The door was close to his left hand; he reached over in an instant, gripping the edge of the door and slammed it shut.

Warder Doherty was by then on the ground. It was as if the door had slammed right inside the heads of both Kelly and Storey who were in the circle area at that moment. It galvanised them into action. They saw the closed door, immediately thought of the number of intercoms, telephones, two-way radios and alarm bells in the H7 control room. One leapt towards the door. He put his hand on the door-knob and in one motion turned it and hit the heavy door with his shoulder. The door opened about two or three inches only. The guard was obviously pushing against the door. While he was not very tall he was heavy, weighing maybe 200lbs. The prisoner put a foot in the door to stop it from closing further and started to push hard. He got another one or two inches out of it. It was hard work. There was little give. The only comfort was that he knew that while the guard was concentrating on trying to close the door he couldn't be near the phones or intercoms. He squeezed the gun round the door and fired a shot at waist level on the blind. The gun went off with a bang but the door didn't give. Shifting the angle of his wrist up very slightly, he fired another shot.

The H-Blocks of Long Kesh was said to be one of the most secure jails in Western Europe, with each block designed to be a jail within a jail

The door gave way and he pushed it open wide enough to squeeze through. The guard was lying on the floor in a heap. He opened the door to its full extent and looked at the guard face down on the floor. He was completely still.

This was a defining moment in the escape. Everyone who had embarked on it knew that something like this could happen. It had been agreed that verbal aggression should be used liberally by the Volunteers so that as little physical aggression as possible would be necessary. Up to this point the psychology had worked well. However, Volunteers were clear that if it was necessary to use force to physically protect Volunteers or to safeguard the escape then there could be no hesitation.

The two Volunteers were fairly sure that the guard had not had the time or space to set off the alarm but they couldn't be totally sure. However, everyone in H7 now knew that the guns were not toys and that the escape was for real.

Storey had been moving the M.O. across the circle area towards the canteen when the door of the toilet opened and Kelly spun round to face Warder Doherty. The imperative now was to pass the M.O. to Tony McAllister and to check the other rooms of the circle. McAllister had moved to the canteen door. He had heard the shots and wanted to know what had happened. There was no time to explain. McAllister was told to hold his position. Warder Doherty was then moved over to the canteen.

When Doherty was safely in the canteen the door of the other toilet was opened by another guard. Kelly could not believe it. A guard was lying on the floor bleeding and still in the control room. Thoughts were racing through Kelly's head. He wondered if Adams would recover. He also knew he needed to be replaced just in case any alarm went off. He had already called for assistance from medical officer Nevins who was now in the guards' canteen. While he was working this out the door of the toilet opened and out came Reggie Leeks, an Englishman and an ex-British soldier. He was buckling his belt as he came out. He obviously hadn't heard the shots and didn't realise what was happening. Very quickly, as he raised his head, the scene told the story.

Kelly turned, pointing the gun straight at him. He repeated what he had shouted at others that day, clearly but with some exasperation, *"Put your hands in the air. Get down on the floor or I will fucking shoot you!"*

Warder Leeks instantly assessed the situation and raised his hands in the air. He was instructed to get down on his knees and then down on his stomach, which he did. At that stage Storey had come out of the canteen and took Leeks across on his hands and knees past the control room. As he moved past the control room Leeks looked in and saw his colleague lying there. He moved on more certain of the new realities and dangers. He was taken into the canteen to join the other guards who were being gathered in increasing numbers.

When Storey emerged again to talk to Kelly and assess the situation he heard noises from behind the closed door of the Principle Officer's room which lay directly across the circle from the canteen. He had sent Mead in earlier to take the room because P.O. Smilie had been a problem standing in the circle area. Mead's job had been to secure this room containing the P.O. and S.O.

When Storey opened the door there was a row going on. It was obvious that the shots had been heard and had triggered a reaction. P.O. George was on the floor but S.O. Smilie was refusing to go down. Rather than use his weapon, Mead, who was one of the fittest Republican prisoners in the camp had punched him hard. Smilie still refused to go down and had himself landed a punch to Mead's face. An ex-paratrooper, Smilie was sizing up the situation and wondering if the weapon was real or if Mead would use it. Storey could not tolerate the delay. Other rooms had to be secured and already he had triggered Sean McGlinchey and Rab Kerr into action between the two wings by simply walking into their line of sight in both corridors leading to A and B Wings and C and D-Wings. *"Get on the floor,"* Storey spoke clearly to Smilie as he pointed his gun at him. Smilie didn't move or answer but Storey, entering the scene armed, had an impact.

With both Mead and Storey pointing guns at him in his own office in the middle of a top security prison, a new reality was dawning. Smilie stared stubbornly back. Storey couldn't wait. He took two steps over to P.O. George, put the gun to the back of his head and without turning around to Smilie said, *"Get on the fucking floor or I will blow his head off."* Smilie lay down on the cold polished bitumen.

The circle in H7 following the escape — on the left of the
picture is the bumper which was the signal for the
takeover of the block

The incident had taken seconds but to Storey, the OC in charge
of the whole operation it seemed like many lost minutes. *"We
can't afford this shite,"* he said loudly to the room in general while
addressing Mead, *"If either moves again shoot them both!" "Do
not hesitate!"* He added sharply for effect. He moved out of the
P.O.'s office into the circle area again. He noticed that
McGlinchey had floored the guard between A and B Wings and
hoped all was going smoothly. He glanced over his left shoulder
to observe Kerr in a similar position with the guard between C
and D-Wings.

At this point, in a matter of minutes, the circle and nerve centre
of H-Block 7 had been taken over by the Republican POWs.
When Storey had walked from the canteen, Kelly had moved to
take the control room. By simply walking past the grille, Bik
McFarlane had known to take the guard at the entrance hall of the

79

block. When Storey walked towards the medical room he passed the two corridors leading to the wings.

The two Volunteers in these corridors, Rab Kerr and Sean McGlinchey, knew that it was their turn to move. Kerr moved into the sightline of both Wings and without speaking, produced an automatic pistol. Kerr arrested the startled guard in the small area between C and D-Wings. He grabbed his head with his left hand and pushed the gun into the temple with his right. The guard froze and was pushed to the floor. Kerr produced a pillow-case and put it over his head. At the same time he reassured the guard that providing he did what he was told, he would come to no harm.

When Kerr moved to arrest the guard, that was the signal to the other volunteers in both C and D-Wings, to move to take their targeted guards. One or two of the guards down the wings had of course seen the actions of Rab Kerr and Sean McGlinchey but it was too late for them to react. As Kerr and McGlinchey were taking the guards between C and D-Wings and A and B-Wings volunteers in each wing moved to arrest their guards. In C-Wing McCann leapt towards his guard, gripped him in a tight head lock and forced him down onto the ground. Gerry McDonnell and Robert Russell did the same. In D-Wing one guard initially resisted and received a slight stab wound to the shoulder, but the wing was secured within seconds with the minimum of injuries.

Sean McGlinchey did not have an automatic weapon; he was armed with a chisel because there had only been six guns. Between A and B wing he moved towards his guard, and overpowered him. In A and B-Wing the other POWs had moved on the guards and pushed them to the ground, putting pillowcases over their heads to subdue them. The Block was now in the control of the political prisoners. One other guard had resisted and received a blow with a hammer but again the injury was not life threatening.

Each of the eight H-Blocks contained in the prison acts as a jail within a jail and while all the internal doors, gates and guards were held, there remained one obstacle to securing H7 completely. Every Block leads into the wider jail and there is a guard manning the security airlock at the bottom of the yard. This is the entrance gate to the H Block. This had to be taken and this job was left to McFarlane and two other Volunteers, Sean McGlinchey and Joe Corey.

It had become common practice for McFarlane to go out to brush the yard and also to go down into the entrance airlock and brush around that area. But he couldn't do it on his own. He was always escorted by at least one guard. To cover this on the escape, Corey and McGlinchey had already dressed up as guards and were standing at the entrance door to the Block, some 40 yards away from the front gate. McFarlane made his way down the yard. The other two prisoners walked down behind him, as if they were there to guard him. They stayed far enough away from the guard on the gate, however, in case he might recognise them. They stopped a good distance from the gate to talk to each other, all the time being aware of where McFarlane was and what he was doing.

When he got to the airlock, the guard opened the small pedestrian gate thinking there was nothing unusual happening. He had seen McFarlane on a daily basis and had also seen his escort. He let McFarlane in. *"Are you here to brush up?"* The guard asked rhetorically. McFarlane immediately produced the weapon, put it into the guard's side and retorted *"No! I am here to arrest you. Let's go."*

He then handed the area over to Corey and McGlinchey. The airlock had to be held until the escape vehicle, the kitchen lorry, arrived with its daily delivery. Other deliveries could have arrived such as newspapers or Block supplies. There had to be a guard on duty to assuage suspicion or to take necessary action. These

81

Volunteer's could not wear hoods of course, so all they had were the guards' uniforms as a disguise. McFarlane moved the guard back into the block and passed him over to the team who were handling all the other guards.

It was 2.50pm. Bobby Storey, the leader of the escape had entered the circle area of the H Block just after 2.30pm to start the operation. In less than 20 minutes Irish Republicans had taken control of H Block 7. The scene was well set for the most spectacular escape in recent British penal history. But there was some way to go before it could be a successful one.

H-Block 7
Taking Stock

It was time to take stock. Storey read down his checklist on the clipboard he had prepared. He called to the wings to find out what the injuries there were, if any. Those now in charge of all the wings reported back: -

"A-Wing under control. One injured slightly."
"B-Wing under control. No injuries."
"C-Wing under control. Two injuries - minor."
"D-Wing under control. One slight injury."
"Do any need medical attention," Storey shouted in each case.
"No," was the consistent answer.

However, the guard in the control room had regained consciousness. He was talking, and he certainly needed medical attention. Storey called for two Volunteers to come to the circle. Medical officer Nevins was escorted back out of the canteen and told to examine the control room guard. Before entering, Kelly told him that he would have to move on all fours because of the alarms, phones and intercoms.

He carried out his examination and said that he believed that the guard needed to be brought to a hospital immediately, as he feared that he might go into shock which could be a dangerous complication. Both the M.O. and the injured guard were assured that they would be given all necessary medical assistance.

However, they were also informed that he could not be removed from H7 until after the operation was completed.

The M.O. was escorted to the medical room to get supplies. A medical futon was put into the control room and the injured guard was helped on to it. He was then pulled out lying on top of the futon to the nearest available room where the M.O. attended to him. A member of the Rearguard watched over them.

When Storey got all the reports from around the Blocks and people were moving into positions, he turned to the problem of replacing the guard in the control room. Warder Adams was thought to be a bit volatile and unpredictable and a guard called Bobby Harra had already been chosen to replace him. Storey moved down the Wing, shouting Harra's name. Harra feared for his life. He already had his shirt removed because all the guards' uniforms were being collected for use in the second phase of the escape. When Storey spoke to him the guard was very, very nervous. But after explaining to him exactly what he had to do, Harra knew there was no point in resisting and moved towards the control room.

Gerry Kelly once again went through the instructions that he had given Warder Adams in the case of any inquiries by phone, radio or intercom especially from the emergency control room situated deep inside the administration area of the jail. Harra seemed a bit too nervous for the task in hand so Kelly set about trying to settle him. He needed the guard to be calm. He was told to sit on the floor against the wall and was given a coat to keep him warm. He was told to ease his breathing, to take long deep breaths and that he would be very safe if he did what he was told. The emphasis with Harra was to settle him so that he could speak normally if the need arose. When he calmed down he was instructed to lie prone on the floor again. The alarms were temptingly close.

At this stage none of the guards knew what was to happen. In

84

fact the Volunteers who had not already been briefed did not know there was an escape either. In the minds of both guards and some prisoners it later emerged they were worried that this may have been, the beginning of a revenge attack on the guards. Many of them had, after all, been part of a regime which had systematically beaten prisoners during the blanket protest which had gone on in the jail for over five years. For some of them this thought was uppermost in their mind. The report back that Storey had asked for from the various wings had a number of purposes: One was a situation report and to check if there was any unforeseen developments. Another part of it was to calm the situation down, to let everybody breathe easy. Most important of all was to let everyone in the Blocks, Volunteers and guards alike, know that the Republican POWs were now in charge.

Of the 24 guards on duty inside H7, 11 were in the Wings and the rest were in the circle or administration area. All of them under the control of the Volunteers, all of them guarded and all of them on the floor, with pillowcases over their heads. The only exception was one heavy-set guard called Harry Reynolds who was well over 25 stone. When an attempt was made to tie his hands behind his back, it caused him so much strain that Storey told McAllister to tie his hands in front of him and let him sit on a seat as it would be too hard for him to get down and up from the floor.

The silence that had settled on the wings was broken in one instance by a prisoner called Duffy, who knew nothing of the escape and had heard none of the commotion from his cell. He had been listening to heavy metal music on a radio. He emerged from the cell walking up the wing, arms swinging, whistling away, without a care in the world. Oblivious to what was going on around him, he raised his head as he moved towards the toilet area. His eyes widened and the swing diminished. He slowed down and then stopped in complete disbelief. He stood about 15 feet from the scene at the top of the wing. Amid laughter which broke the tension, Joe Simpson pulled him gently by the arm and led him into the wing food hall.

All cell windows had been closed, so the guard who was on duty at the main gate of H7 could not hear what was going on. The canteen windows had also been closed to keep any possible noise within the confines of the H-Block itself. After McFarlane arrested the guard at the gate of H7, McGlinchey and Corey took over the front gate duty. Normally only one guard was on gate-duty at any time but two prisoners in guards' uniform were put on just in case any difficult situations might arise.

The entrance to H-Block 8 was situated directly opposite to the H-Block 7 entrance, which was only 30 yards away. Fortunately it was unoccupied at the time. Therefore no guards were on duty, a fact which had played a part in choosing H 7 as the escape block.

Bobby Storey again checked the clipboard list he had meticulously prepared. The next thing to do was to bring all the guards who had been arrested in each wing into cell 26 which was known as the 'big cell' or 'double cell' in each wing. The guards needed to continually be reminded that the prisoners were in control. They were all brought in one at a time. As each one was brought in they were stripped to their underwear as their uniforms were needed. They were all given a poncho made of blankets so that they would not be left half-naked or cold. All the uniforms that had been taken off them were put into brown bags. Each bag was marked 'small,' 'medium' or 'large' depending on the size of the guard so that Volunteers who had to wear them could more easily choose the right size of uniform to fit.

At this point other POWs came out to the circle. Seamus McElwaine and Seamus Clarke took up positions behind the bins at the front gate, in order to escort anybody back to the block who might have been arrested by McGlinchey and Corey. Peter Hamiliton tied up the P.O. and S.O. in the P.O.'s office and Robert

Russell and Denis Cummings tied up the other guards. Marcus Murray stood at the door to watch the front gate and alert Storey to any developments, including the arrival of the food lorry.

Paul Brennan in A-Wing had been one of the three Volunteers watching Warder Billy Ward. Ward was of a slight build but was reputed to have a black belt in karate. The Volunteer's had instructions to move on him fast and together. In the event, Ward was quickly subdued.

Brennan's next job was to assist at the control room. Events in the control room had prevented him entering it so instead he wandered from wing to wing, observing.

When he had been approached originally by Seán McGlinchey it was to take part as a member of the Rearguard because he had only three years left on his sentence. Once he was made aware of the escape, however, he insisted that he be allowed participate. When he heard the shots he started to regret fighting so hard to be an escapee! He was convinced the escape was over and had failed. It was obvious that the guards could not believe what was happening. However, as the minutes passed and there was no counter reaction to the shots, Brennan became more confident again seeing his comrades continuing with the plan. In any case, he had committed himself and he certainly wasn't going to let his comrades or the IRA down.

Once all the guards had been arrested and pillowcases put over their heads to prevent future identification of prisoners, the next part of the escape was to bring out the Rearguard. They were dressed in makeshift hoods and ponchos. Amongst other things they were instructed to keep talking to a minimum and were not to refer to each other by name. They were to take over the duties of watching the guards, thus freeing up the escapees. This allowed the escapees to prepare for the arrival of the food lorry and to allow time for those prisoners who needed to don guards' uniforms, to search out the right sizes.

No one who volunteered for the Rearguard had more than three years left on their sentences to serve. In fact, some Volunteers had only days or months before release and had everything to lose if they were caught. They had no guns. Only when British soldiers or the RUC came into sight would they know to lock themselves up.

Yet they had not hesitated, such was the bond of comradeship. As the Rearguard moved into position they all knew that a guard had been shot and that the stakes and danger had increased tenfold. It was likely that any prisoners left behind would feel the wrath and brutality of a vengeful prison administration. Still they volunteered.

It took about fifteen minutes to move all the guards from cell 26 in each wing to the education room, which was off the hallway connecting C and D-Wings. They were tied together in pairs at the wrist. All the guards at this stage had pillowcases over their heads. While they were very loose, some of the guards found it hard to breathe, so the Volunteers guarding them lifted up the pillowcase with one hand and waved small table tennis bats like a fan with the other. One person took all the guards' names in the order in which they were sitting. This was just in case any one of them had to be called for, if a phone call came from outside or inside the prison for a particular guard. There needed to be immediate access to keep things running smoothly.

The P.O. was tied to the chair in his own office and one of the Rearguard was watching him in case there might be an incoming phone call he would have to answer. He had been warned, as other guards had been warned, to answer as instructed by the Volunteer guarding them. Meanwhile in the circle, 13 prisoners donned the guards' uniforms. Nine of them were to take the Tally Lodge at the main gate, one was to be in the front of the cab and the others were potential replacements in case of an emergency.

The circle was awash with Republican prisoners. The Rearguard was taking over positions from the escapees and some escapees were changing into confiscated uniforms. There were clothes, boots, belts, braces and shoes lying all over the place. It had the appearance of chaos, but in actual fact people knew what they were doing and they were making sure they were getting their part of the overall work done.

Peter Hamilton and Brendy Mead had been detailed to question guards about their cars' exact location in the car park using maps prepared earlier. The car park in question was situated outside the perimeter wall of the prison complex, but still within the British Ministry of Defence perimeter. Peter Hamilton warned the guards again that if they told lies, they would be shot. He told them that they would be able to cross check this information with comrades and other guards, and if information came back different they would be in deep trouble. This scenario took place with a number of guards so there was the possibility of having a selection of car keys for the 'Tally Lodge squad'.

The squad who were taking over the Tally Lodge and who were planning to hold it while the main bulk of the prisoners got away in the lorry, could then take the cars and follow them out some minutes later. Kieran Fleming went into the classroom and read out a prepared statement designed to deter any guard from brutalising those prisoners left behind in the Block after the escape, or at least to help lessen any potential attacks post escape.

To all prison staff who have been arrested by Republican POWs on Sunday, 25th Sept.

"What has taken place here today was a carefully planned exercise to secure the release of a substantial number of POWs. The Block is now under our control. Anyone who has been assaulted or injured was a a result of his refusal to cooperate with us. It is not our intention to settle old scores, ill-treat or degrade

any of you regardless of your past. Though should anyone try to underestimate or wish to challenge our position, he or they will be severely dealt with. Anyone who refuses to comply with our instructions now or in the future will feel the wrath of the Republican Movement.

Should any members of the prison administration ill-treat, victimise, or commit any acts of perjury against Republican POWs in any follow up inquiries, judicial or otherwise, they will forfeit their lives for what we will see as a further act of repression against the Nationalist people.

To conclude we give you our word as Republicans, that none of you will come to any harm providing you co-operate fully with us. Anyone who refuses to do so will suffer the ultimate consequence - death! Allow common sense to prevail. Do not be used as cannon fodder by the prison administration or the faceless bureaucrats at Stormont and Whitehall."

Camp Staff Republican POWs.

The written statement was then left deliberately for the prison authorities to find.

Subsequent to this, after the escape, unfortunately, there were systematic attacks on prisoners left in H7. However, it may have cut the edge off some of the worst brutality.

To all Prison Staff who have been arrested by Republican P.O.W.s on
Sun 25th Sept.

What has took place here today was a carefully planned
manoeuvre to secure the release of a substantial number of P.O.Ws
The block is now under our control. If anyone has been assaulted
or injured it has been a result of his refusal to co-operate
with us, it is not our intention to settle old scores, ill treat
nor degrade any of regardless of your past. Though should
anyone try to underestimate or wish to challenge our
position, he or they will be severely dealt with. Anyone who
refuses to comply with our instructions now or in the future will
feel the wrath of the Republican Movement.

Should any members of the prison administration ill-treat,
victimise or commit any acts of perjury against Rep. P.O.Ws in
any follow up inquiries, judicial or otherwise, will forfeit their
lives for what we will see as a further act of repression
against the Nationalist people.

To conclude, we give you our word as Republicans that
none of you will come to any harm providing you co-operate
fully with us. Anyone who refuses to do so will suffer
the ultimate consequence - death! Allow common sense to prevail
do not be used as cannon fodder by the prison administration nor
the faceless bureaucrats at Stormont & Whitehall.

                    Camp Staff Rep. P.O.Ws

Copy of handwritten statement

3.30pm
September 25th
H-Block 7
The Food Lorry

T he food lorry was expected at the gate of H7 at about
3.15pm. It was late. At 3.30pm a prison van delivering
Sunday papers arrived at the front gate. McGlinchey and Corey,
the two Volunteers manning H7 gate, tensed in anticipation.
McGlinchey tightened his grip on the pistol in his uniform coat
pocket. They were near the pedestrian gate which appeared
locked but which they had unlocked for ease of access if needed.
He spoke to Corey, also adrenalin fuelled, who had his back to
the gate. To all the world it looked like a casual Sunday afternoon
chat between colleagues, as McGlinchey watched the dark blue
transit van intently from under his peaked cap. *"It's doing a U-
turn in front of the gate Joe. I'll do the business if it needs it ok?"*

"No problem Sean," replied Corey not knowing exactly what
McGlinchey meant but ready to go along. All Corey knew was
that his comrade could see what was happening and he would do
back-up if required.

The van contained a guard driving and a prison orderly. After U-
turning, it barely stopped for the orderly to open the door and
throw the small pile of Sunday newspapers to the ground. As they
quickly drove off McGlinchey waved his free hand but they paid

Front Gate of Block

no attention to him. *"The Sunday scandal sheets Joe,"* grinned McGlinchey and slapped him on the shoulder. *"Here look at the headline: 'Corey leads mass escape from Kesh!'"*

"Aye. Well don't count your chickens just yet," Corey retorted. They wouldn't have to commandeer or shoot - for the moment at least. It occurred to the Volunteers that it was just like any other newspaper delivery to a shop in town.

Just as the van disappeared the food lorry came into sight. McGlinchey and Corey opened the first gate to allow the lorry into the airlock – the area between the outer and inner gates at the entrance of H7. The two volunteers tried to keep things looking normal. As the driver positioned the food lorry in front of the gates he turned to Desy Armstrong, the orderly sitting in the passenger seat and said, *"That's odd, isn't it. There is only one officer supposed to be in the airlock, but there are two of them."* Armstrong had noticed it as unusual as well, but just shrugged.

"Maybe it's changeover or one's just down for a yarn," he said

feeling compelled to make a comment. By then the first set of gates were opened and the guard moved the lorry forward. As it drove in between the two gates one of the uniformed prisoners locked the outer gate again while the other walked round, opened the other gate and let the lorry pass on through. Both Republicans made their moves while trying to face away from the driver in case he recognised either of them. The kitchen orderly sat quietly. He was a Republican from another block. From the spot at the front door of the block, Marcus Murray saw the lorry and told Storey that it was on its way up the yard.

As pre-arranged Storey, Kelly and McFarlane took up position and walked out to meet it. The lorry as always did a U-turn in the yard and reversed back to the hall entrance door to make loading and unloading easier. Storey opened the driver's door and Kelly pulled the driver out. McFarlane arrested the orderly, Desy Armstrong, at the passenger's side.

In the discussions about this part of the operation, it had been decided that Storey would do the talking and that Kelly would take an aggressive stance while saying very little. So Kelly put the gun to the driver's head while gripping his arm tightly and frogmarched him into the circle. The whole idea was that the guard would see that the block was in the total control of the armed POWs.

This guard was crucial to the escape. The kitchen lorry had to be driven out of the jail. It wasn't supposed to go out of the jail, even in normal circumstances as it was an internal vehicle only. However it had become the habit of the prison staff to use the lorry to do 'homers.' Basically that meant using the prison vehicle to move house or shift furniture, or carry out various odd jobs. Most of the guards accepted and welcomed this as normal practice.

Warder McLaughlin, the driver, was crucial to the success of the escape. He had to be frightened into believing the prisoners were in charge and to realise he had no choice but to do as he was told. Of course he also had to be calm enough to do the driving. There was no point in him being a nervous wreck or showing his nerves. Like the prisoners involved in the enterprise, he would have to pass other guards as if he hadn't a care in the world. So the psychology involved in this was to let him know Republican prisoners were in complete control, but to let him know that if he did anything wrong that retribution would be immediate. If he acted as he was told then everything would be O.K. The scene was being set for him. That was why only Storey would speak to him initially.

As the driver was marched into the circle he saw a number of masked Republican prisoners and a number of others in uniform that he assumed to be Republicans. He saw a number of pistols and ammunition lying about on tables. The idea was to overawe him and he was overawed.

Storey was talking to him all the time as they walked, *"The Irish Republican POWs have taken over the Block. We are in charge. You need to know that if you do what you are told you will be O.K. Any of the officers who did what they were told are safe. One who did not was shot. You do not want to face the same situation!"* He nodded towards Kelly. *"The man who is holding you at gun point is serving a number of life sentences. He will have no hesitation in shooting you should you disobey any order he gives you at any time. He will be in the cab of the lorry with you and be sure, even among Republicans he is known as a ruthless bastard!"*

Kelly, who had been listening to this unscripted monologue had not expected to hear Storey describing him in this way. He could think of nothing else to do but growl menacingly. *"Alright,"* Kelly deepened his voice and gave his darkest myopic stare, since normally he wore strong spectacles. Warder McLaughlin stared back at him in some shock and horror. The grip tightened on the drivers arm as he was led over into the medical room. As he pushed McLaughlin through the door, Kelly looked back at Storey *"Ruthless Bastard??"* He mouthed with raised eyebrows. Storey winked at his comrade and entered the room.

The medical room had been transformed into an operations room. There were four homemade maps up on the wall with lots of detail on them. One was of the entire prison camp. Another showed the route that the lorry was to take to the car pool, where the lorry was to be parked, near the Tally Lodge. Yet another map revealed the carpool itself, showing exactly where the lorry was to be parked. The final one showed the route the lorry was to take exiting the jail.

The driver was placed in front of the maps. Storey started talking again. *"This Block is now in the hands of the Republican prisoners. We will not let this escape be messed up by you or anyone else. Be sure and certain of that. If you do what you are told you will not be harmed. John Adams has been shot because he did not do what he was ordered to do. Do you understand?"* The lorry driver replied in a stronger than expected voice, *"Yes."*

"Do you want us to show him to you as proof of our intent?" The driver answered with a subdued, *"No."* Storey pointed to Kelly again, *"This Volunteer will remain with you throughout the escape. He will travel with you in the cab. He has nothing to lose. In a few minutes you are going to be brought out to the lorry. You are the one who is going to drive the lorry out of the jail. Your foot will be tied to the clutch. Under your seat will be a hand grenade. A string will be tied to the pin. Your door handle on the driver's side will be smashed off and this man will be lying on the floor of the cab during the whole journey. If at any time he believes you are even attempting to alert anyone, if you act in the wrong fashion, if you deviate from the escape route through the jail – and he knows the precise route you have to take – if at*

anytime you try to drive the lorry anywhere else off this route, he will shoot you and pull the pin. He will have seven seconds to get out of the lorry. In the confusion of the shot and the explosion we will continue the escape. There are two ways that this escape is going to succeed. It is going to go ahead either way. One is that you and all your colleagues will be unscathed if you do exactly what you are told and none of the guns have to be used again. The other is that you and some of your colleagues and possibly prisoners may be injured or worse."

After listening and observing the driver, Kelly believed that the driver understood the predicament he was in and would make the necessary choice.

Storey left for a couple of minutes to let the driver think about this, and he had other work to do. Kelly stayed with the guard. Under gunpoint he put him on the floor face down and told him to take it easy. *"I am just going to frisk you to make sure you are not carrying anything you shouldn't be,"* said Kelly and proceeded to search him. Kelly felt it odd to have roles reversed in such a dramatic way that the prisoners were searching the guards. Most of it was to let Warder McLaughlin know that the Volunteers would be competent and professional but also ruthless if they thought it necessary.

Everyone knew that the guards never carried weapons inside the jail. The British army patrolled the perimeter and the military posts were manned and heavily armed, but the prison staff had to leave their personal weapons in the prison armoury while they were on duty. After a few minutes Storey returned, and asked him how he was doing. The driver replied, *"Look, I don't want anything to happen to me or anyone else. I will do exactly as I am told."* This was what Storey and Kelly had been waiting to hear.

They exchanged glances, but there was still some more

psychology to be sorted out. The driver needed to know that they had the full knowledge of the lorry's routine. Storey said to him: *"We know the lorry is not searched when it is passing through any internal gates even though it should be under regulations. So there is no need for you to get out of the lorry at any point. Isn't that right?"* The driver didn't want to answer. *"We also know that although this is an internal vehicle it is quite often used outside the jail by staff to do homers. Isn't that also right?"*

"Yes, but it will be searched if it's going out the front gate," replied the driver.

"Let us worry about that one," replied Storey.

Storey then went over the maps in front of the driver explaining what his instructions were and what exactly he should do. The driver listened carefully. They went over it two or three times and he indicated that he clearly understood what was expected of him. Glances were again exchanged between the Republicans. Storey decided that the guard was ready.

At this stage Kelly was the only prisoner, supposed to be wearing a uniform, who had not actually put one on because he had been guarding the lorry driver. He spoke to Storey quietly and someone else was sent in from the Rearguard to replace him with instructions not to have any conversation with the lorry driver whatsoever.

As Kelly exited the medical room he almost bumped into a guard at the door. He jumped back startled and started to raise his handgun. *"It's me Gerry, Ciaran"* said the guard. *What do you think?"*

Kelly relaxed, going red with embarrassment at mistaking his comrade for a guard. It was Ciaran Jones. *"You definitely look the part Ciaran especially with the moustache!"* And so he did.

Jones was not an escapee but was part of the Rearguard who were starting to take over positions from escapees as they prepared to get on the lorry. In Jones' case, he was in full uniform in preparation to take over from McGlinchey and Corey manning the entrance gate to H7. Someone had to hold the gate area while the escapees made their way out.

It was in fact the most vulnerable position for anyone on the Rearguard as he could not wear the handmade hoods that the rest of the Rearguard were now wearing. He would be there to accept any delivery or vehicle that might arrive while the lorry moved towards the perimeter of the camp. The false moustache was his only disguise along with the peaked cap of the guard's uniform. He had argued vehemently with the OC to be allowed on the escape but he had been refused on the basis that he had a very short time left to serve of his sentence. Yet he had still volunteered to take this most vulnerable post to assist his comrades to escape. *"I couldn't get the moustache to stay on so I had to use superglue,"* Jones laughed.

"Well you fooled me big effort and I have known you for years," Kelly said encouragingly.

Kelly went off to get a uniform. Unfortunately he couldn't find a uniform that would fit him well because he was the last one to dress. The shirt was torn down the back so that it would fit at the front. The tunic was slightly tight and the trousers were about four sizes too big but the bottom half of the uniform did not matter a lot. So long as he looked the part to anyone looking into the lorry, it should be okay. He managed to get a cap that fitted and then he returned again to take control of his captive.

Marcus Murray from Fermanagh had taken over at the front door from McFarlane once H7 was secured. He had let Storey know when the food lorry arrived. Then he unloaded most of the food containers to make room for the escaping prisoners. Following that, he broke the handles of the driver's door so that the driver could not easily get out of the cab.

After Kelly had put on a guard's uniform he, and Marcus Murray then brought the driver out to the lorry. He was told to get in at the passenger's side as the driver's door had been closed and the lock had been broken. He could also see a string coming out from underneath his seat. The lorry driver's foot was tied to the clutch. The uniformed Kelly got up into the cab and lay on the floor along the well of the cab. While the lorry driver had been briefed by Kelly and Storey in the medical/operations room, the other escapees were being loaded into the back of the food lorry. The count was 37 POWs in the back, plus Gerry Kelly in the front, making a final count of 38 potential Republican escapees leaving *"the most secure prison in Europe."* And by the front gate!

The prisoners who were not going on the escape or were not involved in the Rearguard had all been locked in their cells. The cell cards that indicated who inhabited each cell were all removed by the Rearguard so that there would be confusion as to who had escaped and who had not. This would force the administration to go through a process of individual identification which would cause a considerable delay. It would give the escapees outside extra time before their photographs would appear on the media.

Only the Rearguard was out on the wings when McFarlane went down to his cell to get changed into the uniform he had picked up earlier in the operation. The cell had been locked. He called for the keys to be brought down and changed quickly. He then grabbed a bag of clothes that he had also prepared earlier. While he was on his way back, one of the Rearguard approached him. He had not recognised who it was because he was fully disguised, until he spoke. Then he recognised the voice. His comrade said, *"Good Luck, Bikso."* He replied, *"Thanks mo chara, I hope to see you again some day outside of here of course!"* At that he moved off. Time was moving on. The Block had now been in the hands of the prisoners for over an hour. It was almost a quarter to four.

Storey knew the shift change in the Tally Lodge was at 4pm and it was going to be a busy time. He was standing in the circle checking every name as they got into the lorry. Those wearing uniforms were kept to the back and put into the lorry last because they were going to have to come out of it first. Everyone was shaking hands or slapping the backs of the Rearguard as they left but very little was said. The Rearguard was anxious about the safety of the escapees and the success of the operation. The escapees were also thinking of what kind of revenge the guards might take on the Rearguard and the rest of the lads who had stayed behind.

McFarlane brought the orderly round and put him in the passenger side. He was already well briefed and told to do exactly what Kelly said. Desy Armstrong was to sit up on the seat. The journey started when the hydraulic tailgate was raised and the back of the lorry closed.

"No talking, not a single sound!" Was Storey's instruction as the shutter closed off the light. Everybody settled down unto the floor of the lorry and Seamus McDermott, the rearguard OC, rapped the side of the lorry in a heartfelt gesture to his comrades.

The driver turned the ignition key and for a number of seconds the lorry turned over without starting. All 38 Republicans held their breath. The ignition key was turned a second time, again it turned over but didn't start. On the third attempt all hearts were thumping with anxiety when the heavy diesel engine shuddered into life. On the floor of the cab Kelly sighed with relief. The prisoners in the back were having a similar collective experience.

The lorry moved off towards the airlock at the front of H7. The gate opened swiftly and the escape entered another phase. The

Aerial view of Escape route

lorry turned left as it normally would and then, at the corner of the block, it turned left again. After travelling about 150 yards it turned right towards the airlock which contained two gates and a guard on duty between them. The first gate was opened and the tension mounted in the back of the lorry. Storey was listening intently.

One uniformed escapee was ready to take the guard's place if anything went wrong. Joe Corey was praying under his breath because he had volunteered for the job. From his position on the floor of the cab Kelly was also listening to see if the guard would come over to have a conversation with the lorry driver. As it happened, nothing was said. The guard recognised Davy McLaughlin driving and let the lorry through the gate without hesitation.

As the guard opened the second gate the driver swung the lorry to one side. Kelly, lying in the well of the cab could see this as he looked up through the windscreen. He tensed immediately, as he knew the escape route was straight ahead. He pushed the gun into the driver's abdomen, worried that they were going off route. The driver corrected the swing and straightened the lorry up. He had pulled off a bit too enthusiastically, before the gate was fully opened and was simply giving the gate a wide berth. *"It's OK,"* the driver whispered quickly to Kelly, *"I am going straight to the main gate."*

To the relief of both Kelly and the driver, Kelly pulled the pistol back along the seat a few inches. All those in the back of the lorry were oblivious except for a few moments of nervous glances between Storey and McFarlane who had also been momentarily startled by the swing of the lorry.

Joe Corey let his breath out long and quietly. He was delighted with himself. His grin was lost in the darkness. He had got past that point without a hitch. If Corey had had to take over at the gate he was then to make his way back to H-Block 7 if possible once the alarm had gone up, to help with the Rearguard and go back into his cell. For Corey that would have been a disastrous plan B.

The next obstacle was the 'administration gate', which led into the main gate area which was a 'prisoner-free area'. Normally after going through the second gate the lorry would have turned right, towards the kitchen but this day he was going straight on. While it was not the normal route it was not so extraordinary a direction for this lorry to take on a Sunday. As Davy McLauglin drove down Kelly reached up and tugged the orderly Desy Armstrong by the coat. Armstrong moved down onto the floor. The orderly was not permitted beyond the administration gate. No unauthorised personnel could pass that point as it was entering a restricted area. Kelly realised that they were passing the prison hospital where ten comrades had died on Hunger Strike in 1981, just two years previously. He remembered a particular, vindictive prison governor saying to him in its aftermath, when he was in the punishment block, that the only way Republican lifers would leave the prison would be in a brown box. They were about to, not just prove him absolutely wrong, but to cause a huge political crisis within the British administration by their actions –he hoped!

Others in the back of the lorry were feeling a mixture of heightened anticipation tinged with dread. They were all now past the second set of gates. Another obstacle overcome, they were into a different phase. In the back of the lorry their eyes had got used to the darkness. It wasn't totally black. There were small shards of sunlight getting through the gaps in the sides of the lorry. People could see each other's faces at this stage. Peter Hamilton, who was a Leonard Cohen fan, was whispering one of his songs. "Like a bird on the wire, Like a drunk in a midnight choir, I have tried in my way to be free." smiling all the while. *"What?"* whispered his comrade sitting opposite *"Nothing,"* he mouthed back, realising that he had been whispering audibly.

Excitement was building among the 37 prisoners in the back of the lorry. They knew that they were getting closer to the outside, even though most of them didn't know exactly where they were at that point. The next gate was into the Main Gate area, and the car park known as the 'van pool.' When the guard on duty saw the lorry coming, he started to open the gate. He noticed that there was another guard sitting in the passenger seat. He was whistling and joked with the driver whom he knew, *"You're always doing Sundays Davey, you must love this job."* The prisoners in the back listened for anything which was out of place but the gate swung smoothly open and the lorry passed through turning left up into the car park not far from the Tally Lodge.

Kelly moved off the floor to sit in the passenger seat and ordered the driver to reverse up towards the inner perimeter wire fence next to the wall so that the back of the lorry could be obscured more from the British Military post because of the angle of the fencing. This allowed the prisoners with uniforms to get out of the back of the lorry which they duly did, quietly. There were a few things that had to be done before the lorry drove off again towards the Main Gate airlock. The Tally Lodge team which vaulted over the back of the tail gate were Bobby Storey, Bik McFarlane, Brendy Mead, Sean McGlinchey, Rab Kerr, Eddie O'Connor, Denis Cummings, Jimmy Burns and Harry Murray. They straightened their uniforms and got ready.

The metal shutter was then pulled down again. Since there were only six pistols, the one that Kelly had was needed for taking over the Tally Lodge. So while Storey went to the other side of the cab and spoke quietly to the driver, distracting his attention and reminding him what his job was during the rest of the escape, Kelly slipped the pistol out of the passenger window to one of his comrades who replaced it by giving him a wooden replica weapon. This had been made by Gerry McDonnell in the handicraft room in A-Wing. The replica actually looked more real than the genuine .22s and .25 calibre weapons. This passed off smoothly and the huddle of prisoners dressed as prison guards gathered at the side of the lorry. The next phase of the operation was about to begin.

Harry Murray's nickname was 'Norman Wisdom' after the comedy actor, because at times he got on like the comic and he was always cracking jokes. When Storey moved back to his comrades and away from the cab Harry said to Storey, *"Is there not supposed to be nine of us?"*

Storey replied *"Yes there is."*

"Well," he said *"there is only eight of us."* Storey could feel the blood drain from his face. He didn't need any further delays. Thinking there had been a mistake made he started to count them, *"one, two, three, four, five, six, seven, eight, nine,"* he counted. Harry looked at him and said *"No. There is only eight!"* And started counting himself again, *"one, two, three, four, five, six, seven, eight,"* and then with sudden realisation he said *"Oh fuck! I forgot to count myself. You're right, there is nine."* Storey was relieved but too tense to laugh. There was however one or two nervous giggles among the others.

Storey focused everyone's attention by simply saying *"Is everybody ready? Right, into designated groups."* They moved off across the car park towards the Tally Lodge. At this stage all of them knew that the twenty minutes or so delay in the lorry coming into H7 had put the schedule off. They knew they were running close to a staff shift change. The original plan had been based on there being about six guards manning the Tally Lodge and perhaps one or two others coming in and out as was normal. It all went to plan, there were plenty of prisoners and indeed weapons to be able to take control.

4pm
The Main Gate Area

Half way across the van pool area Storey tipped his hat, which gave the signal. Kelly ordered the driver to slowly drive the fifty yards towards the Inner Main Gate. As the prisoners and the lorry headed towards the first of the two huge gates at the main airlock a very tall prison guard came out of the Tally Lodge. Bobby Storey was 6ft 4 inches but this guy was about 6ft 7 inches. It was a new experience for Storey to be looking up into someone elses face. He stared at Storey who, realising that he had been recognised, immediately put his gun to the guard's abdomen and told him that he was under arrest. Storey knew he could not be seen from the closer of the Brit watch towers by the Tally Lodge itself. The guard couldn't believe what was going on. Storey insisted by pushing the gun harder into the guard's stomach. He was arrested and then handed over to McFarlane who took him back towards the Tally Lodge.

All nine of the prisoners in the Tally Lodge squad were now taking in the detail of the jail plans that they had studied and were marked indelibly on their minds. The Tally Lodge contained all the security passes necessary for going in and out of the prison. It was the main security check for everyone and it was crucial that it should be taken quickly and cleanly. All of them were getting into character and starting to behave like guards.

A view of the Tally Lodge and inner main gate from the inside of the jail

Inset into the huge perimiter wall of the jail was the green Outer Main Gate. This was a large, heavy hydraulic gate. Beside that, there was a pedestrian gate through which most of the guards would walk. The hydraulic gate was only for vehicles to enter the air-lock between it and the Inner Main Gate. Here a guard was expected to come out of the Tally Lodge and unlock the gate as the lorry pulled up. The Tally Lodge was nearly the full length of this airlock, sitting on the other side of the 18ft wire fence along with the transport office. There was a corridor on one side of the Tally Lodge through which the guards came in. On the opposite side there was another corridor through which the guards would exit. It operated on a one-way system. All the prisoners involved in its takeover had studied the layout. They knew the PO's office, the tea-room, the tally-room and the search areas. They knew exactly where to go. Once they entered they would split up into two teams to take control, both inside and outside of the Tally Lodge.

The Tally Lodge Team of Republicans were standing along the outside back wall of the portacabin as the lorry trundled over. As it approached the Inner Main Gate, a guard came out of the portacabin and Kelly surreptitiously nodded. McGlinchey, waiting for the signal, then moved out from the cover of the portacabin's wall with a newspaper covering the gun he was carrying. He moved towards the guard, greeting him casually. The guard had already automatically started to open the gate at this stage. While McGlinchey spoke to him, he was very aware that at the other end of the airlock, just above the main gate, there was a British soldier in a watch tower. The soldier was armed and his job was to scrutinise all that was going on around that area.

McGlinchey moved the newspaper carefully and showed the gun to the guard, using his body as a barrier to the line of sight of the British soldier. *"Do what I say or I'll shoot you. Behave normally."* McGlinchey spoke stern-faced and followed up with a huge grin just in case his facial expression could be seen from the watch-tower. He went on to emphasise to the guard that if he didn't do exactly what he was told he would be shot. McGlinchey then escorted the guard back inside the Tally Lodge. Murray, who had followed McGlinchey, took over the post. He allowed the kitchen lorry into the main gate airlock and closed the Inner Main Gate as would be normal practice. Thus began this important part of the escape which involved taking over the Tally Lodge and the entire Main Gate security area.

The plan at this point involved arresting all of the guards in the Tally Lodge and at the main vehicular gate and the pedestrian gate. Any guards going off or coming on duty were to be arrested and held in the Tally Lodge. Kelly was then to get on the floor of the lorry again, and Harry Murray and Robert Russell in uniform, and with three external passes, were to sit on the passenger seat. The lorry with 33 escapees on board was then to go through the main gate and drive about 600 yards to the external gate in the

British Army Camp perimeter. Five men – Rab Kerr, Dennis Cummings, Jimmy Burns, Eddie O'Connor and Brendy Mead – were to hold the Tally Lodge until the lorry was clear of the camp.

Outside the prison which is surrounded by a two mile long 18ft high concrete wall, there is British Ministry of Defence land. About 30 yards from the prison perimeter wall and running roughly parallel most of the way round it, there are coils of barbed wire which stretch some 12ft wide and 4ft high. Armed British soldiers and guards with dogs patrol these areas.

A huge area, immediately outside the prison to the south and east is taken up by a British army camp. It was a secure or sterile area and only people with passes could travel through it. The procedure for leaving this area was also known by certain members of the escape team. The guards going off duty would drive along the road beside the perimeter wall until they came to a pole-barrier, which was usually open during the busy period of staff shift-changes. They would stop their car and walk to what was called the 'External Tally Lodge,' which was part of the British Army camp area. There, a guard would hand in his external pass in return for an ordinary playing card. The suite of the deck of cards changed every day according to the daily code. The guard would then get into his car again, drive the short distance of about 20 yards to the external B.M.O.D. gate which was staffed by a prison guard and a British soldier armed with a pistol. He would hand in the playing card and drive through the gate out of the camp and onto a public road.

The lorry was to follow the exact same procedure on the day of the escape. If, at the External Tally Lodge, a search of the lorry was attempted (which would have been an unusual occurrence) or a guard on duty recognised Russell as he exchanged his external passes, then the guard was to be arrested. Russell had volunteered in such a situation to stay behind to be picked up by the Tally Lodge Team who were to leave the camp five minutes after the lorry   They would be in a car which would be commandeered from a guard on duty in H7 who was still captive there.   The plan was to rendezvous some miles away with a heavily armed group of IRA volunteers from the South Armagh Brigade. The hope was to be in safe houses by the time the news of the escape broke publicly. But as often happens with the best laid plans, things don't necessarily go according to plan.

3.55pm
Tally Lodge at Main Gate

T he Tally Lodge Team split into groups as they crossed the van pool area. McGlinchey and Murray were to take the first gate and the guard staffing it. Storey, Kerr, Cummings and Burns entered the Tally Lodge through the exit door of the incoming corridor and Burns went into the first room which was the P.O's office.

On entering the Tally Lodge Storey immediately encountered two other guards. He arrested them and brought them into the tally-room where Kerr and Cummings had already arrested a number of guards. The staff in the Tally Lodge initially thought it was a training exercise and Storey, in a guard's uniform at the time, removed the peaked cap and spectacles he was wearing to convince the S.O. that it was for real. Storey was immediately recognised.

Mead, McFarlane and O'Connor entered the outgoing corridor of the Tally Lodge. O'Connor took up position at the door to arrest any guards coming off duty. The guard who Storey had arrested in the van pool was put face down on the floor. The Tally Lodge had the normal six guards in it plus about six extra guards. They were taken quickly. Mead and McFarlane then moved swiftly out of the Tally Lodge down to the pedestrian gate to arrest the guard on duty there.

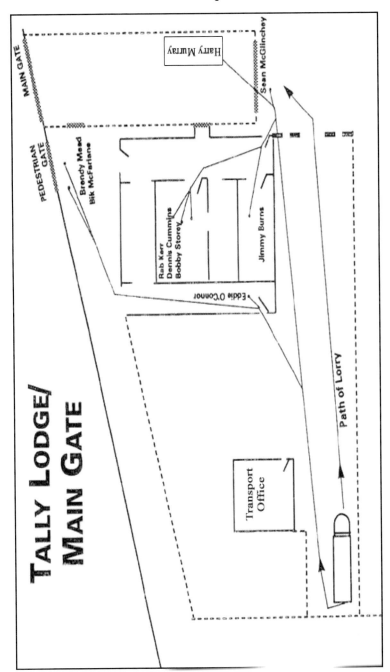

Storey went to the transport office, a smallish hut which sat behind the Tally Lodge. There he arrested the guard and brought him in to O'Connor. McGlinchey brought in the guard that he had arrested at the inner main gate and he was put into the tally room with the rest. Murray reported that there was no-one in the vehicle-check hut. The orderly, Desy Armstrong, who had been in the lorry was brought into the tally room and left there in captivity with the guards.

The door to the PO's office was directly across the narrow corridor. Burns entered, withdrawing the pistol from his tunic pocket. The Senior Officer was alone sitting at his desk. As Burns entered the S.O. raised his head and found himself staring into the barrel of the pistol. *"Irish Republican prisoners. Get on the floor, facedown,"* Burns intoned clearly. The guard froze so Burns repeated the order. The guard moved into a press-up position on the floor of the small office but did not go fully down. Burns, impatient now, said, *"I said, get down on your fucking stomach,"* and pushed into his shoulder blade with his free hand. The guard was rigid and mumbled something, Burns now exasperated, lifted his foot and planted it heavily between the guard's shoulder blades forcing him down on his stomach. He realised that the guard was either in shock or working out a possible move, either way he needed to show who was in charge. *"Your shirt isn't too white now big lad,"* he said removing his foot from the guard's back and closing the door over enough that he could watch the guard and outside at the same time.

The Tally Lodge and main gate area were now under the prisoners' control at this point. When Mead and McFarlane had moved to arrest the guard on gate duty at the pedestrian entrance at the perimeter wall, the guard realised something was wrong at the last moment. He threw his keys onto the floor of the guard-hut. He had however already unlocked the pedestrian gate knowing that it was a staff shift change period and scores of guards would be passing in and out of the gate. It was Mead's brief to take his place and he did so while McFarlane escorted the guard into the Tally Lodge to join the others who had been arrested. Mead was working out how to make opening the gate look normal without the ability of locking and unlocking it. He had no key but did have one of the long heavy key chains that prison guards carry as part of their uniforms.

There were TV monitors at the front gate through which Mead could see who was coming to the pedestrian gate. Mead wedged his foot firmly against the gate, holding it shut and giving the pretence that it was locked. Four guards arrived. He took a deep breath, rattled the long, metal key-chain against the gate and then opened it. The guards just moved on past him, ignoring him as their daily routine unfolded. He kept his cap down and they took no notice of him as they walked into the Tally Lodge. There, they were arrested and put on the floor. Rab Kerr was tying the hands of all those who were arrested with strips of bed sheet.

Mead was repeating his actions, becoming practised at it. At the start he had actually asked them for identification and some of the guards were slegging each other about this guy being a *"super screw,"* looking for I.D. Mead saw the double-edged humour of it but decided not to smile. He stopped asking for I.D.s after that. The numbers were getting greater but as they entered the Tally Lodge, everything was running smoothly. However, groups of guards were appearing on the monitor at regular intervals. After a short while, Kerr had to give up trying to tie their hands together: it was becoming impossible because of the growing numbers being arrested.

The late arrival of the food lorry at H7 was telling now. The delay meant that the Tally Lodge was being held at the start of a major shift change with substantial numbers of guards moving on and off duty. Within about ten minutes, Kerr and Cummings had up to thirty guards under arrest. At first they had them just lying on the floor, then sitting on the floor. They were starting to pile up and this was in the tally room alone, which was a small room the size of a town house kitchen.

O'Connor, McGlinchey, Murray and Burns were arresting guards going off duty and they were having the same problem. Storey and McFarlane were arresting guards coming through the pedestrian gate.

At one point a guard, entering the Tally Lodge, who was told to lie down drew his baton and attacked the Volunteer. He was stabbed once in the side with a narrow chisel. Two others behind him saw the fracas and also drew their batons. They too were stabbed. All three were quickly arrested and put on the floor. The captured guards were starting to become emboldened because of their increasing numbers. They were shouting and making attempts to get up. There was a growing belief amongst the guards that the prisoners were small in number and could be overrun.

Shortly after the tally room was full beyond capacity, a phone rang. Immediately Storey and McFarlane grabbed P.O. (Principal Officer) Wright who was in charge. They told him to answer the phone. He was warned to be very careful in what he said and to ask what the caller wanted and, if there was any problem, to give very sensible answers. They then moved close so they could listen to the conversation. The P.O. lifted the phone. It was the Emergency Control Room (ECR) which is at the nerve centre of the overall jail complex. If any alarm goes off anywhere within the prison, this is where it shows up on a control panel and they must follow up on any problem.

The guard on the other end of the phone asked, *"Who's that?"* P.O. Wright identified himself. He was told an alarm had been set off in the Tally Lodge. P.O. Wright said, *"No. I don't think so. Which alarm was it?"* The guns that both Storey and McFarlane had touching his temples pressed into his head a little tighter as a warning. The guard on the other end of the phone replied that it was the one under the television. Storey and McFarlane scanned the room to find the alarm button. Sure enough, there were guards clearing an area around the alarm bell which was under the television in the corner. They were crawling away from the wall-mounted alarm, cartoon like, not wishing to be blamed for setting the alarm off.

P.O. Wright spoke calmly into the phone: *"I see it now but it's OK. Someone must have triggered it accidentally."* When the guard in the ECR then instructed him to re-set the alarm. He spoke slowly and deliberately, *"How do you reset the alarm?"* When he said this McFarlane and Storey immediately knew that he was trying to warn the ECR, because everyone, including prisoners knew exactly how to reset an alarm. They automatically pushed the muzzles of their guns tighter against the guard's temples.

Instead of picking up on this last ditch effort at warning, the guard in the ECR said dismissively, *"Push the alarm button back in, you stupid bastard!"* and hung up the phone. P.O. Wright turned white and sank sweating into the chair. Storey and McFarlane were too relieved to smile at this ironic twist. Instead Storey spoke loud enough for all to hear, *"Count yourself lucky you are not fucking dead after that little conversation!"* At which point they hauled him back onto the floor.

However, the prisoners in the Tally Lodge were under growing pressure, they were now knee-deep in guards sitting and lying about the place. The guards were getting cockier, shouting and starting to rise up. They had to be threatened on a number of occasions. At the same time out at the pedestrian gate, Mead had to continually let more in. Sometimes he was turning his back while they passed him as if he had something else to do.

At one point when he turned back round there was a guard

standing there looking at him. Mead said, *"Do you want something?"* *"Yes"* he said back, *"I am your relief. Give me the keys and away you go."*

Off the top of his head Mead said, *"Look I am in a bit of bother with the Chief. Could you go to the Tally Lodge and if he's there let me know. He was looking me earlier."* The guard who basically didn't care said, *"That's your problem mate not mine."* Mead stepped towards him and in another attempt to wrong foot him, said sharply, *"Were you drinking? If you don't go in and see the chief for me I am going to let him know that you're drunk."*

Just then the door of the Tally Lodge opened and a guard came tumbling out, followed by Kerr wielding a gun. The guard who had been talking to Mead, looked at him, looked at the gun and recognition came over his face. He began to shout, *"Don't shoot me! Don't shoot me!"* and tried to run out through the gate but Mead grabbed him and pushed him back. He tried again so then Mead punched him hard. McFarlane and Storey had come out. *"Get him into the Tally Lodge,"* Mead said urgently, Storey lifted him bodily and carried him in.

The British soldier sitting in the lookout post stared down and Mead wished he could do something sensible to allay his suspicion. The original plan was quite obviously running into trouble because of the earlier delays. Instead of having to deal with a small number of guards in the Tally Lodge and then letting everyone move on, the Tally Lodge squad were involved in fights and arresting guards. Trying to guard them and keep the escape going was becoming increasingly more difficult. Trying to make sure alarms were not raised seemed much more unlikely but they still hoped to restrain all the guards.

Kelly was sitting in the front of the lorry, holding the driver. He had got him to manoeuvre the lorry into a position that would cover a lot of what was happening in front of the Tally Lodge.

However, there was a fenced-in passageway outside the Tally Lodge that led to the pedestrian gate. There was some serious fighting going on in that passageway. The British army watchtower was within 15 yards of it. The British soldier had seen the fighting going on within the pedestrian walkway. Kelly was constantly and surreptitiously looking up to see what the soldier was doing. He had as yet done nothing drastic. The explanation of that became clear later on in the court case when the British soldier gave evidence that he had only seen guards fighting guards, as far as he was concerned. No shots had been fired at this stage within his sight or hearing, although there had been some fist fights.

However, Kelly's job was also to keep the driver calm and focused. In trying to keep him calm he was engaging him in a conversation about jobs and family, however surreal the situation appeared. Ironically, Kelly believed, the driver was also trying to keep him calm, because he had been told by Storey earlier, that Kelly was a mad man likely to shoot him. Recognising this, he spoke, *"What's your name?"*

"Davy McLaughlin."

"Are you married?"

"I am."

"Have you kids?" He said

"Yes, I have."

"How much do you earn?"

The driver turned to him and answered with feeling, *"Not near enough for this craic!"* Kelly gave an involuntary laugh despite himself.

At this point McFarlane had come down to test the hydraulic lever on the main vehicle gate. The huge gate shuttered in momentary movement. Satisfied and without opening the vehicle gate further he returned to the Tally Lodge. A short time later while McFarlane was out in the pedestrian passageway the small wicker gate opened and one of the guards coming on duty recognised him immediately and started to blow his whistle. Others then joined in. McFarlane walked past the opened window on the passenger side of the lorry and said quietly to Kelly, *"The balloon's up,"* and walked on.

South Armagh Brigade
IRA
Scarva, County Down

Burns jumped down from the cab of the lorry and said to Moley that he thought he'd seen a walker just down the road a bit. Moley found a position near the road where he could see more clearly while the others stood close to the radio they had brought to listen to the police messages on any incidents.

Then a few minutes later Moley appeared beside the other three. *"There's a guy down at the gate. He has seen the lorry and I think he's coming in. I think it's the same guy we passed earlier. He's an older man but looks a bit military and definitely nosey. Here he comes!"* Moley interrupted his own flow. *"We have to take him."*

The man was getting closer as Moley watched his progress peering under the lorry. *"As soon as he turns past the front,"* he whispered. He motioned Lynch to make his way under the lorry to the other side to cut him off. Lynch removed the Browning 9mm from his belt as he moved. *"Here he comes,"* whispered Moley as the unwitting stroller came around the driver's side of the car to be confronted by three strangers. All the IRA men were now wearing balaclavas which they had been wearing as woollen hats up until the stranger had entered the gateway. They manhandled him unceremoniously into the back of the lorry through the custom made door cut in the side, as the tailgate had been strengthened and welded shut.

The new captive was placed sitting on the floor in a corner. Moley had gone back into position to make sure the stranger had no company and Magee set about calming him down as he was in an agitated state.

The man's eyes had got used to the dark and he was taking the scene in more calmly now. Magee watched him, suspicious that he was military or ex-military. He had been able to calm him almost too easily. His age would've made him ex-military if anything. He was taking no chances. *"I am going to search you just to make sure you aren't carrying any weapons. Don't panic."* He then searched him and said to Lynch and Burns, *"He's clean."*

Magee noticed the man's well boots. His suspicion deepened. *"What's your name?"* The man told him. *"Where are you from?"*

"Just up the road a bit."

"What do you work at?"

"I'm a carpenter."

"Nice shine on your boots there. Are you military?"

"No, I fit kitchens."

"Are your boots always this shiny? You're RUC or UDR!" Magee persisted.

"I am not, its Sunday so I'm in my Sunday kit," he half shrugged. He had a local accent and wore neat corduroy trousers and a

Burberry coat. Magee was convinced he was a member of the local Ulster Defence Regiment (UDR) of the British Army, or a member of the RUC. He looked at Lynch and Burns who had been listening quietly all the while. They all knew that they had other business to do. Lynch lifted a large mail bag which they had transported some of the weapons in and pulled it down over the man's head and body. Magee spoke again, *"Do anything silly, anything at all and I'll shoot you on the spot! Do you understand?"* The man nodded his understanding.

Time dragged and the high excitement and anticipation waned. They had agreed they would stay in situ for an hour but the hour had passed. Nothing was coming up on the police messages.

At about 3.30pm they had a short discussion on possibilities. Had it been cancelled? Why no police message? Had they got away clean? All agreed to sit it out for another half hour or so and 4pm came and went.

Moley returned, again from his road-side position. As they gathered to have a whispered conversation the radio crackled into life.

"Operation Vesper! All units Operation Vesper." They had never heard the term before but knew from the excited tones that they were referring to the breakout. Almost immediately came two separate queries on the airwaves. *"Is this an exercise?"* *"Exercise, or real?"* The base operator appeared uncertain, *"I don't know,"* she replied but then in the background someone was shouting. *"For real! For real!"* She repeated several times.

The four IRA volunteers looked at each other excitedly. *"Yes,"* Lynch practically hissed. *"Yesss!."*

4.10pm
The Jail Main Gate

Bobby Storey knew critical decisions had to be made and made now. He went to the back of the lorry to have a quick consultation with McFarlane. Storey ordered the uniformed escapees to board the lorry, except for Kerr, Cummings and O'Connor who were to hold the Tally Lodge. He then had to explain to Kerr that he needed him to hold the Tally Lodge as long as possible so as the lorry could clear the camp without interference. *"Tá brón orm"* (I am sorry), he said to Kerr. Kerr replied, *"Fadhb ar bith a Chara, lean ar aghaidh, agus gabh anois."* (No problem comrade, go ahead and go now).

McFarlane had then moved to open up the main gate fully. There was a fair crowd of guards outside it. It was an exciting moment as the huge 18ft high gate lumbered slowly open to reveal green fields within 30 yards. Of course, there was a road and the governor's car-park with parked cars, not to mention the frantic activity of navy blue uniforms. But as the gate opened, Kelly could see freedom, almost taste freedom, and smell freedom in the Irish countryside. He was quickly refocusing on the job in hand when he heard someone speak. McLaughlin the driver had obviously heard McFarlane telling Kelly that the balloon was up. He turned to Kelly and said, *"Can you still make it?"* Kelly, who was taken by surprise by the comment of the driver, showed no change in his facial expression. He said instinctively: *"We will wait for orders."* Kelly was thinking. *"We have either psyched this guy completely or he is trying to psych me out now!"* In fact he has forever been referred to since, as the "39th Volunteer" by the escapees, because he was the man who was driving them down through the jail and out - allbeit reluctantly.

At that point, the shouting outside the main gate and the crowd of guards that were there had grown considerably. Two of them drove cars in and parked them diagonally to block the lorry so it couldn't be driven out. Then a number of the guards who now knew that there was an escape in progress moved forward towards the lorry.

In actual fact they thought that they were only dealing with a small handful of prisoners dressed up as guards. They didn't know how many there really were as the bulk of Republican prisoners were still out of sight in the back of the food lorry. One guard in particular, drew his baton and moved towards the lorry. Kelly watched him as he tried to rally his colleagues. He was shouting to bring some order to the seeming chaos, *"Right lads, lets sort this out!"* All of them knew the driver Davy McLaughlin, and as the other guard came closer to the windscreen of the lorry, slapping the baton off his hand, he looked up at McLaughlin and said, *"What's the craic Davy?"* The driver, who at this stage didn't want to say anything, with Kelly holding him at gunpoint, didn't answer. At which point, the guard turned to Kelly, studied his silence momentarily and then said, loud enough for all around to hear, *"Right we will start with you then."* At this point he moved aggressively towards the passenger door of the cab followed by a few other guards.

Kelly had been sitting motionless except for his eyes which were scanning the scene outside, wondering if he had been recognised or not. As the guard came up to the open window Kelly threw off the coat which he had been using to hide the replica gun. He thrust it out the open window and said with considered aggression, *"Fuck off or I'll blow your head off."* At which point the guards immediately turned and ran back out the gate shouting, *"They have guns! They have guns!"*

To the prison guards coming on duty who had not yet entered the Tally Lodge, this was a revelation and something they had not expected. In that moment, the guards' attempt at advancing turned into a retreat of sorts. Kelly stepped out of the cab believing it would only be moments before they regrouped. He made his way down to the back of the lorry.

Storey had re-entered the Tally Lodge to try to help control the situation but the guards were getting cockier. At one stage one of the prisoners brandishing a weapon with a silencer had it grabbed by a guard. The weapon fired. There was a moment of shock as the guard felt the weapon jerk forward in his hand. It was a dull thud rather than a bang. He let go of the barrel. In shock and panic-stricken, he checked to see where he had been hit. The prisoner too was following the guard's eyes scanning his torso. But the round had actually lodged in the silencer as the guard had bent it where it joined the barrel.

Things were getting out of hand. Kerr had accepted his team were going to have to hold the Tally Lodge while the others made their escape. Storey leaving them, knew that they were going to face certain capture. The lorry was no longer an option. It had been blocked. The main entrance gate out of the jail had been captured and opened. The perimeter wall was well breached and freedom was in sight and still within grasp in the countryside only yards away. It was time for plan B.

McFarlane, on Storey's orders, lifted the shutter and released the tail gate of the lorry and the other prisoners stared out, not knowing what was happening. Most of them were wearing civilian clothes. Because the lorry almost took up the width of the airlock area, the prisoners seemed to be much more numerous as they poured down either side of the lorry. It made them look like a huge crowd as they came down each side and out to face the guards. The Republican prisoners with uniforms, some of them armed with guns or replicas, including Kelly, Storey and McFarlane moved out in front to form a spearhead to confront a group of about 35 guards coming on duty.

Everyone was acutely aware of the British soldier, heavily armed, sitting within 20 feet above them but he was obviously still uncertain about the situation. However, they didn't want the soldier to see the weapons.

The empty food lorry

In trying to push guards back, the guns were lifted up to firing positions at shoulder height and then withdrawn back again out of sight, keeping an eye on the British soldier. It had some effect in that the sheer numbers and shock of all the other prisoners appearing created a wedge, which split the crowd of guards up the middle. It opened up a temporary corridor through the guards, who at this stage didn't know how many of the prisoners were armed, though they now knew it was a mass escape attempt.

In front of the main gate there was a governors' car park. It was a small car park but there were a lot of cars in it. Perhaps 40 yards away was the BMOD (British Ministry of Defence) barbed wire fence and beyond that were green fields and freedom. The prisoners, were deciding what to do and they had limited choices. Most made their way towards the barbed wire and fields beyond.

Cummings and Kerr were standing in the middle of the tally room back to back. Both were armed but were knee-deep in prison guards. Cummings could smell the alcohol off two of them in front of him. *"That gun's a fake,"* one of them addressed Cummings.

"Yeah?" He stared back, *"Maggie Thatcher doesn't give a fuck whether it's real or not but I guarantee your family don't want me to prove it's real!"*

At the same time against all odds, Cummings, Kerr and O'Connor had maintained control of the Tally Lodge. The guards who had been outside then surged in after the gap was created by fleeing escapees. The three POWs ended up with almost twice as many guards as they had had to deal with just a few moments earlier. The guards who had been sitting and lying on the floor were starting to get up. The guards who were coming in were trying to attack them thinking they were Republicans as they had seen Kerr and the others with weapons.

It was a confused melee. The number and force of the guards trying to get up off the floor was knocking Kerr to the side and pushing him down. Those who were trying to attack him were actually hampered by the fact that other guards were trying to get up. Kerr fell on top of the guards. As he fell he flicked on the safety catch of his weapon. He believed he was going to be executed if they were able to get the weapon and he tried to flick the weapon as far away from him as possible so it wouldn't be taken off him and used immediately in anger.

The guards regained control of the Tally Lodge and a guard gave the order to get Kerr, O'Connor and Cummings out to the lorry. Kerr was being dragged face down along the corridor with his face scraping the floor, he was semi-conscious and bleeding heavily. A guard was pressing his foot down on his neck as he was getting dragged out. The only thing he could see was the ground and the guard's feet, and people taking swipes at him and kicking him. It felt like the guards were everywhere and in the middle of it he could hear someone else screaming. He only learnt at a later date that it was the food-lorry orderly Desy Armstrong who had been earlier arrested by the prisoners.

Desy Armstrong was a Republican prisoner from H6 who was working as orderly with the food lorry that day. Kerr had taken him from the lorry and put him in with guards under arrest on the floor of the tally room. When the guards had overpowered Kerr and Cummings, Armstrong thought it was all over. The lorry driver Davy McLaughlin came in and told him to stay where he was in the corner of the room sitting on the floor.

But another guard came in, *"Get to your feet! You're part of this,"* he shouted. *"Ask the lorry driver,"* was all Armstrong could think of to say back. He could hear different guards shouting above the pandemonium. *"Open the armoury! Shoot the bastards!"* *"They call themselves POWs so we can shoot them as escapees!"*

More guards arrived demanding to know where Armstrong was. He was then trailed out by his ankles, face down. Some guards were kicking and punching him and beating him with batons. He pleaded innocence but to no avail. After blacking-out a few times he came to, stripped naked, on the tarmac outside the Tally Lodge. A guard lifted his head by his hair and hit him across his mouth with his baton breaking several teeth.

Eventually he heard someone shouting that he should be taken to the prison hospital but the guards were arguing amongst themselves about his guilt or innocence. In the end he was taken to the hospital and put in a cell. Even then, different guards were coming in and asking where he was.

They washed his face and gave him headache tablets. Later that night the prison chaplain arrived and gave him the 'last rites'. He didn't see a doctor or dentist for two days but was later transferred back into H6. Guards continued to accuse him of being involved throughout the remainder of his sentence.

When the guards in the back corridor scrambled to their feet, O'Connor ran out of the door hoping to circle round to the pedestrian gate. It was locked and guards were coming at him in dozens. He threw the chisel up over the roof just as they reached him. He was knocked unconscious and woke up lying naked on the tarmac road surrounded by a sea of navy blue uniforms. A guard kicked him in the head and he lost consciousness again. Cummings had his clothes ripped off him also. As the guards beat him they were questioning him, *"What Block are you from?"* Another asked, *"Are you Republican or Loyalist?"* To which his other tormentor retorted *"They aren't Loyalist ya clown ya or we'd have heard about it months ago."*

Shortly afterwards Kerr, Cummings, O'Connor and Gorman were thrown into a van face down on top of each other. They were transported to the Segregation Unit or 'Boards'. In the middle of the aches and pains and kicking in the van, O'Connor was thinking, *"I hope somebody has got away to make all this worthwhile."*

Plan B
Outside Main Gate

Brendan Mead was a strong athlete, a soccer player with good prospects before his arrest. He burst out through the main gate with an eye to the fields but saw a guard in the driver seat of a yellow Toyota Celica car. Jimmy Donnelly had also seen the car and had reached it just in front of Mead. Without hesitation Donnelly opened the door and yanked the guard out of the car. As he looked to the ignition he realised the guard had already withdrawn the car keys. He threw them towards a group of his colleagues a few yards away. Both Mead and the group of guards moved to get the keys. Mead assessed, as he moved with speed, that the guard out front might reach the keys at the same time as him or shortly before. The last thing he needed was a wrestling match at this point. As he reached the keys, just marginally ahead of the guard, he bent down as if to pick them up. Instead though he moved past them, coming out of a stooping position to hit the guard in the throat with his fist, the guard was knocked instantly to the ground as Mead turned, secured the car keys and sped back to the car.

The Celica was full of his comrades as he jumped into the driver's seat and slammed the door. Aware that other guards would be surrounding the car he shouted: *"Lock the doors!"* to the others as he locked the driver's door and put the window up.

The car wouldn't start. *"Shut up!"* He shouted to the others who were cackling away in nervousness and excitement. *"Is there a cut off switch?"* He was wondering to himself reaching frantically with his left hand. He was an experienced lorry driver. He tried putting the gearstick into the neutral position.

He heard a sharp tap of metal against his window and when he turned he faced a gun inches from his face. A guard had got hold of one of the escapee's guns and was trying to fire it. Mead tried the ignition again as he jerked his head away automatically. The engine roared into life and he accelerated off just as the guard reversed the gun in his hand and smashed the butt hard against the windscreen. Other guards' batons rained down on the car and the side windows shattered.

A red car overtook them at speed and thumped over the road ramp below one of the British Army watchtowers that peppered the jail's perimeter wall. Mead slowed to drive over the ramp a bit less suspiciously. The red car's horn had been sounding to draw as much attention as he could and all the escapees were wondering why the Brits had not fired on either car. Mead sped up again and as he took the second ramp and watchtower, everyone in the car tensed for shots being fired. The soldier leaned out of the tower and looked down but did nothing. The watchtowers were dotted every couple of hundred yards along the perimeter wall. As they passed the third one without incident, they could see the red and white pole-barriers pointing skywards. If they could make it before they came down, there were no other barriers between them and the main British Army camp gate which sat outside the prison. Mead floored the accelerator.

The red car skidded to a halt as he passed the pole barriers. The guard leapt out shouting and waving wildly. Mead's skin tingled as he saw him running towards the gate. The yellow car was now travelling at full pelt towards the gate. The gates were being closed. It was heart rending for those in the car watching the openness of hedges and fields diminishing behind the grey metal gates.

Mead did not go for the brakes or ease his foot off the accelerator. The metal gates were made of corrugated tin, strengthened only by a light-framed skeleton of three inch box metal. It was worth a try! *"Hold tight lads,"* was all he could shout to signify his decision before he gripped the steering wheel tighter and closed his eyes.

The soldier and guards had barely managed to close the two gates and drop the vertical bar into its keeper on the ground. As the car rocketed towards them they dived left and right to get out of its path. In the car there were six escapees. Along with the driver was Jimmy Donnelly, Paul Kane, Jimmy Burns, Barry Artt and Jaz McCann. When Mead had shouted they all braced themselves immediately and variedly for the impact.

Their brace positions were less than scientific. Mead was momentarily knocked out. He awoke to the pain of being trailed out of the car by his hair. But his adrenalin was flowing. He was immediately alert. *"Right, right! I'm caught!"* He shouted as he stumbled out the door of the car. *"Take my arm,"* he said stretching it out *"let my hair go, you've caught me. I'll go back with you!"*

"Too fucking right you will ye bastard," retorted the guard who had him by the hair.

The second he felt the guards grip loosening Mead hit him hard in the ribs forcing him to stagger back. Before closing his eyes Mead had pointed the car directly at the centre of the gates where they met, hoping to smash through. He hadn't succeeded entirely but he had forced one of the gates open. The car was jammed in the entrance. He leapt onto the car bonnet in an instant and after jumping off, turned right and ran down the road as fast as his feet

The Toyota car, hijacked by the escaping prisoners, lies jammed in the main gate

could carry him. He could see a housing estate in the distance and instinctively headed in that direction, thinking about getting another car.

Kelly and Storey were standing side by side, both looking up with others at the British Army watch tower, each with their own thoughts. They had opened a gap through the guards and were now facing back towards the jail. They had not spoken to each other. They were technically free. They had escaped but had not yet got away. Kelly had witnessed the fight between the guards and Mead and had decided that that was not the way for him to go. All it needed was a guard to be able to grab hold of him tightly and it would all be over. He looked down to the right as he was facing the jail and knew that the M1 motorway to Belfast was in that direction. It was about a quarter to a half mile away and he suspected that it would be the first route that the British Army and RUC would pick to set up roadblocks. Thoughts were flooding his mind at high speed. To the left where Mead had gone he knew there was the British Military camp. He assumed that the balloon was already up and it would be very hard to escape in that direction now.

There was only one option left. He turned and looked round at the BMOD fencing. It was made of coils of single strand barbed wire. While he knew it would cut him, he didn't think it would entangle or hold him.

Kelly and Storey both were thinking about the soldier and why he hadn't opened fire at this stage but Kelly had already made up his mind. He was heading across the fields. He could see freedom; it was within yards of him and this was the moment to go. He didn't want to do anything to spook the soldier or show his intentions. He simply turned round saying to Storey in a casual voice, *"Ádh Mór Bob, slán a Chara"* (Good luck and goobye friend) which Storey didn't hear. Kelly was running towards the fence. He ran at it as hard as he could, throwing off the guards cap with a motion of his hand. He was fairly fit, as most Republican prisoners were. The entanglements sat at chest height. He jumped as high into them as he possibly could and fell prone as he had expected.

All six foot of him fell face down in the wire but while it cut him a bit it also eased his fall. He was stretched belly down. As he started to pull himself up and forward he was shocked to be suddenly forced down again with someone running over him, then another, then another. He had created a gap in the barbed wire and was being used as a bridge by the other escapees. After the first couple ran across him he shouted in some exasperation, *"For fuck's sake lads!!"* After another two ran over him who had obviously been queuing up, he felt himself being lifted out of the wire. It was Marty McManus and Gerard Fryers, apologising profusely and with understandable haste, but showing just a hint of a smile.

Carpark – facing the main gate through which most of the escapees burst

It was only much later that Kelly recollected that in war films, in no-mans land, this was apparently the technique used to breach barbed-wire entanglements by infantry. The first soldier flattened the barbed wire entanglements and his comrades would follow. Some of the escapees clearly thought it was a pre-planned action – or so they claimed!

At this stage he found that he had lost a shoe and sock and that the tunic and the shirt of the guard's uniform were ripped open. There was some blood and scratches on him, but not a lot. The incident had turned out well for him.

The whole crowd was running off to the right. They were running up a fairly steep hill. But they were in open fields. This was actual freedom and Kelly was very aware that they had got past all the fences and were now in the outside world. He was standing in a green field after a decade of hard concrete and tarmac surfaces.

He was still thinking about the Brit and when he might open fire. He thought that it was always better to go off on your own, away from the crowd. So he darted off to the left and started to run up what felt like a 45 degree gradient. Also to the left was a number of large warehouses and he hoped to get them between him and the Brit watchtowers as quickly as possible, before the shooting started.

He ran up the hill, not straight but in a narrow zig zagging motion, using all the power that he had in his legs and whatever fitness he could muster. At one stage he looked over his shoulder for a quick glimpse while still running to see what was happening. Up to 15 escapees were following him. They thought Kelly knew where he was going, that it was plan B. In fact he hadn't got a clue other than he was making distance between himself and the prison. So in the end there was quite a crowd going in that direction as well.

A view of the car park, and behind, the barbed wire fence through which some of the escapees ran

He made it to the top of the hill in moments, though it seemed like a lifetime, and dived headlong over the crest. There was an almost cliff-like gradient down the other side for about 20 feet and he slid down it to the bottom. Then he had to climb another very steep bank to get to the same height in the next field again. By the time he got to that point he was totally out of breath and exhausted.

He sat on the damp grass for a moment deciding whether to take the time to remove the guard's uniform or not. He had his own clothes on underneath the uniform and it felt increasingly heavy. Although he was fit he obviously wasn't used to wearing two sets of clothing or running up hills and especially not in this kind of pressurised situation. He was also looking towards a gate over on his right hand side which led to a road where the bulk of the escapees were heading.

About 150 yards up the field, on the left he could see a farm, but the road also led to the farm. The shortest distance was through the field, however, it would have been hardest to run. As he was contemplating what to do he heard a rifle shot. He knew he was over the ridge of the hill and felt confident that he was safely out of sight of the British watchtowers. He made the decision not to take the time to remove the heavy uniform. Kelly ran down towards the gate because he wanted to get onto the hard tar of the road. He had been used to running on hard ground in the prison exercise yards and the field seemed too soft underfoot with too many potholes. He was worried about twisting an ankle or a worse injury. As he ran, he managed to take off the tunic and toss it to the side. He felt lighter even if most of the weight loss was psychological. He had already discarded the wooden replica gun at the wire fence, feeling that it was of no benefit to him, and possibly a danger as the soldier would think it real if he spotted it.

H-Block 7
The Rearguard

W hen H7 fell to the control of the Republican escapees, the next move was to lock-up anyone not involved with the escape for their own protection. All prisoners were brought into the food halls in each of the four wings.

A preselected escapee in each wing read out a prepared statement, more for the benefit of the captive guards than the prisoners:

A Chairde,
Very few of you are aware of what is now taking place. This is due to security and the possible refusal of some of you to go on this escape. Since it is the duty of all POWs to escape I now instruct you to go to the yard to board the food-lorry. Regardless of your feelings we are taking you with us. We have no time for arguments. Just do as instructed. Any refusals will be met with force.
Operational OC

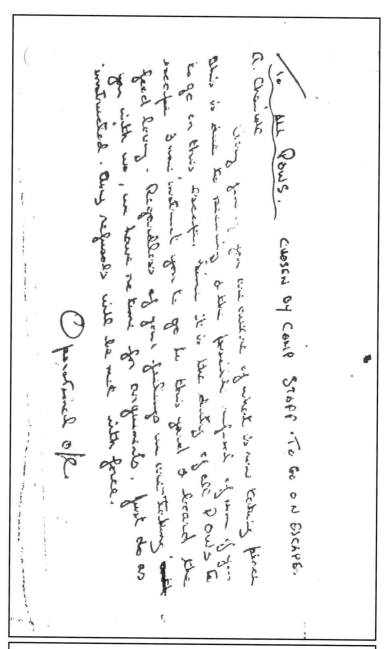

Copy of handwritten statement

The Volunteers involved in reading out the statement pointed at the guards on the ground to indicate that the statement was for their benefit. Quietly then and out of earshot they were ordered to lock-up in their cells and to turn their radios up to full volume. The reason for this was to give some protection from prosecution because those prisoners could truthfully say they heard nothing other than the radio blasting. It was a small but important statement to help those comrades who were staying behind. The written statements were left purposely to be found by the Prison authorities.

They all went to their cells. However, those involved in the Rearguard did not lock their cells. Instead they had already set about disguising their identities by dressing up in homemade hoods and ponchos. They also put socks on their hands to avoid fingerprints being left in the wrong places.

As they were staying behind and were all shortly due for release their anonymity was imperative. They helped move the guards to Cell 26 in each wing and divested them of their uniforms before herding them all into a single classroom situated in the corridor between C and D-Wings.

By the time the lorry had been filled with their comrades to leave H7, the Rearguard, under its OC, Seamus McDermott, was in control of all the necessary points that had previously been held by escapees. They were guarding the guards in the Control Room and the PO's office, as well as all the others in the classroom. They had lit a fire in the circle and were destroying all the prisoners' photos and security details. Volunteers including Cormac MacArt from Short Strand were going through the filing cabinet in the Governor's office. People were set in different parts of the Block as an early warning system for soldiers or cops trying to enter. There were no phones or radios that they could use to have any warning of the arrival of State forces.

141

Storey and then McDermott each had made it clear that their captives must be treated with dignity despite the brutal regime during the protest years. When speaking, those in the Rearguard, were instructed to only refer to each other as 'Óglach' (Volunteer).

When McDermott heard the two shots being fired he got worried, in common with most other prisoners in the Block. It was still some minutes before the escapees controlled all the key points in H7 and during that short period he had convinced himself that he should join his escaping comrades despite his short sentence. He went to the circle area to find that a guard had been shot but seemed to be recovering. He decided, with some reluctance that he would stay and oversee the Rearguard operation as planned. To change now or even raise it with OC Storey in the middle of the operation could cause its own confusion and difficulties.

As Pádraig McKearney queued to get on the lorry he spoke to one of the hooded Rearguard, *"Good Luck Cormac and thanks for everything."* Cormac MacArt could only laugh. *"Not much of a disguise if you know who I am."*

"It's the nose Cormac," McKearney answered as he climbed into the lorry. *"No hood could hide a nose that size!"*

"Bastard!" MacArt said, quietly pleased that he had been recognised as he felt very proud to be part of the endeavour.

It was about 3.50pm when McDermott slapped the side of the kitchen lorry and sent it on its way. Francy Donegan noticed that Grand Prix racing was on the TV in the food hall. He and Cormac McArt had trailed a heavy work bench from the hobbies room in C-Wing round to the door of the classroom which contained the captive guards. *"When the balloon goes up I want to make sure we've enough time to get safely to our cells before those guards go on the rampage. I wouldn't want to be fighting off two dozen angry bears just yet."* Donegan explained to McDermott.

"Good thinking. We need to start bringing our numbers down anyway. All we need is one Óglach covering each wing, one in the Control Room, a couple in the classroom, one on the medic and wounded screw, and us four floating," McDermott said referring to himself, McArt, Cassidy and Donegan. *"All they need now is cell door keys in each wing. Bring all the other keys out to me here leaving all gates unlocked and wide open to the circle."*

They all went off to organise and get ready. They continued to shout reports about the Block to let the guards know they were still in charge and to give the impression there were more prisoners in corridors than there actually were. When the lorry had departed, the level of activity and general noise had dropped immediately. All the guards were tied together but some were starting to talk and ask questions - less worried now that they knew they would not be ill-treated.

At 4.10pm McDermott could hear Pink Floyd's album 'Wish You Were Here' above all the other radios that people had been told to turn up to full volume. At 4.12pm the alarm went up. In H7 there was a cacophony of buzzers, intercoms and telephones which were all active for some minutes. The small group stood in the circle area. *"The balloon's up and much too quick for my liking. Tell the lads in the wings to lock-up. Tell everyone to do it. Bring the cell door keys here. Make sure their doors are locked, folks."* They returned within minutes satisfied. *"We need to put the 'white shirts' into the classroom along with the control room screw,"* Cassidy said referring to the PO and SO still tied up in their office. *"Make sure the MO is well tied as well."*

When it was done Donegan and McArt blocked the door with the heavy work bench. *"It will slow them down a bit anyway!"* McDermott was going through a checklist in his head. *"What about the man on the gate?"* Donegan said, remembering suddenly that he was, most vulnerable of the Rearguard. He ran

143

out through the grille into the front yard between A and D-Wings. He whistled loudly between his teeth and started to run down waving. He still didn't want to shout.

Ciarán Jones had heard the siren going off but had stayed at his post despite his nervousness. He had locked the outer vehicle and pedestrian gate of the airlock as well as the inner large vehicle gates in preparation. He jammed small wooden wedges into the locks and broke them off to slow the State forces down. When he saw his comrade running towards him he moved out into the front yard of H7 locking the inner pedestrian gate after him. He met Donegan in the middle of the yard, aware that there were eyes in the cells to either side watching. *"Fuck me - I thought you were gonna leave your oul mate stranded there."*

Donegan put his arm around his shoulder saying, *"Now what did I tell you about volunteering for anything ye mad gitt! Time for bedsie byes!"* He joked, relieved that everyone was now accounted for – well those left behind in the Block anyway.

As they passed the classroom the guards were banging at the locked door. *"Shut up in there!"* McDermott shouted. *"Get away from the door,"* added Donegan. There was silence but they knew it would be short-lived. All they needed now was minutes. Jones and Cassidy were safely locked away after they quickly divested themselves of the guards uniforms, hoods and socks. They moved quickly to the end of the wing at the back of the block and reaching through the gate, threw all the keys except the cell-door key away to the side of the gate. Any delay on the guards getting access to the cells would be time for them to calm down a bit – hopefully.

Donegan and McDermott stuffed the socks they had on their hands as far down the S bend of the toilet as they could. They then entered their cell and pulled the cell-door closed. The bolt shot. Their biggest nightmare would've been if the door had failed to lock - which is why they brought the cell key in with them. McDermott checked out the window, used a pillow case to wipe the key and then threw it as far as he could.

Ciaran Jones, safely in his cell again was trying to remove his false moustache in front of the mirror. It wasn't budging. *"Well it was Super Glue,"* he mouthed at his reflection. *"Should have called it Super Duper Glue!"* He gave up and had to leave it for several days before he managed to remove it. Happily for him the prison Administration and the Royal Ulster Constabulary were concentrating on more important, though connected issues.

Donegan and McDermott both stood listening for a while. Donegan turned on the radio for news. It seemed a long wait until 5pm when the newsreader on the radio announced the escape. H7 erupted with cheers and then they could hear other H-Blocks cheering as well. Listening to the news was a daily ritual in jail.

Harry Murray and Billy Gorman

arry Murray was in uniform and armed as one of the escape team who were to secure the Tally Lodge at the main gate. The tailgate of the kitchen lorry had been dropped and all the rest of the escapees in civilian garb were piling out. Bobby Storey was leading the way down the side of the lorry and out the gate. The prisoners with uniforms, some armed, spearheaded the large group of prisoners.

Murray turned to form a makeshift buffer with others because he was armed. He was trying to advance through the guards and cover other comrades as best he could. They all moved through to the governor's carpark facing the gate. He watched Mead knock a guard off his feet, pick something off the ground and jump into a car. It was immediately surrounded by guards and they were trying to break the windows. Murray raised his weapon, aware of the Brit watchtower above him, and got ready to shoot if the guard succeeded in getting to Mead. A moment later the car sped off.

At that he turned to see Bobby Storey and Billy Gorman making their way over the barbed wire entanglements. He moved to join them. It was a bit of a scrambling match but Storey got over followed by Murray. They started up the field, but Murray heard Gorman calling and looked back. Gorman was caught in the wire.

He was wearing a red fleece and it seemed like the more he tried to free himself the more entangled he became. Murray turned back and was trying to free his young comrade when one of the guards who were charging towards them stopped and pointed a gun at his head.

"It's over Murray, you're under arrest," shouted the guard. Murray pointed his own weapon at him in turn saying dismissively *"Fuck off."* The fact that the guard hadn't already fired any shots registered, as did the fact that the pistol the guard had was one of the ones used in the escape. *"Maybe he thinks it isn't real,"* Murray thought. Keeping his own weapon pointed at the guard Murray continued to try to free Gorman. It was extremely difficult. *"Drop your weapon or I'll shoot!"* Said the guard. Murray lowered the weapon as if to do what he was told and shot the guard in the leg.

The guard fell to the ground and Murray swung the pistol in an arc to cover the group of guards who were scrambling into the wire to get at him. It had the desired effect. Murray thought it was like the keystone cops from a Charlie Chaplin movie with all the uniforms running about covering their heads with their arms, ducking and bobbing about bumping into each other. Billy Gorman knew it was useless. He had been keeping half an eye on the Brit in the watchtower. After Murray had shot the guard in the leg Gorman had pushed into the grass to make himself a smaller target. He had expected the soldier to open fire but he hadn't. As he looked again he saw the rifle barrel pointing out. Murray was still trying to free him. *"Harry, you need to run a chara. I'm banjaxed and that Brit is going to open up!"*

Murray insisted on trying to help Gorman. The guards had started throwing bits of rubble at them both. Eventually Murray took off up the hill. When he was half way up, he looked over his shoulder and saw Gorman still lying at the wire surrounded by guards. Murray pressed on.

He had a few steps left to crest the hill when he felt a dull thud on his thigh. He had not heard any shots but the next he knew was that he was on his back and his pistol was lying a few feet away. As he turned to retrieve it, he saw his foot was way too close to his shoulder. He didn't feel much pain but he knew then that he had been shot.

Murray felt himself going numb. He was watching a horde of guards running towards him. It was like a dream as he was seeing the motions but not hearing the sounds even though he could see they were all shouting and enraged. With some relief he recognised the first guard as a 'Born Again Christian' from the jail. Better to be arrested by an avowed Christian he thought rather than some of the others he knew. He was trying to remember his name as he reached him. His Christianity however was somewhat diluted by this stage as Murray found out to his cost.

Others joined in as they arrived. Harry was trailed down the field and yelled out with the pain of it. One of the guards said to the others, *"Listen to him whinging, Super IRA man."* So he clenched his teeth and stopped yelling. Some guards who passed were kicking and punching him. Some were screaming at him, *"Turncoat bastard."* Nearly all of them knew that Harry Murray had been raised a loyalist in the working-class Tiger's Bay area of Belfast. He had become an Irish Republican as an adult but still had the pro-British tattoos on his body from his youth.

Murray was trying to muster the energy to physically fight back but he was overwhelmed and exhausted. The only respite he got from the beatings was when a British Army medic came on the scene and gave Murray First Aid. When he finished, the beatings resumed.

He was transported to the Lagan Valley Hospital in the nearby town of Lisburn. Ironically, the guard he had shot, Campbell

Courtney, was on a stretcher next to him in the hospital. They traded insults with each other for a while but Murray was the worst injured having been shot by a high calibre 7.62 SLR rifle. The soldier in the watchtower had eventually been able to fire on a target once he had witnessed Murray shooting a guard. He was also being vociferously urged to open fire by dozens of guards shouting at him.

As Murray drifted off he could hear a guard explaining to a nurse that although they were both in uniform that he was actually a prisoner. *"If I'd have known that,"* she said with some venom *"I'd have left him lying there for a week."* *"Thank you Florence Nightingale,"* said Murray, not caring if he could be heard but thinking, *"Thank God he didn't tell her before my leg was sorted!"*

Billy Gorman saw the guard fall to the ground as Murray fired. He was almost through the barbed wire but it was tangled in his trouser leg. He quickly turned about to see dozens of guards heading in his direction. Realising the consequences he tore frantically at the wire but the harder he tried the more entangled he seemed to become.

The guards came to a halt some yards away and he realised their hesitation was caused by the fact that the pistol was lying on the ground between the wounded guard and himself. They very quickly spotted that Gorman was trapped by the wire, however, and moved in. The crack of the shot which wounded Murray pulled his attention away from his struggle with the wire momentarily.

Gorman was pulled back out of the entanglements back into the Governor's car park. They then trailed him quickly back inside the jail's perimeter gate. He was spread-eagled on the ground. Nearby he saw his comrades Rab Kerr, Eddie O'Connor, Dennis Cummings and the orderly from the food lorry, Desy Armstrong. All were face down on the ground as well.

There was mayhem and anger. The guards seemed out of control. Reports and rumours were coming in from H7. A report or rumour would be the catalyst for another surge of fists and boots hitting the naked prisoners. At times there were so many trying to hit them that they were hitting each other. Some of the guards were trying to calm the situation down but other guards were calling them, *"IRA-lovers."* So the beatings continued sporadically.

6pm
September 25th
H-Block 7
Post Escape

Back in H7 on the six o'clock news it was announced that a guard was dead. Those in the Rearguard thought it was John Adams but gave no indication to any of the other prisoners as it would identify them as members of the Rearguard. In fact it wasn't John Adams (who made a full recovery). It was James Ferris who had taken a heart attack while on duty in the Tally Lodge at the Main Gate area of the prison. *"We're fucked,"* McDermott said simply. When the state forces arrived they were a mixture of British Army, RUC and prison guards. The Republican prisoners started to psych themselves up for the expected onslaught as they listened to the commotion in the corridors. The imprisoned guards had been released and some were looking for vengeance. One of them was shouting, *"Give me a gun. I'm gonna shoot them all."*

Donegan had a thought. *"Tell me this. Did you check this cell to see if anything was in it? I'm only asking because I saw a couple of our escaping comrades spending quite some time in here earlier."* There was really only a tall locker and a small bedside locker but the two of them quickly checked under beds, pillows, mattresses and cupboards.

As Donegan moved some clothes he realised that a sock contained what felt like bullets. With his back to the door he opened it to reveal about 30 rounds of small calibre ammunition. He showed it to McDermott, being careful of the spy-hole in the door.

It was not a time for discussion. McDermott moved to the door to listen and then peered out through the slit at the side. There was activity but no-one was opening doors just yet. Donegan moved to the window. There was a small opener at the top. He scanned left and right as best he could. There was a police woman patrolling the yard alone. She was in the middle of it. He waved to McDermott to see if it was all clear at the door. He gave him the thumbs up.

Donegan stood awkwardly on the top bunk. It was getting dark but their cell light was not yet lit. As the RUC woman turned to look towards the other wing he put his arm out and threw the sock full of ammunition as far as he could. He withdrew his arm quickly knowing the cop would hear the bullets hitting the ground. Both prisoners then did a second and very thorough search of the cell. They were satisfied that they had recovered all incriminating evidence.

In C-Wing Seamy Finucane, – a brother of Dermot Finucane who had escaped - and his mate Brian Gillen had been listening to the commotion. They had been toughened by many beatings in the protest years, but tonight they didn't know what to expect. They were in cell 24 and they had just turned their faces to the door on having heard the butterfly lock turn. The cell door flew open and a British soldier ran in pointing his rifle followed by another and then two armed RUC men. One of the cops was shouting, *"Put your hands up. Turn around and face the wall!"* A third cop was restraining an Alsatian in the doorway of the cell. The two Republicans already knew from the radio that a prison guard was dead so they faced the wall when told to do so. The cops searched what little furniture and bedding there was. They then carried out a thorough body-search of both men. When that was done they then backed out one at a time and slammed the door shut. Both had taken bad beatings in the past but instinctively knew they were in dangerous circumstances. However, experience taught them that the British Army and the RUC didn't trust each other so it was better that it had been a mixed group. It might prevent the most extreme reaction from any individual.

"Do you think they're upset?" Gillen said sardonically.

"Not half as much as the screws will be when they arrive," answered   Finucane, smiling unconvincingly.

One of the Rearguard in A-Wing had watched the front gate of H7 from his cell. He had lit fires in the washrooms of each wing and set ponchos, hoods and some captured documents alight. The British Army and RUC were wary on entering at first because they didn't know if there were any weapons still in the block. After gaining entry into the Block, the RUC and soldiers formed a gauntlet from the Block entrance down the centre of the yard to the entrance gate. But then suddenly they fell back to allow prison guards to take their places.

Then a prison Governor arrived. He had prided himself on being a 'Born Again Christian'. The first cell they hit in A-Wing contained Cormac Mac Art and Kevin McCracken. McCracken must have been the skinniest prisoner in the blocks. He looked like a kid. The Governor told McCracken that if they found anything in the cell he would "pay dearly". He was not to know that McCracken a key member of the Rearguard and more importantly was soon due for release.

When the prison guards took over they came in force and with force. The first voice that Sean Murray heard was a guard, nicknamed Big T who had been particularly brutal during the protest years. *"Get ready for a move. Take nothing with you!"*

He shouted down C and D Wings. The guards were moving methodically from cell to cell. Murray could see John McGrillen out the side of his door. He was small in stature but tough. *"He said, take nothing with you ye Fenian bastard,"* the guard roared as he knocked McGrillen's radio and personal photographs out of his hands. Two other guards grabbed him by both arms and trailed him towards the food hall. *"Ná bígí ag rith a chairde!"* (Don't be running lads!) Murray shouted out.

His cell door opened almost immediately. He came out eating an apple and walked casually for a few steps before getting a heavy slap to the back of his head. He resisted the pushing and shoving as best he could, still stubbornly walking.

In the food-hall the prisoners were stripped to the waist, searched and left bare-footed. Each was then hand-cuffed and a guard assigned to grip them by the handcuffs and run them the short distance to the circle area. All the Republicans resisted the effort to make them run.

When Anthony Hughes arrived bare-foot and handcuffed in the circle of H7, there was a prison guard reception party. He was asked his name and number. *"I don't have a number and you already know my name,"* he answered defiantly to the guard who knew him well. Irish political prisoners had never answered to or identified themselves with prison number, seeing it as criminalising. He was, in any case more interested in the sound of barking dogs in the front yard of the Block and the fact that the grilles to the front door were being held open.

At a nod, the guard, still holding him by the handcuffs, started running and trailing Hughes out to the yard. As they exited the Block, Hughes could see the gauntlet of guards and dogs. He thought they must have emptied the prison dog kennels. He decided his best plan was to run despite his bare feet as guards were swinging batons and the dogs were snapping at him. He got close to the guard and then overtook him. Reversing the planned scenario, he was now pulling the guard who was forced to keep hold of the handcuffs.

The gauntlet stretched the whole way across into H8 opposite H7. He no longer felt the pain of the rough tarmac or the small sharp stones on the soles of his feet. His concentration was on speed and staying upright.

When he eventually arrived in the circle area of H8, he was asked again for his name and number. Ignoring the question Hughes asked his own. *"Do you know that Alsatian dogs are being seized on half naked prisoners running a gauntlet to H8?"*

The response was, *"A Prison Officer is dead!"* after which he was trailed to a cell down one of the wings. There he was strip-searched and left naked in a bed-less empty cell.

Each of the 88 prisoners was put through the same trauma as they were moved from H7 to H8. They were left without anything overnight and then up to four days without clothes. It was a nightmarish return to the protest years or worse. But after the initial violence settled, the POWs reorganised. Communications with other Blocks and the Camp OC were re-established. The Republicans then started to demand their entitlements. The fight-back, post escape, had already begun.

The Hillman Car

Kelly surveyed the landscape for a moment to catch his breath. In a way it was every man for himself at this stage, although escapees were taking a lead off others and moving in groups. People had similar thoughts of course. They were free; they were in the fields. It was a moment of great exhilaration even though they were still close to the jail. They were still running and there was a realisation that no matter what came next, freedom had been achieved. Adrenalin was driving them on, even though exhaustion was in every muscle and breathing increasingly laboured. They were pushing themselves beyond the limits of their own fitness.

Kelly looked to the field gate onto the road. There was a line of running men in front of him. He ran down towards the gate and all the time he was trying to plan ahead. Get to the farm. Would there be any vehicles there? His mind was a staccato of ideas. He remembered when he was a kid that what he used to do was run down, put his foot on the bottom rung of the gate and vault over the top, landing neatly on both feet. He had it in his head that he was going to do just that.

But he hadn't considered how tired he actually was and how much pressure he had put on his body. So when he got to the gate he put his foot on the rung, tried to rise up to vault the gate, but instead hit the top bar with his stomach and flipped over unceremoniously. He landed on his back, badly winded.

Kieran Fleming was some twenty yards ahead. He stopped when he heard Kelly swear loudly. Kelly was completely out of breath. He felt like his lung was outside his body. He was gasping for breath and couldn't get up for a moment but he knew this would pass fairly quickly. He was just badly winded. He could hear Kieran Fleming shouting back, *"Gerry are you ok? Are you ok?"* Kelly was trying to wave at him to go on because he couldn't really talk for gasping. But Fleming who had obviously seen the incident and was worried that Kelly was hurt, ran back.

In the circumstances, this was a very brave and very comradely, act. In any escape bid, 20 yards is a great advantage. By the time Fleming got back to Kelly he was already on one knee, trying to get on his feet. He was gesturing at Fleming to run on, to let him know he was OK. Fleming coming back, was in itself encouraging Kelly to get up. As Fleming came within a couple of yards Kelly was able to stand and shout, *"I'm ok run on."* Fleming, satisfied that he was up and moving then turned and ran with Kelly following him at pace. They ran with the others up to the farm with hope in their hearts.

When Kieran Fleming had turned to check on Kelly he had been in a group which included Seamus Campbell and Pádraig McKearney. Both were from Tyrone and were good friends. They had been part of taking over C-Wing earlier, and they had locked other POWs, who were not involved in the escape operation, in their cells. They had then removed identifying cell cards to confuse the guards and others during the inevitable searches. Campbell had found some coins which he pocketed for possible phone calls.

At one stage, before the operation had started, another Tyrone prisoner had shouted, *"Who has all the tools"* and McKearney moved him quickly back into the handicraft room to silence his protests. During the lock-up another friend, Ned McPeake, was arguing to go on the escape. He had lost a leg during the conflict but that was not the issue. He had very little of his sentence left to serve so he wasn't included on the list of escapees.

When the shutter at the back of the kitchen lorry was opened at the main-gate they didn't know what to expect but when Bobby Storey ordered everyone to get out he didn't need to say it twice. The open gate framed a melee but Campbell and McKearney focused on the fields beyond. They scrambled over the barbed-wire entanglements without hesitation.

First to feel the softness of the grass under their feet, the Tyrone men felt comforted with the feel of the open countryside. They were the first to turn the corner into the farm yard where they saw a young man in the driver's seat of an old Hillman car. Campbell opened the door and pulled the startled teenager out by the arm in one motion. He jumped into the driver's seat as McKearney opened the front passenger seat to join him.

The engine was already running so Campbell moved down the lane. By the time he got to the road the car was bursting at the seams with his comrades. He pressed the accelerator and eased off the clutch. Very slowly the car moved off. To see the car was like getting an injection straight into the blood stream. There was an energy burst in everyone.

When Kelly and Fleming spotted the car there was a momentary panic that the car was going to take off and their chance could be lost. Fleming and Kelly gave an extra burst and got into the already overcrowded car. Kelly got in behind the driver and managed to close the door despite the packed sardine effect.

The car started to move off again, Kelly could feel the car was sluggish. It was an old car and carrying more weight that it should ever have had to. He smelled what he thought was the clutch burning under pressure but the car was starting to move off, so he relaxed.

The Hillman was starting to pick up some momentum when someone shouted suddenly from the back seat, *"There's Goose Russell! There's Goose Russell."* Right enough Kelly looked round and there was Robert Russell trying his hardest, his lungs bursting, to keep going. When he had seen the car moving he had got his second wind. Everybody was shouting, *"Stop!"* to the driver. Kelly, who was worried that the car wouldn't be able to stop and start again, was talking, his hand cupped over Campbell's ear, *"Don't stop Spanner, just keep it moving slowly."* The car was going at a very slow pace. *"Just keep the momentum, Goose will catch us."* Russell ran up and Kelly was shouting, *"Jump in Goose, Jump in!"* Russell tried to open the passenger door at the back but couldn't get it open because of the pressure of the packed bodies. However he did get the driver's door open and jumped in pushing in behind the driver and then settling himself down in the front seat, along with one or two of the others. The car had kept its momentum and was picking up some speed.

4.15pm
September 25th
Jaz McCann

Jaz McCann was badly shaken but conscious after crashing into the gates of the Brit camp. He was stunned but instinct drove him out through the passenger door. He was oblivious to others around him. He felt he was moving in a slow motion film. Running left onto the Halftown Road he became more aware of his surroundings and felt his energy returning.

He was outside the jail. This fact alone lifted his spirits and he lessened the pace slightly. He was a keen runner and wanted to pace himself as he knew he had been running too fast to last any length of time. He looked over his shoulder to see if any of his comrades from the car were following him. He saw a bunch of guards around the car and two other guards and a soldier running after him.

Quickening his pace again he was thinking that he was the only one who had escaped from the car. As it was also the only vehicle that had reached the perimeter gates of the camp. He believed he was the only one of all the escaping Republicans to have made it outside. So he felt the success of the escape now fell on his shoulders alone.

The sentry box at the camp main gate had a good line of sight along the right hand side of Halftown Road so this prevented McCann turning right on to Blaris Road and directly away from the jail towards Lisburn town. He looked over his shoulder again to find the soldier had overtaken the guards in the pursuit.

"Stop or I'll fire," shouted the soldier. McCann did not slacken his pace. It was a good sign that the soldier had warned him because it meant he wasn't trigger happy. But McCann also heard the excitement in his voice. He was about 30 yards behind him and he knew if the soldier started to fall behind further he would shoot. He couldn't let a prisoner go. The soldier was carrying a handgun. At least, thought McCann, a short-arm is less accurate than a rifle.

He started zig-zagging slightly to put his shot off. He didn't want to stop but he was hoping if he was hit that it wouldn't be in the head or spine. A shot rang out. It was loud but not ear splitting. He found himself ducking but not slowing. He wondered had the Brit fired in the air. The second shot left a ring in his ear but he wasn't for giving up.

He dug deep for energy and headed towards a turning to his left. It was the Bog Road. Although the road skirted the visitor's car park to the jail he was elated as he turned the corner. The respite was dampened somewhat when he realised that the road ran in a straight line into the distance –too clear a shot. He hoped that the soldier's heavy breathing from running would affect his aim. McCann continued running and crossed to the hedging on the other side of the Bog Road.

Anything to obstruct the line of fire would be helpful. As he searched for a break in the hedge he realised that the field was flat and unbroken. Worse still it was freshly ploughed. It would slow his pace too much and leave him a sitting target. He stuck to the road where he was more confident of his footing.

As the British soldier took the corner into the Bog Road he had the escapee in sight again. Both he and McCann were breathless and exhausted. He called on him to halt again. The prisoner had nowhere to run but was showing no signs of giving up. The soldier didn't particularly want to shoot the men while he was running away but he couldn't let him escape.

McCann was having the same thoughts. He was in easy range now for the Brit but he couldn't bring himself to stop. The straightness of the road was relentless. Exhausted now he was forced to a walk but still wouldn't stop. Behind him the soldier had levelled the gun on his back ready to shoot. He felt relief when the escapee broke his run. He closed the gap to within a few feet still keeping him covered with a pistol.

Only when the soldier had moved past him did McCann stop, bending over and resting he hands on his knees with pure exhaustion. His chest was heavy in a battle for oxygen. The soldier told him to walk back in the direction of the front gate. A car stopped near where the Bog Road joined Halftown Road and a prison guard disembarked. It was one of the original guards who were chasing him and he was running towards them. When he reached the escapee he tried to grip him in a headlock and then an armlock.

There was no way that McCann was letting the prison guard take over his capture. He fought back and threw him off. The guard appealed to the armed soldier for help but was rewarded with *"Fuck off mate and keep out of my line of fire!"* He had watched the scuffle still concentrating on keeping the escapee covered. After that, the guard gave up and simply accompanied them back to the jail.

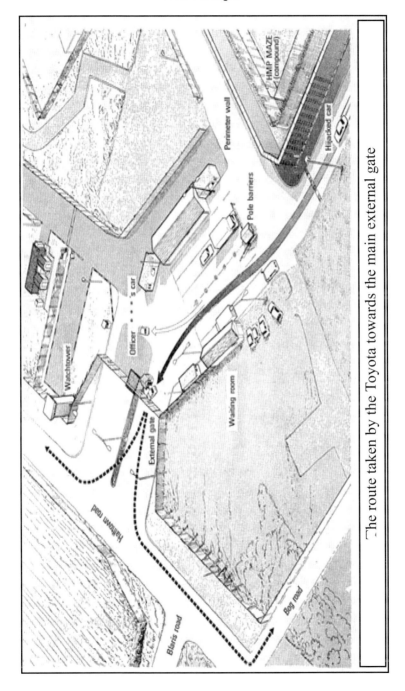

The route taken by the Toyota towards the main external gate

Paul Kane and
Brendy Mead

Paul Kane had scrambled out of the car crash at the gates. He had watched, fascinated momentarily as Mead had accelerated towards the soldier. As the soldier dived to avoid the Toyota, Kane prepared himself for the impact. He braced his arms against the dash board in the passenger seat and ducked his head between his arms. The car struck the gate off centre, concentrating the impact to the left. The gate was open but not fully and the impact had spun the car sideways.

Kane kicked the passenger door open. He saw the soldier unholstering his sidearm and noticed it was attached to the thin lanyard rope. The soldier was on the inside of the gate so Kane turned immediately and ran in a crouched position to his right.

He headed along Halftown Road. He passed the sentry box situated beside the gate but saw no activity inside. Was that where the Brit soldier had come from, he wondered? He hugged the side of the road as he ran, to make the angle awkward for any soldier who might decide to shoot from that position. When he looked over his shoulder he saw Brendy Mead running in the same direction and slowed briefly to let him catch up. They were well suited as both were amongst the fastest sprinters on the jail football pitch.

Mead waved down the first car that appeared. The prison guard's uniform he was wearing did the trick so they hijacked the car. The only occupant was the driver and they ordered him to drive on. He was in his late teens and Kane searched him for weapons just in case. He found a driving licence and studied it. There was something familiar about the guy. It was his father's driving licence. *"Do you race dogs?"* Kane inquired. *"My father keeps greyhounds,"* was the nervous reply. *"Your Da races his dogs at Dunmore Stadium in North Belfast. I know him,"* continued Kane triumphantly. The driver nodded. *"Just take us where we want to go and you'll be all right Big Lad,"* continued Kane winking at Mead.

They both knew there would be British Army and RUC checkpoints on the roads so they gave themselves five minutes of drive-time before they would have to ditch the car. They talked to the young man some more about his father. They talked about the escaped prisoners. They were psyching him out. If he wanted his father to be safe then all he had to do was to take orders. When they got him to stop they told him to return home and tell no-one of his experience and everyone would be safe. The teenager assured them he wouldn't even tell his father.

Kane and Mead took the chance. They got out of the car and watched him turn and head back. As soon as he was out of sight they went off the road. Mead found a rusty pitch fork in a hedge. Outside of rust it was in good condition so he used it as a walking staff. At one of their rest breaks he sat rubbing a stone over the bridge end of the fork. There was an inscription with a date. The date was 1883 – exactly 100 years ago. He thought it was a good omen. They took to the fields, feeling it was a safer bet and walked and jogged where possible, always keeping to the cover of the hedgerows and ditches until night fell.

They didn't know for sure what direction they were walking in. They thought it was south or southwest but really all they wanted was to use the darkness to increase their distance from the jail. They walked with exhilaration and excitement giving way to determination and stamina. No obstacle was too great. They climbed fences, waded through rivers and ploughed through boglands. After about five hours they saw the lights of a small town or village in the distance and headed towards it.

It wasn't long until they realised it was the distinctive parallel lines of lighting that was needed for security in the Long Kesh Prison Camp. They had walked in a wide circle and landed back near to where they had left the car, not far from the jail.

It was about 10pm they guessed. Dejected but determined, they turned and set off again. This time they used roads and ditches as a guide, to at least make sure they didn't travel in a circle. Now and then they walked the road for a short distance. On one such occasion they walked over a bridge rather than get soaked in the river. As they crossed, a car's headlights appeared. They quickly hopped over the stone wall of the bridge. Mead wedged the pitch-fork shaft behind a couple of small protruding rocks on top of the wall. Both then hung down the river-side of the bridge. They were literally clinging to the shaft by their fingers. Although both were strong it seemed like an age before the car passed. Both scrambled up on to the bridge again after the vehicle passed. Their fingers and forearms were aching. But another set of headlights appeared almost at once and they repeated the exercise. After it passed, Mead climbed back up but Kane was nowhere to be seen. Mead looked down to the stream and could just see his comrade lying on his back about 12ft below. He giggled nervously but clambered down the bank to find Kane moaning in pain. He helped him up but it was obvious he was hurt. Kane however insisted on moving on. The pace slowed considerably but they were determined to make more distance away from the jail.

After another few hours, cold, wet and exhausted they started searching for somewhere safe to hide during daylight. Mead left Kane in search of a place. He found a wall covered in Ivy and other shrubbery. He dug in and burrowed out enough room for both of them. He had managed to find some heavy duty plastic bags which he laid on the ground. He then brought his comrade to it. They lay down behind the thick camouflage and tried to sleep - or at least to rest. The cold was biting deep.

The River Runs Through It

J oe Simpson had experienced a deep and dreamless sleep the night before the escape. Although he was serving a 20-year sentence he was known for always being in good spirits. He was a bit of a comedian, continuously playing tricks on his comrades. So when Seamy McDermott had approached him he thought he was being wound up.

When it became obvious that he was being offered a part in a mass escape his first feeling was of a deep pride in being trusted. He did his brief with a good heart, taking over D-Wing, arresting guards and removing their uniforms. As he climbed into the back of the lorry, his only worry, was for those being left behind and what might be visited on them by a vengeful administration. Even when he looked curiously at the trays of boiled eggs and cheese in the kitchen lorry he couldn't help winding Bobby Storey up by putting an egg in his pocket after Storey had warned them to – *"leave the food alone,"* as if anyone was hungry at that stage. Storey just didn't want any noise whatsoever in the back of the lorry.

As soon as he got out of the lorry he was away like a hare, out of the gate and up the field. He was nearing the crest, like many others, when he heard the shot and thought he was the target and crouched down. Looking around he saw Harry Murray lying on the ground nearby. As he started to move towards him Harry was already waving and shouting, *"Go on, go on! You can't do anything for me!"* So he took off again and after jumping a hedge saw a packed getaway car speeding past. It was too late to wave it down. He spotted Sean McGlinchey and then Bobby Storey and Peter Hamilton in the next field.

The four moved on together, trying to make distance from the jail. They spotted farm buildings in the distance. Storey suggested there might be cars at it but the river Lagan stretched across their path. As his gaze found a stone bridge a few hundred yards away British Army and Police jeeps stopped at it. Storey instinctively hunkered down and said, *"We'll have to go into the river lads"* just as the whirr of a helicopter became audible.

They had no choice and slipped quietly off the river bank and into the cold water, it was deep and fast. The water came up to Storey's chest. At 6ft 4in he was by far the tallest. With the others it was up to their necks. They were oblivious to the cold as they moved under the overhang of grass and soil pulling the grass down further to disguise their presence. They were about half a mile from the jail and it was around 5pm. In a whispered discussion Storey suggested they stay put until darkness fell before crossing more open ground.

After about 10 minutes they could see a number of police and prison guards on the other bank. The river was about 20 yards wide and they could hear the conversation. There was one RUC man and one Reserve RUC man. They walked from left to right past the prisoners hiding place and crouched down at a 3ft diameter storm drain. *"They could be up there" "Go in and check then" "No way! Fire a few shots up" "Fuck off! You fire them then."* They sent for a flashlight.

The escapees collective hearts sank as it seemed obvious they had been seen in the field and reported, but they continued to listen intently. The adrenalin rush was diminishing and with it the cold was deepening in their bones. They were starting to shiver and causing small ripples. Storey whispered to Simpson as they were standing in a row, *"Tell them to stop shivering."* Joe passed the message down the line but in truth they were all shivering and couldn't stop. It was all they could do to stop their teeth from chattering, this adding sound effects to their shivers

The Reserve cop was a country man and had noticed the ripple effect. He pointed over, *"There's movement in the water there."* His colleague was less convinced. The Reserve cop insisted and he went prone in a push-up position. He spotted the four heads of the escapees in a row above the waterline and leapt to his feet, grabbing his weapon. A shot was fired. None of the four escapees were hit so they thought that nervousness was affecting his aim. Hamilton shouted, *"Hey Fuck Off, we aren't armed!"*

As he prepared to fire again Bobby Storey shouted, *"We're not armed and we're coming out."* The other cop had unholstered his own short-arm and shouted, *"Swim across the river to me."* *"I can't swim,"* said Storey and McGlinchey in tandem but started to move out of cover.

The cop radios were hopping with activity and more British soldiers and cops were arriving. The four escapees were caught but they had succeeded in escaping – if only for an hour or so – and the elation buoyed them up. The weight of disappointment would not fall on them just yet.

Storey and the others were ordered to lie face down on the grass and were quickly frisked for weapons. They were then stripped at gunpoint to their underpants. Storey wasn't wearing any so was frogmarched totally naked the 300 yards to the vehicles at the bridge. They had been cuffed and forced to walk with their hands above their heads. Spectators were appearing on the road now as well as military and police personnel, but the escapees were indifferent to their gazes.

They were told to stand on the bridge and face the river. Hamilton thought they were going to get pushed off the bridge into the middle of the Lagan. Instead they started questioning them on who they were and about others involved in the escape. Not surprisingly these questions were met with a dismissive, *"Are you serious?"* *"Catch yourselves on!"* and then silence. The interrogators gave up.

McGlinchey was wearing a crucifix on a chain which his mother had brought him back from a pilgrimage to Lourdes. A British soldier ripped it from his neck and smirked, *"Was that supposed to bring you good luck mate?"* McGlinchey maintained an angry silence but couldn't help a smile when Hamiliton whispered out of the side of his mouth. *"Luck, fuck–if I was a duck I'd drown!"* It wasn't the first time trying to escape for either of them. McGlinchey repeated the story of the crucifix – leaving out Hamilton's remark to his mother on the first visit after his recapture. Her simple response was *"Sure didn't it save your life Son."*

The four escapees were then literally thrown into the jeeps – two to a jeep. McGlinchey was on the floor and Hamilton thrown prone on top of him. Military personnel then sat on the benches with their boots on Hamilton's back for the short distance to the jail.

By the time Storey, Hamilton, Simpson and McGlinchey neared the main gate in the jail wall through which they had escaped, a baying crowd of prison guards was waiting.

They were unceremoniously flung out of the jeeps onto the tarmac road and the reception committee. The pent up rage of a humiliated prison regime made brutal contact immediately. They had organised a long two-line gauntlet with batons drawn.

When Storey picked himself up and looked down the tunnel of

dark blue screaming bodies he took a deep breath but did not move. This enraged the guards and he and his comrades were pushed and dragged into the middle of the gauntlet turned melee. Boots and batons came raining from all directions. There was no-one in charge. Management had been taken over by vengeful mob. All they could do was to curl up in a ball and hope that the guards would exhaust themselves.

Storey realised that, in fact, what was saving him from death was that there were so many trying to beat him that they were getting in each other's way. He concentrated on protecting his head as best he could. The beating continued for what seemed like hours but could've been half an hour when he became aware of a loud voice above the pain and the din. *"Put the batons away. Just use your boots or fists lads. If you kill one of these scumbags we'll all be in trouble. Avoid the head."* Storey recognised the senior guard who was standing over him with a foot on either side of his head.

Storey believed the guard was protecting him from head injuries but was also trying to slowly de-escalate the anger and reintroduce some control into the chaos. The guard himself was making no moves to strike him. In the midst of his pain and nakedness he felt gratitude.

McGlinchey, Hamilton and Simpson were taking the battering of their lives at the same time, but a gap appeared in the bunch of guards beating them and Governor Duncan McLaughlin appeared. He didn't look at any of the prisoners but spoke clearly to the guards. *"Anymore of this and you will be held to account."* He too was trying to re-establish a semblance of control. *"Get these prisoners to the punishment cells,"* he said as he turned away, aware of the deep resentment his words had triggered. A few kicks followed the Governor turning his back but they were then manhandled into vans with three or four guards. Again they were prone on the floor – two to a van.

172

The escapees were hoping for some respite once they reached the cells. However, at the cell block, once the van door was opened, they were all trailed out by the ankles and dropped face-down on gravel. Peter Hamilton was in excruciating pain and trying hard not to show it. When two guards gripped his ankles he knew he was getting trailed the 10 yards or so to the segregation block and it would shred his skin. Despite being handcuffed he spun himself onto his back in the belief it might be a bit less painful and that his back and buttocks could survive the abuse much better than his ribs, face and private parts. He was wrong about the pain. But at least it was over fairly quickly as he was thrust onto the floor of an empty cell. The coldness of the concrete floor was actually a relief.

Making Distance
The Squad in the
Hillman Car

As hope was disappearing in the segregation unit back at the jail, hope and excitement in the Hillman was growing the further the car travelled away from the jail. Kelly was thinking things out like everybody else. The problem was there were too many people with too many ideas.

'Operation Vesper' was on Kelly's mind. At that stage he didn't know its title but knew the British would have contingencies. This was the British Government operation which kicked in automatically in the event of a prison escape. It involved road blocks being set up in concentric circles around the jail; each circle, further from the jail. It was set to create a series of obstacles to prevent escapees getting any distance away. He reckoned they would be a little rusty since there hadn't been an escape from the H-Blocks before. So with his mouth cupped close to the driver's ear, he spoke in clear syllables to be understood above the babble. *"Make distance: Stay off the main road: Stick to the small roads until we get distance. We need to break the circle."* Campbell was nodding as the advice tallied with his own thoughts. He was trying to build up some speed in the car which he was doing fairly effectively.

Kelly thought that the car was sluggish. *"It's like an attempt at the Guinness Book of Records in a Hillman,"* he said to no-one in particular. People were settling down a bit and not shouting as much. There were ideas and discussions going on about where to go, and what to do. McKearney, from Tyrone, was talking about going to the Lough Shore meaning Lough Neagh which he knew very well and which wasn't too far away.

Campbell drove down a couple of the narrower roads. Kelly was saying, *"We need to take another car. There are too many in this one. Look out for a car."* At one stage a car came up behind them, Tony Kelly at the rear window was shouting instructions to Campbell of how to cut them off. But the Hillman was unresponsive. Campbell tried to cut it off but the other car swerved round it and sped away.

After what seemed like a half hour but was probably five minutes, they spotted another car, a large one parked beside a small housing estate. There was a young guy, perhaps in his late teens or early twenties speaking with two young women. They were dressed in their Sunday best. The escapees' car pulled up. Some of the prisoners, including Russell, were still wearing guards' uniforms. As Russell jumped out and walked over to the guy who was standing there, Kelly was trying to open the back door of the car. He had noticed stencilled along the side of the car the word 'Turbo'. While he didn't know much about turbo engines, he knew that 'Turbo' equated to high speed.

Most other prisoners were staying in the car, because they didn't want to take any chances. Nobody really wanted to lose that security. Kelly couldn't get the door open because there were so many people in the back squeezed against the doors. He wound down the window and could hear the conversation. It was like watching a film or a pantomime because Russell, with all the authority of the uniform he was wearing, was in interrogative mode. *"Who owns this vehicle?"* To which the young man who had obviously been taken by surprise replied, *"I do."* Russell said in a clipped military tone, *"Well I am going to commandeer the vehicle sir."* He opened the driver's door and climbed in.

At this stage Campbell, who had been driving, Russell and Gerard Fryers were all out of the Hillman. For some reason Russell couldn't start the vehicle. It had some sort of new starting mechanism in it which Russell didn't recognise. So he got back out of the car and said to the owner, *"Start the car!"* Which he duly did. Russell then said brightly, *"Thank you."* And pulled him out of the car. The young man remonstrated in a mild enough voice while trying to stand up for himself saying, *"I know my rights; what are you doing?"* Russell pushed him effortlessly to one side saying, *"Sorry about that son"* and the car sped off with Russell, Fryers and Campbell in it.

Because no-one else got out of the Hillman, there were only three in the new car which disappeared into the distance. There were now nine in the Hillman which was still too many. McKearney got into the driver's seat and drove off. Kelly was then talking into his ear, *"Get off this road. He'll make a phone call and they'll know exactly where we are,"* he said referring to the owner of the car that had just been hijacked. *"We need to get off into a side road and take a different direction."* Mc Kearney pulled off at the next left turn and drove down a fairly narrow road. There was a little more room in the car now and everybody was looking around them, passing houses and looking across fields for any danger signs. They were scouring the sky for British Army helicopters. The whole idea however was still to make distance. They had yet to see any road signs to give an indication of their direction of travel.

After a couple of miles, the car gave up. The clutch burnt out and the car wouldn't go any further. For a moment there was pandemonium.

Kelly had spotted Dermy Finucane in the car. He knew Finucane, by reputation, was a fast and competent driver. He caught his eye, then shouted, "*Right everybody out of the car, get into the ditch. Dermy come on with me.*" Turning to the rest of the escapees, he spoke "*Lads, if we aren't back in 10 minutes you're on your own. Don't wait any longer. We passed a house a couple of hundred yards back there. I saw a car. They may have weapons, so you need to listen carefully for any shots or anything. But you also need to stay in the ditch. If we aren't back in 10 minutes then make your own way. Good luck.*"

Jimmy Burns

Jimmy Burns dived out the side window of the Celica glad to survive the crash at the front gate of the jail. As he scrambled to his feet he saw two guards and a British soldier a few yards away. Burns was still in the guard's uniform so he shouted to them that he was pursuing the prisoners. He didn't really expect to fool them but was hoping a little confusion did no harm in the circumstances. It may have worked because although they stared at him for a moment they ran off in the other direction after Jaz McCann who was in civilian clothes.

Kane, Mead and Artt were in front of him. They had turned right onto the Halftown Road outside the gate while McCann had gone left. He watched Barry Artt jump left through a hedge a short distance ahead of him but decided to pursue Kane and Mead. They were a good distance ahead of him but still in sight when he spotted them waving down a car and hijacking it. Burns shouted at them to wait for him but he realised they couldn't hear him and watched dejectedly as they disappeared.

The road was deserted and Burns was exhausted but he set off again. He tried to wave cars down. The first two drove on past but the third one stopped. He opened the passenger door to discover a man was driving and a woman was in the back seat with a child. He got in and spoke to the man who was driving. *"Will you follow that car; they've just escaped from the prison."* *"Go ahead John, Get after them!"* Enthused the woman, spurred on by the drama she had happened into.

But John was having none of it. He stalled the car, pretending he had run out of petrol. His suspicions deepened when Burns put his hand into his pocket. He was searching for his pistol to take control but it wasn't there. With dismay Burns realised he must have lost it in the car crash. The driver moved when he saw Burn's hand in his pocket. He trapped Burn's hand in the overcoat pocket of the guard's uniform.

Burns was now trying to get out of the car again as he had lost the advantage. The husband thought there was a gun involved and was tightening his grip so that the intruder couldn't get the gun out of his pocket. His wife, now realising what was going on was trying to hold on to Burns as well. The child in the back of the car was screaming. Burns had had enough and broke free from their grip managing to escape.

He ran up the road and waved down another car which had appeared on the scene. This time the car stopped about 50 yards ahead but as he got closer the first car had pulled up alongside it and John had obviously warned the other driver of the danger. With that, both cars sped off.

Desperation was building in Burns. He cut through the back gardens of some houses and ended up on a street. A car horn sounded and he looked around to see a British army jeep with a number of soldiers out on the road. Burns immediately waved frantically at them and pointed straight ahead shouting, *"They went that direction. Get after them."* To his amazement the soldiers piled into the jeep and drove off in the direction he indicated. He on the other hand, took off in the opposite direction.

He continued on through fields, determined but exhausted, just wanting to get further away from the jail. At one point he leapt over a gate and landed almost on top of two Alsatian dogs. The dogs were as startled as he was, at least at first. Had anyone been watching this encounter from a distance they would be forgiven for thinking he had landed on a trampoline as his exit was so immediate!

Burns was exhilarated by the escape as soon as he had exited the main gate of the Brit camp. After years of hard imprisonment and protest he had beaten the system. His victory couldn't be taken off him but he wanted to enjoy a lot more of this freedom.

Just then he saw a small housing estate. He made his way to the first house with a car parked outside it and rang the bell. A man opened the door. This was still close to the jail so the guy recognised the guard's uniform. But he was taken aback as to how dishevelled and rough the guard appeared. Realising this, Burns used it to his advantage explaining that he was a prison officer and that he had been in an accident. He asked the house owner could he drive him to the nearest police station.

The man was apologetic but explained that his wife was going to use the car. There was however a taxi driver living across the street who might help. He pointed out the house to Burns who thanked him and walked to the taxi man's house.

Burns dusted himself down as he moved towards the house. He had decided on a different tack this time. When the door opened he explained to the taxi man that his wife was very ill and that he had missed his lift from the prison and could he drive him to the hospital as it was urgent. *"No problem,"* replied the taxi man as he lifted his coat off the banister behind him.

They set off but as they turned on to the main road Burns could see what he thought was a roadblock in the distance. There was certainly activity on the road and it was in the direction he had sent the British soldiers. *"Are we heading for Lisburn or Belfast,"* he asked the driver. *"Lisburn,"* he replied. *"Sorry,"* said Burns *"My fault. We need to go to the Royal Victoria Hospital in Belfast."*

The taxi driver almost immediately did a u-turn but they had been getting closer to the vehicle checkpoint all the time. They were about 50 yards from it when they turned and the hairs on the back of Burn's neck were standing in anticipation of the soldiers opening fire. Nothing happened and Burns kept a surreptitious eye on the wing mirror to see if they were being pursued.

Turning another bend they found themselves at a checkpoint on the road immediately outside the jail again. Burns heart sank. He should've been miles away by now. Two soldiers ran over and told the driver they couldn't get through so they turned about and drove towards the first checkpoint. When they reached it Burns was ready for a nervous breakdown but he wound down his window, leaned out to make his uniform obvious and waved to the British soldiers who in turn waved them through thinking he was prison staff.

Burn's spirits rose again as he had succeeded in getting past some checkpoints and was now definitely travelling away from the prison. *"What's all that about?"* The driver broke in *"Don't know,"* Burns replied. *"Maybe it's a terrorist incident,"* he added thinking he should have something more to say. *"It was very quiet when I left a while ago. It looks a bit mad."*

He was trying to work out when and where to abandon the relative security of the taxi. He certainly had no money to pay for the trip so he needed to pick a good spot where he could get a head start on the driver. The taxi man didn't look too fit so he just needed that bit of distance at the start. As they crested a hill they came upon another checkpoint near a crossroads but just off the road that they were travelling on. Burns suggested to the driver that they should go on or they'd be there all day. The driver, who was now starting to resent the disruption to his Sunday routine said, *"We can't move until we're told."*

Just then an RUC man looked over. He screamed at Burns, pointing his rifle at him, to get out of the car. Burns kept his cool and disembarked. *"I am a prison officer,"* he said in an indignant tone instead of raising his arms as ordered *"stop pointing that*

Escape

weapon at me." The cop calmed his pace and aggression but said, "Ok show me your warrant card" Burns made a show of searching his uniform pockets and then said, "I must have left it in my other jacket." He thought he saw the twitch of a smile on the RUC man's face as he said, "No problem Sir. Have you got any ID at all?"

Burns knew his luck had definitely run out as soon as a warrant card was mentioned. It meant the cop knew that no staff get in or out of prison without carrying ID cards. "I'm afraid not," replied Burns as the RUC man pushed him up against the car and started frisking him as other armed RUC men gathered around the car.

At this point the taxi driver jumped out of the car. Burns, face down on the bonnet could see his agitation. To his amazement the taxi man exploded, "Leave that officer alone. His wife is very ill and I'm taking him to see her." At that, he was pounced upon and wrestled against his taxi. The RUC obviously thought they had caught an accomplice.

Both were put into the RUC vehicle and transported to the barracks. Burns was handcuffed in the back and the taxi driver was in the front. He now knew the score about his passenger. After a while he looked at Burns over his shoulder and practically hissed, "This is a fine mess you've got me into!"

Despite the circumstance Burns found it hard not to smile at the Laurel and Hardy moment. He felt sorry for the guy but the taxi driver was going to be released later that day – Burns would be back doing a life sentence.

182

Kevin Barry Artt
and the Bicycle

Kevin Barry Artt couldn't believe his luck when he was offered a chance of escape on September 25th. He had only been in the H-Blocks a matter of weeks starting a life sentence. Better still, all he had to do was get in the back of a lorry and be a passenger. He had not hesitated. It was a no-brainer. If he got caught, what could they add to a life sentence! He was only on the starting line. And if he escaped – well it was fantasy come true. It was Steve McQueen in Ireland!

When he boarded the kitchen lorry he hunkered about half-way down among his comrades. It looked like the whole Block was on board. He sat in the dark quietness feeling the vehicle's motion and trying to guess, from the starts and stops of gates and left and right turns, how close they might be to the front gate.

He had heard the growing commotion outside along with the others, but nobody dared to speak. He had started to resign himself to capture when the shutter at the back of the lorry shot up and light silhouetted a tall uniformed guard. Everybody's eyes were adjusting to the new light when the guard spoke. Only then did he and many of the others, he guessed, realise the guard was actually Bobby Storey in uniform. The urgency in his voice galvanised them into a scramble on to the tailgate and down either side of the lorry to the open gate.

Artt saw the open fields and then the yellow Toyota car with prisoners piling in. He was last in and made it just in time before Mead drove off.

From the back seat he could see comrades scrambling over barbed wire. A red car overtook them sounding the horn. They were travelling along in the shadow of the high perimeter wall. He knew they were out – but not out of the woods. A set of gates lay ahead and he saw a British soldier and a warder drawing them closed. The car accelerated and he found himself shouting along with the others, gripping the seat in front and wedging his shoulder against it for the impact. The car was forced sideways but he felt okay and still exhilarated. Mead and McCann in the front seats were already getting out. He followed Kane out the passenger door scrambling between seats and onto his hands and knees on the ground.

He spotted Kane running to the right with a guard chasing close behind him. He was about to change direction when he realised that the guard was actually another prisoner, Brendy Mead. They were too fast for him to keep up with. He wanted off the road and turned down a farm lane and into a farmyard. He had hoped for vehicles but it was empty. He moved through quickly and ran down an embankment towards a small housing estate. He crossed a ditch and crawled to a hedge near the road. He was out of breath from running at full pelt and crawled through long grass and weeds into the bottom of a hedge to get his breath. As he was trying to work out the next move a number of vehicles could be heard coming along the road. He knew the sound of jeeps and his worst fears were realised when they squealed to a halt about fifteen yards ahead of him.

The slamming of doors and thud of boots along with the English accents made him worm closer into the hedge. He burrowed underneath brambles. He reached out and pulled weeds and brambles closer over his prone body. He was glad that the denim jeans and shirt he was wearing were a dark blue and not light as he lowered his head onto his arms to wait.

It was a long and intense wait until dark. As the adrenalin wore off the cold deepened but he was still free and patience cost nothing. It wasn't a busy road and after a while the excited soldiers voices and movements calmed. Eventually, the British army moved on after dark but still he lay in the quiet for a further half an hour.

He was stiff with cold as he crossed the road to the housing estate and into the back garden of the first house. He was looking for transport and warm clothes. The first shed was padlocked as was the second. He checked the lock on the third house shed and found it wasn't fastened. He slipped inside.

Immediately his eye caught the shadowy outline of a number of bicycles against the wall. As he moved towards them a light went on. He moved back to the door. Someone was in the bathroom gargling loudly. He left the shed door ajar and used the light from the bathroom window to check the tyre pressures on the wheels and chose the largest bike. Carefully he separated it out and moved to the door. Noticing a woollen jersey he put it on grateful for the extra warmth it promised. After closing the shed door he quietly moved down the side of the house and out onto the street. There were a few young people in the street but he waved as he passed them out onto the road.

He was still very close to the prison which became obvious as he found himself cycling past the main gates a few minutes later. He reckoned it was about 9pm and there were still workmen repairing them. He swung onto Blaris Road which he knew led to Lisburn Town and soon found himself approaching a main road. There was an RUC vehicle checkpoint. It was blocking his way but as it was too late to turn or take to the fields, he cycled on.

The Hillman Squad Continue Their Road Trip

Kelly and Finucane started up the hill away from the car, working up a plan. They were piecing it together, running and talking. *"OK did you see the house there?"* *"Yeah, yeah there was a car at it, I think."* *"Yeah there was a car, that means there is somebody in, hopefully."* *"It's a country house, they might have shotguns or something. We need to be careful."* *"You don't have a gun?"* *"No I don't have a gun. I threw that stupid wooden one away. It would have came in handy."* That was the type of conversation that was going on. *"Ok what way will we play it?"* Kelly said, *"Play it like an accident."* Kelly was wearing a prison officer's shirt which was torn and had blood on it from climbing through the barbed wire. *"I'm wearing a uniform, let's go to the house as if we need an ambulance and want to use the phone."*

As they were talking a car came over the brow of the hill. Without conversation, each acted in their own way. They had thought of the accident idea: Kelly had put his arm round Finucane's shoulder and said, *"Look you assist me as if I've been injured."* Now Kelly dropped his arm off Finucane's shoulder and started staggering as if injured. Finucane fell to the ground without a word and lay on the verge of the road motionless. Kelly didn't know if the occupants of the car had seen Finucane going down or if they had just seen him lying there. He saw the car come to a halt as it crested the hill and then saw it reversing a couple of yards before stopping again. He decided to play the hand he had been dealt. He held out a limp arm in a begging fashion as if he needed help and staggered in the direction of the car some 30 yards away.

Kelly was making it up as he went along. He didn't know what Finucane was doing so he rolled his head as if dazed and fell deliberately unto one knee. When he did this he glanced back and saw that Finucane was lying on the edge of the road playing dead. He pulled himself back up off his knee and started in a pleading voice saying, *"Help! Help! Get the police, Get me to the hospital, Please help."* When the car had reversed a little, he thought he had lost the moment. He could see there were two people in the car. He didn't care, he just needed to get the car. He didn't know at the time but it was a woman in the driver's seat of a small sports car. A man got out on the passenger side and Kelly rose to his feet again and unsteadily moved forward. Staggering weakly as if he was badly injured, he continued to plead, *"Please help, Please help. Get the police. Get me to a hospital."* He fell again for effect as if very tired and confused. He stole another glance and saw that Finucane hadn't moved a muscle.

He was trying to work out Finucane's plan and his own plan. Finucane was obviously pretending that he had been in an accident or he had been shot. He could see just down the road, as the driver and passenger could also see, that there was a car with all the doors lying open. This of course was the car that they had abandoned. He was creating possibilities in his head.

He got unsteadily to his feet again and staggered forward. He was very near now and was wondering if he could overpower both people. What way could he take control as he had no weapon. Kelly was trying to work out some way of getting them both out of the car. The woman had not moved out of the driver's seat. The man, who was in his forties, was behaving in a nervously sympathetic way. Kelly turned round again, pleading with a crying voice, *"Help me, Please help me - my mate...."* Just pointing back at Finucane with an unfinished sentence made its own statement. The driver still did not get out of the car but the passenger pulled forward the passenger seat and said, *"It's okay mate. We'll get you in and then we'll sort your mate out in a minute."*

The man and woman hadn't worked out what was going on. They were nervous but at the same time they had a man in uniform who was obviously injured. His shirt was torn and bloody and Kelly assessed that the uniform was allaying their worst suspicions.

Kelly staggered alongside the car and the man made way for him. He had the seat pushed forward to allow access to the back seat. As Kelly got into the back seat, he saw through the windscreen that Finucane was up and sprinting the short distance to the car. Kelly had been used to saying all day in a very forceful way, *"Don't move or I'll blow your head off."* So he repeated this mantra again despite having no weapon. However the shock of what he said was enough to stun both the man and the woman who watched Finucane's advance mesmerised. In a matter of seconds Finucane was at the driver's door, which he opened and pulled the woman out. The couple didn't know what they had stumbled into.

The two escaping Republicans had been determined to take the car. Kelly pulled back the front passenger seat and climbed into it. He then leaned over to grab the inside handle of the door, nodded to the man and said matter of factly, *"Thanks for that,"* closed the door and they drove off. They drove the short distance to the other vehicle which had been abandoned. It must have looked like a crowd of people when in fact it was only seven others coming out of the hedges and over the ditches. They all piled into the car. There was a sunroof in the car and as they piled into the back and front, Kelly was forced further and further out through the open roof.

As the last escapee got in and the door was closed, Kelly was out through the sunroof from his waist up. He could see a considerable distance. Finucane took off at high speed, in the small sports car. They were on a minor road but there was a major road some three or four hundred yards up ahead. Kelly could see over the hedges and spotted a garage far up on his left hand side about six or seven hundred yards away. He was doing navigator to Finucane, *"Straight ahead. There is a garage up on the left. You're going to hit a main road. Go into the garage and you'll see two cars in it. We'll be able to get another car and split up."* He was pointing dramatically with his arm at full length and it struck him in the middle of doing this he was a bit like 'Oddball' (Donald Sutherland) the eccentric tank commander sitting out of the turret. The corners of his mouth twitched into a smile. It released some tension. He was starting to enjoy himself. They were all realising that they had broken free and overcome another obstacle.

The wind pulling at his face was exhilarating but he realised also that it did not look at all normal, so he wriggled his way down through the sunroof and pushed his way down into the passenger seat. It was time for decisions again. *"Half of youse are going to have to get out at this garage. There are a couple of cars at the petrol pumps. We need to take at least one of them and then we split our forces."* Nobody answered. Everybody was listening but no-one was answering because the thought of getting out of the security of this car into another car while things were going so well was not a happy thought. Nobody knew who was going to make the move.

As they drove into the garage there was a large saloon car sitting at the pumps. The owner was a huge bear of a man. They were told later he was a nationalist from Fermanagh. Kelly pulled the front seat forward and said, *"Right lads half of youse get out and take that car."* Four of the nine got out of the car and ran over to hijack another one. The owner, seeing the group coming and

189

realising that it was some sort of hijacking, fought like a Trojan. He didn't know exactly what was happening but he did have money in his car as he worked at insurance and had been collecting payments from some customers. He had stopped to get some petrol and now he was getting attacked by four or five people. More confusing still was that some of them were wearing uniforms.

Finucane had driven on just as far as the exit from the garage forecourt once the four others had disembarked. He wanted to be ready to go back out on to the road. Kelly watching events unfold from the passenger seat touched Finucane's arm and said, *"Let's wait and make sure."* But Finucane had already stopped the car and the five in the car watched as the others fought with the man, who seemed to be fighting for his life.

Kelly cupped his hands around his mouth and shouted to egg his comrades on. Joe Corey, produced a baton from the prison uniform he was wearing and threatened the guy in an attempt to get the keys off him, but it was to no avail. Actually at this stage he had thrown away the keys. Kelly and Finucane exchanged glances.

Kelly shouted over, *"Right everybody back in."* He opened the passenger door, raised his seat again to let everyone into the back. There was a bit of a panic, as you might expect, in case anybody was left behind. There was a pile up at the door. Gerry Kelly who had been forced over towards the driver again, watched as the youngest escapee Tony Kelly from Derry ran and jumped straight over the others at the door and dived head first in through the sunroof nearly knocking Gerry Kelly out when their heads clashed. Within moments everyone was safely back in the car. Gerry Kelly did a head count just in case. They drove out onto the main road and sped off, turning right, not knowing in what direction they were travelling at this stage.

The conversation was toing and froing, So they were watching for road signs to see where they were heading. As they came to a roundabout they saw a sign for Belfast via the M1 motorway. There were two cars parked on the hard shoulder of the roundabout. They drove past them playing for time to think up a scenario. At a glance Kelly had seen two people in the front seats of one of the cars. He said to Finucane, *"Play it the same as before like an accident. Pull up but block off the car when you're stopping."*

When they stopped alongside the car after doing a full circle of the roundabout Kelly went into his routine, *"There's been an accident..."* He saw there were two women sitting in the one car. The woman in the driver's seat had started the engine as soon as the escapees' car had pulled in and tried to drive off but her route was effectively blocked. Kelly and a few others got out of the sports car which included Paddy McIntyre, Joe Corey, Jim Smyth and Tony Kelly and took the keys of the car.

All pretence had disappeared as Smyth said in a broad Belfast accent, *"Listen Missus we're taking your car, simple as that!"* The four escapees climbed in. The younger woman then spoke *"My mummy is sick."* *"Not as sick as we will be if we don't get outta here!"* Smyth retorted facetiously as he revved the engine and checked for the handbrake. The daughter continued. *"At least can she have her handbag?"* *"Handbag for the lady lads!"* Smyth half-shouted while searching. Corey found it and handed it over. The women were ushered out to the side and the car was commandeered. The women were left standing beside the other parked car. Once it was obvious that the car had been secured Kelly got back into the first car and Finucane drove off with the other car following. At this stage there were five in the sports car and four in the other car.

It was quickly decided there was no point going onto the M1. The logic was that the motorway would be the first route the British

Army would block off. There was no point going to Belfast even though it was only 15 minutes drive away. It was too obvious. They decided to travel away from the Republican stronghold of West Belfast in a different direction. They went down another road and turned to the left at the first crossroads.

About a hundred yards up this road there was a sign for Hillsborough town. Kelly shouted, *"Stop the car,"* startling Finucane, *"Don't be going to Hillsborough it's a bad town."* He explained unnecessarily as everyone in the car knew it was a militarised town. As they turned round the other car came up. They waved it down, and Kelly shouted across to Smyth, *"Look don't go into Hillsborough. It's heavily militarised. It's a Unionist town. Go back down to the crossroads. We're going to go left. You take any of the other routes, but we need to split up. It gives us double the chance, at least to get half of us away, rather than staying in convoy."* Smyth nodded his agreement. So when they got down to the crossroads again Finucane drove left which took them towards Lurgan. The other car travelled in the direction of Castlewellan.

They were keeping to the speed limit at this stage. Finucane was driving. Kelly was in the front passenger seat and Kieran Fleming was in the back along with Pádraig McKearney and Seamus Clarke. Things had settled down and it was a bit more comfortable. The excitement continued but the conversation was calm. They returned to the obvious theme of what to do next and where to go. McKearney suggested going along the Loughshore. When the sign for Lurgan appeared, he said that he knew someone there and was trying to remember the address and directions to it. The conversation continued, *"Let's see how far we can get."* *"We have been in this car far too long. We need to get rid of the car."*

At one stage as they drove into Lurgan town, two British Army Jeeps passed, travelling at speed, on the other side of the road. The three republicans in the back automatically ducked below window level when they spotted the jeeps. When the first one passed the second jeep flashed its lights repeatedly. This caused a bit of animation in the car. People were cross talking, *"Nobody look round!"* Finucane shouted automatically. Finucane and Kelly were watching the mirrors to see if anything untoward happened. To their relief the jeeps sped on.

One of the few advantages of having been in jail for so long was recognising the place names of nationalist and republican areas. Prisoners were always talking about their own districts in jail. Kelly remembered some of them. *"Look out for Kilwilkee, Taghnavan or Shankill"* Everybody was watching out for these or for signs of Republican emblems or graffiti. Ironically the only native Lurgan man on the escape had gone in the Mercedes car from the farm with Brendan McFarlane. Kieran Fleming sitting in the back shouted suddenly, *"That says 'Shankill'! That says Shankill."* Kelly asked, *"Where?"* and he pointed over to the right. Finucane swung the car sharply round and drove into the estate that Fleming had indicated.

At this point doubt started to creep into Kelly's mind, *"Was 'Shankill' entirely Nationalist? Was it mixed?"* He knew it had been mentioned. He couldn't remember any particular republican prisoners who were actually from Shankill. The Kilwilkee estate was uppermost in his mind. While he was musing, they passed a small corner shop. They decided to check out the shop to see what sort of reaction they would get. McKearney got out. As he walked to the shop Finucane turned the car ready to exit the estate quickly if necessary. They surveyed the surrounding area while keeping an eye on McKearney. There were no union jack flags, there was no sign that it was a unionist estate. But they were still very nervous as there were no Irish republican emblems or graffiti, that they could see, either.

McKearney entered the shop and spoke to a teenage girl waiting to be served. He said that he had been involved in an escape from

Long Kesh and that he needed to talk to republicans. The young girl didn't know what to do. She was about 16 years old and a bit frightened. McKearney had spoken a few words in Irish to convince her that he was a republican. Most young nationalists had at least school Irish.

She came out with him. In the meantime a man had walked past the car, carrying a garden spade. Kelly stepped out of the car and spoke to him, *"Listen we have just escaped from the Kesh can you help us."* The man hesitated and then looked at Kelly as if he was a complete lunatic and hurried on without comment.

Kelly realised he was dressed partly in a uniform and must have frightened or confused the man, who probably thought he was a cop. When the girl came out Kelly got out of the car again and himself and McKearney jointly tried to persuade her that they were indeed escapees. *"Do you know any republican ex-prisoners,"* Kelly started by saying, *"Look I know this is hard to believe, but we have escaped from the H-Blocks!"* He went through names of ex-prisoners he had known from the Lurgan area.

He had named about ten people and was running out of names when the girl said she didn't know any of them but: *"Do you know 'Clancey'"* Kelly immediately recognised the nick-name. Kelly said, *"Yes, we need to see him. I was in the 'Cages' with him."* The 'Cages' was a well-known term to describe the compounds of Long Kesh Prison Camp before the H-Blocks were built. She was nervously trying to give directions. A bit too impatiently, Kelly asked her would she get into the car and show them. He was worried about time passing and whether or not they had been spotted on the way into the estate and possibly reported. In fact there was very little doubt that they had been seen since going into the estate.

The girl absolutely refused to get into the car as she was too nervous. However a few children had gathered at that stage and had listened to the conversation. One of the kids who was about 10 years old said, *"That's my brother, I'll show you where he lives."* The escapees got back into the car. They couldn't believe their luck. The boy led the way on his bike and pointed out the house. It was decided on the spot that the driver should remain in the car with Clarke and Fleming ready for a quick getaway and that Kelly and McKearney should go in. The door was open.

There was a man in his thirties sitting on the sofa who was watching 'Match of the Day' on television. Kelly called out his nickname, *"Clancey."* He leapt from the sofa to his feet in shock. He thought it was an assassination bid which were all too frequent at the time. As he jumped ready to run, Kelly raised his hands in an open gesture showing they were empty. He spoke calmly, *"Its Gerry, its Gerry Kelly. Do you remember me Clancey?"* He looked confused and stunned.

Kelly used to have shoulder length long hair in jail but in the build-up to the escape he had gradually cut it shorter in preparation for wearing a guard's uniform. Clancey would never have seen him with his hair so short. *"I got my hair cut,"* Kelly smiled reassuringly. *"We have just escaped from the Blocks. Has it not been on the news?"* Clancey responded with a dawning recognition *"No. There has been nothing at all."*

He could see that Clancey was still a bit bewildered but Kelly started firing questions at him. *"Look we have been seen coming into the estate. You need to get us out of this area and as soon as possible. We need transport. Is there any help you can get? Can you get the OC of the area?"* *"I don't know,"* Clancey replied. *"I know where he lives but he is in a different estate. I'll have to go and check."* *"okay,"* Kelly replied. *"Your house is too well known and we have been seen coming into it. Can you find us somewhere else to wait?"*

So out he went and walked down the street, casting his eyes left to right remembering houses that he had used in the past, when he was involved in the IRA. Eventually he directed them round to the back of a house and ushered them in. Kelly grabbed him tightly by the arm for emphasis and said, *"Look Clancey we are in danger here. There has been an escape and we have been seen coming in here. I am wearing a screw's uniform and it will be on the news any minute, if it hasn't already been on it. They will be raiding this place in a very short period of time. You need to get us out of here and you need to do it fast. You need to get the OC and you need to get him here now – ten minutes tops. Otherwise we will have to take a chance and make our own arrangements. Either way we are out of here in ten minutes."*

Clancey replied tersely but sincerely, *"I will do what I can,"* and away he went. Kelly had spoken slowly and clearly. He knew that he was putting a heavy load on someone who had managed to get some semblance of normality back into his life after imprisonment. He could see his excitement bordering on disbelief but he wanted him to be clear-headed and to understand the urgency.

They hadn't the time at that moment to explain to the owner of the house what was going on. The five moved in and took up position. One covered the back door and one guarded the front door. All the people in the house; a man, a woman and a few kids were hustled up the stairs. Kelly had started to take off the rest of his uniform. The trousers were heavy over the top of his jeans. He felt much lighter divested of them. As he wiped his face of sweat and cleaned a few minor cuts, things were settling down and there was time to look around the room a bit. He needed shoes, *"Does anyone else need anything here? We need to talk to the man and woman of the house. Where are they?"*

"They are upstairs,"

"Who's with them?"

"There is somebody up guarding them."

Kelly went upstairs and into the room where the family was huddled together on the bed. They were petrified. They didn't know what was going on. Clancey, who they would have known, had rushed on without entering to explain the takeover. Kelly spoke reassuringly although his own heart was racing. *"I know this is hard on you and hard to believe. We are sorry for taking over your house but we have just escaped from the H-Blocks of Long Kesh. My name is Gerry Kelly, I am a Republican POW and we need your help. We won't be here very long."* The man could hardly speak. He just kept looking at them.

There had been killings in the area by loyalists and the man was obviously worried for his family. Kelly realised again the significance of the State uniform he had been wearing on entering the house. The owner had been staring at the torn and somewhat bloody shirt of the uniform.

Realising the bewilderment on the man's face because he was most worried about his family, he looked around the room. He spotted a wooden celtic cross made in Long Kesh. It had Noel McGeown's name painted on it. Kelly spoke, *"That's Noel McGeown, I know him. His nickname is 'The Brit'. I was in The Cages with him. I have made these celtic crosses myself."* He could see it was having the desired effect especially when he mentioned Noel McGeown's nickname.

The man's expression changed and some pinkness returned to his pale face. He said, *"Right, right, what do you need?"* Kelly answered, *"A wee bit of food if you have it. We are hopefully only going to be here for ten minutes or so. I need a pair of shoes if you have them, I take a size 9. Do you have any that fit. A larger size would do."* *"Well I take size 9 myself,"* answered the man a bit more enthused.

He went downstairs and brought Kelly a pair of black brogue shoes, socks and a jersey as well. Kelly said to him, *"Thank you.*

These are great. We will return all this to you." "*That's the least of my worries,"* retorted the man with the beginnings of a smile. *"You can keep them." "We don't want you saying to anybody about us being here for some time after we leave okay?"* said Kelly. *"In fact if you never tell anyone, all the better because we certainly won't be telling anyone."* The man moved to put the kettle on and proceeded to make some sandwiches for his surprise guests.

Time was ticking by and tension was starting to rise. Five minutes seemed like an hour. The ten minutes had now stretched to 15 in reality. McKearney was talking about the Loughshore again. He knew where he was now. He could walk down to the Loughshore from Lurgan. He thought it was the best way to go because it was off the roads. Some thought this was a good idea. Kelly was worried that the Brits knew that they were in the Lurgan.

Finucane motioned Kelly to the side and said, *"You need to take charge."* Everything up to then had been instinctive, a mad rush with decisions taken as an automatic response. But now there was time to collect thoughts and time to doubt. They were there for about 20 minutes and Kelly had come to the conclusion they would soon have to go. However he believed Clancey would be trying his best. He wanted to give him some more leeway. He spoke loud enough for all the volunteers to hear, *"Give it another couple of minutes at the most and then it is down to the Loughshore."* All were nodding assent when the OC of the area came through the back door with Clancey who had come up trumps. Kelly clasped him tightly by the hand. He was flabbergasted and delighted.

Sean McCool was firing questions, like, *"How many got out? Who got away? How many of youse are here?"* Kelly told him what he knew in quick succession. *"There were 38 on the escape. Don't know how many are still out and there are five of us here."* But his priority was to get out of that house so he cut the conversation short saying, *"You need to get us out of this estate a chara. The Brits are going to raid it. We were seen coming in here. We won't have a chance if we stay."*

They need not have been worried as McCool was on top of it. Unlike the escapees, who were in an alien arena, he knew his own area and capabilities. As he spoke, the atmosphere of his sure-footedness and decisiveness lifted the tension and brought a certain calming relief. They were in the hands of the IRA. They were nearly home and dry. The OC had not come alone or wasted any time.

The Lurgan OC spoke, *"Right we are getting out of here. There is a van round the corner. What I want you all to do is come out one at a time. Go out the back and turn right. Walk down the lane and get into the Volkswagen van at the end. It is in the next street. Lie on the floor and we'll get youse out of this estate."* *"Give about a minute or so between each man leaving."* *"How long will it take,"* Kelly asked. *"It will take ten minutes at the most."* *"I think ten minutes is too long"* replied Kelly still a bit tense. However the OC was taking charge in his own area. *"Fair enough, I understand, a chara, but this is our area and this is the safest way to do it. You just need to trust us on this."*

"Have you got the keys - the car keys?" Finucane handed over the car keys. The OC explained, *"I will get somebody to take that car away now."* The Volunteer who had come in with the OC immediately went out and got into the car. The car was driven away to Newry town (situated close to the border with the South of Ireland). It was to be left there to make the Brits believe that a number of the escapees had crossed the border already.

One by one the escapees walked out and slipped into the back of the Volkswagen van. Everyone lay down as instructed and the van drove off into another estate. They ended up in the bedroom of a terraced house and the OC came in for a chat. The woman of the house brought up some hot food. They sat with plates on their knees making sandwiches out of the sausage, bacon, eggs and bread and gulping down hot tea, all smiles and excited conversation around their escape. They were starving but they were more interested in moving on.

McCool knew the escapees were bound to be hyper-sensitive. *"Look,"* he said *"We are in another district but we are still in Lurgan. Now you have a couple of choices. We can take youse one at a time, we can put youse into different 'billets'. There probably will be raiding here tonight. There is a chance that some of you will get caught and some of you won't get caught, though it is my view that if they catch one of you they will search every house in the town. The second choice is that we can use an old arms-dump. The dump is empty and has been unused for some time. It was never discovered. Only the house owners and myself know about it. It is under the floor and it can accommodate all of you in it. That means there will be eight of youse together so you sink or swim together."* He winced a little at his own description of the options, but essentially it was as straightforward as that.

Kelly interrupted, *"There are only five of us, mo chara."* The OC said, *"No Gerry there are eight of youse."* Kelly repeated his assertion but the OC explained with some mischievous glee in his eyes that there was another three escapees in hiding at the far end of town. They had arrived in another car.

Even though the turbo charge car had taken off at high speed away ahead of them, they had ended up in the same area later than them and it transpired that they had actually gone into the same shop in the Shankill district and had been directed, by one of the customers, to a Republican's house from there.

In fact the OC had been left with a huge problem, literally, in the shape of the very modern Turbo-charged vehicle. It was too late to drive it to the border as had been done with the other car. He got a Volunteer to drive it to a lock-up garage. The next day the two of them set about cutting the vehicle up into small chunks of scrap. Later still it was distributed in pieces into various bogs, lakes and deep rivers. Other parts were taken to various building sites to be buried by bulldozers and JCBs, never to be heard of again.

McCool explained that part of the delay in him getting to Kelly was that he got word of the other three escapees: Campbell, Russell and Fryers. An ex-POW had already taken Russell away. McCool decided that it was easier to cope with all the escapees as one group and had sent a Volunteer off to retrieve him. He told Kelly that they had made a good choice in choosing the Shankill estate because it was a Nationalist area however just over the wall at the back of the shop they had entered, was a loyalist estate called 'Wakehurst'. That might have presented an entirely different ending to their story.

There was some discussion amongst the escapees and a bit of questioning of the OC as to how safe this dump was. He assured them that it was in a mixed residential area. It wouldn't be looked upon as a republican area and the arms-dump had been safe the whole time it was in use. It had not been used for some time and it was easier for them to handle because they then wouldn't have to move in and out of a lot of different houses.

Finally the OC made the wise point that the choice was the escapees to make, as it was their liberty at stake. For the same reason Kelly was looking for consensus. There was a very short discussion, at the end of which it was agreed that they would all go to the unused arms-dump as everyone expected house-raids in the area. There was some further discussion on security, of how to get there, so as there would be a break in the knowledge trail between where they were at that moment and their destination

Only one person would be used to ferry all the escapees to the hide-away to minimise the possibility of loose talk or of information leaking out. The OC used a teenage girl who would not have been known as a republican and he alone would organise the route in. However he, himself stayed away from the move as he was a high profile republican. He was often under surveillance and didn't want to bring on any heat to the escapees. So, one at a time over a short period, from dusk onwards the escapees moved out. They crossed various roads and streets into another district and one at a time entered the safe house. Once in the house they were reunited with Seamus Campbell, Robert Russell and Gerard Fryers. There was a bit of craic: the escapees were relieved that they had got that far. They knew they were not out of danger; perhaps they never would be, but they had succeeded in escaping and that was a life achievement in everybody's mind.

Kelly was sighing contentedly. It had taken ten years and a number of escape attempts to arrive at this point but there was excitement running through every vein and trickling out through every pore. While the chatter was not over-excited there was a certain quiet euphoria running through everyone there. When they had regrouped in the sitting room there was another cup of tea, something else to eat and then another short discussion which ended with, *"Let's go now. Let's get under the floor boards. Let's get used to this. Let's see what we have to do down there before we settle for the night."*

By this time it was after 9pm. There were two areas underneath two rooms, connected to each other by a narrow gap in the foundation walls. The hidden trap door was underneath the stairs in the hallway. Four crawled under the far room and four settled under the near room. Kelly took up a position near the trap door for ease of communications with the householders. Everybody had gone to the toilet before going down and the Lurgan OC had offered to put down a firearm with them. At first Kelly agreed to take it, but on reflection he decided that there was no point in having a weapon when under floorboards as there was no escape if they were discovered.

As they settled in for the night, they didn't know how long they would have to remain under those floorboards. It was very dusty. All the rubble from the time the house was built was lying about. Flash lights were supplied and they started pushing the rubble and rubbish back to make some sort of room. In the end they only managed to clear enough space between the ground and the floor lying down. There was no space to sit up or even lie sideways, so everyone had to be content to lie flat..

Not long afterwards the man and woman of the house fed down the sleeping bags, a radio and earpiece, and closed the trap door for the night. One person listened to the news and whispered the details which were passed around the hideaway. It was unclear how many of their comrades remained at large but the escape itself had thrown the British establishment into turmoil with calls for resignations. The Prime Minister Thatcher declared it the biggest crisis in British penal history.

They were too excited to sleep much that night and whispered quietly into the small hours. They had been given some empty coffee jars and jam jars in case they needed to pee during the night – which of course they did. The first one to break got slegged mercilessly making it even harder for him in the awkward circumstances doing it while lying down. *"Are you doing your number ones or number twos there?" "Last time you pointed a weapon your aim was just as bad!" "Shush, you'll wake the neighbours with that waterfall." "Don't even think of shaking it!" "You never could hold your water!"*

It was a good break from 'escape talk', but then led on to what they might get to eat and drink the next day. The man of the house offered them cool bottles of beer the night before. They had taken one each and enjoyed the pleasure of something they had not tasted for years. Kelly enjoyed it but was determined that one was the limit. He would only raise it if it became an issue, but it didn't.

The next day they got up through the trap door, had breakfast and used the bathroom. The woman of the house was pregnant. They were Republicans and clearly glad to be part of such an historical event. But they were taking an enormous chance with their future – especially with a baby due. Eight extra people moving about a house is hard to hide from neighbours. The front door which they had to pass to go to the trapdoor had with it the risk of being seen by a passer-by or a casual caller.

After breakfast on Monday, when the couple were out of the room the escapees decided that they would stay below the floorboards despite the discomfort. The house could be hit with a sudden raid by the British who, they figured, must know by now that a number of escapees had arrived in Lurgan.

Kelly explained the logic to the young couple without reference to their own nervousness or danger. Because of the cramped conditions the escapees were very happy to be fed, sandwiches, soups, stew or whatever was handiest, served in plastic cups with just spoons. They would continue to use sealed jars or sealed buckets like paint containers for going to the toilet. The only exception was if anyone needed to do their 'number twos'. Kelly smiled, as did his hosts knowing that none of them were normally polite about their ablutions unless they were talking to very young children.

He thought they were relieved at the suggestion as they knew the dangers but didn't want to raise it themselves. None of them knew how long they would have to stay but all hoped that it would be a matter of a few days at the most.

They were supplied with the newspapers daily by the man of the house and the radio was a great help but nearing the end of the first week eight men under the floorboards 24 hours a day was creating enough odour to attract neighbours' dogs to the air vents under floorboard level. They got sprays to put the dogs off but it was worrying. While the Lurgan OC was in contact every couple of days through the man of the house the frustration was eating away at the elation. There was a rule of absolute silence at night or when visitors were at the house, but it was getting hard to maintain. Pressure was building on Kelly and the Lurgan OC.

9pm
Sunday September 25th
Kevin Barry Artt

Kevin Barry Artt slowed as he came to the RUC checkpoint on the bike, hoping to be waved on but he was stopped. *"What's your name Sir?"* Asked the cop. *"William Johnson,"* replied Artt. *"Date of birth?" "December 6th 1962." "Where are you going?" "I'm going back to Belfast. I'm a student at Queen's University." "Stay there,"* said the cop walking a bit away to where the sergeant stood. After a few moments the sergeant came over, *"What did you say your date of birth was?"* Artt couldn't remember except that the false one he gave was December 62 but without hesitation he answered, *"December 16th 1962."* The cop didn't seem to notice. *"What are you doing out here?" "I'm a student at Queen's and I heard about the escape from the Maze prison so I came out to have a look."* Artt knew as the cop did, that Blaris Road led to the jail. The two of them were standing under a road sign which read "HMP MAZE to accentuate the fact!

The sergeant looked at him for a moment and then said, *"We're taking you to Lisburn Police Station."* Artt wasn't sure what to say that might change the situation but he felt the need to say something, *"Can I take my bike?" "No you can't,"* said the cop. *"Leave it there."* He pointed to the footpath at the junction. Artt pushed the bike over and said *"Watch the bike, its nearly new."*

But he noticed that there was no ove-the-top reaction. No weapons levelled at him. They seemed fairly relaxed.

He was transported to the Lisburn RUC Station by car and brought into the reception-desk area and told to sit down. The two cops who had accompanied him then went further into the building. Artt wondered if they were making an idiot out of him and just playing him along but he decided to play the game as the stakes were high. The reception was chaotic with phones continually ringing and a lot of toing and froing. Nobody came near him for an hour and he spent his time trying not to make eye contact or draw any attention to himself, despite the fact that he thought someone would notice the jersey he was wearing was a woman's. But he was on hyper-alert to all that was going on around him.

After an hour the same two cops came back and one said, *"Come on kid, we're taking you back to your bike."* Artt's mind was in a spin. He had been sitting wondering, could he make a bolt for it or was that what they were waiting on, and now he was wondering were they going to let him go and then shoot him, or were they just playing him for a fool?

In the car he was making conversation about the day's events more to assess the cop's attitude than from curiosity. *"How many escaped? How many were caught?"* The two RUC men avoided his questions and told him nothing. Inside his head he was shouting, *"Do these guys not know?"*

They let him out where they had picked him up. *"Am I free to go?"* Asked Artt. *"Aye, get on your bike Son,"* replied the cop chuckling. Not wanting to pass the Lisburn Station again Artt rode off in another direction into Lisburn. He was comforted by the town lights and traffic but he got lost. As he approached a British Army Barracks, situated in the town, he turned and headed back the way he had come.

He found the Belfast to Lisburn road and followed it passing three more checkpoints before being stopped at a UDR Checkpoint on the Finaghy Road crossroads in South Belfast. He had been a taxi-driver before his arrest and knew where he was. His parents and other relatives lived within half a mile but he had no intentions of visiting that night!

"Where are you going?" He was asked.

"Home," he answered.

"Have you any I.D.?"

"Listen, no I don't, but I've just spent an hour in Lisburn Police Station over the same thing if you want to check?" It was now well after 10pm. The escape had happened at 4pm. The high alert phase for prisoners trying to reach Belfast was over. The soldiers were tired and bored. *"On you go,"* said the UDR man with little interest.

Artt made his way to a taxi depot that he remembered off the Andersonstown Road. Still cautious he asked the deskman could he direct him to any Sinn Féin member. The deskman looked back quizzically and suspicious, *"Connolly House is on the Andersonstown Road Son. Just around the corner there."* Of course he knew the Sinn Féin Advice centre would be closed at that time on a Sunday.

One of the taxi drivers spoke, *"I'll give you a lift."*

When Artt got in to the car he said *"Listen I escaped from the Kesh today, I need to make contact with someone."*

"That was a bit obvious Big Lad," replied the driver with a smile. *"Relax."*

He and dozens of other men and women from Belfast had been driving the roads between Belfast and the jail most of the day, since the news broke in the hope of picking the prisoners up. Whatever about his passenger, his own morale was sky high for having found one of the escaping Republicans.

Artt was brought to the house of a relative of the driver's where he stayed, amazingly, for two months while the British and Irish authorities scoured the country. He was treated like a king but had contact with only one person outside the house – a woman with close ties to the jail. He stayed in the Suffolk area of Belfast and was then transported to Derry where he stayed overnight. The following morning early, he was given a sports kit and runners and put into a squad of joggers who ran across the border roads regularly. He had to jog past a huge British Army Border Post. When the other joggers turned back to Derry, Artt jogged on alone to St. Aengus Chapel – a well known round church on the Letterkenny Road. There, two women picked him up in their car and took him into the seaside town of Buncrana where he felt the beginning of the rest of his life was about to unfold.

4.30pm
September 25th
Dixons Farm, Bog Road

Brendan McFarlane in common with most of the escaping Republicans made his way through the barbed-wire and up the field facing the main gate of the jail. He was still armed and in uniform. Once over the brow of the hill and out of sight he felt the relief of no longer having the possibility of a rifle sight focussed between his shoulder blades. He slid down the steep gravel bank and scrambled up the other side.

As he heaved his head and shoulders out of the small ravine he saw the farm off to his left a couple of hundred yards away. As he got to the farm entrance, a Hillman Avenger car was moving out onto the road. It was packed with his comrades and he could see Seamus Campbell driving. He immediately saw that there were two other vehicles in the yard and other prisoners checking them for keys. Robert Russell was leaning out of the Hillman shouting at McFarlane to get into the car. But McFarlane waved him on knowing that they were already like sardines in a tin. He also assessed that if one car was being driven out, then the two others parked at the farmhouse were likely to have keys as well. So he moved to join the other dozen or so of his comrades in the farmyard.

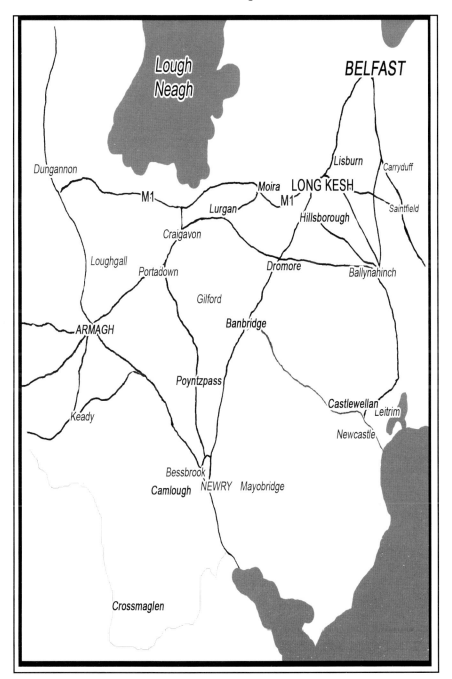

211

In fact, 22 of the original 38 republicans arrived at Dixon's farm in the immediate aftermath of the escape. McFarlane heard someone shout, *"No keys!"* He moved automatically to the farmhouse where the blue van and green Mercedes car were parked. As he entered the porch, Gerry McDonnell was coming out with a teenage boy in tow. McDonnell had keys in his hand and threw a set to McFarlane. *"I think that's the Merc keys Bik."* McFarlane moved into the driver's seat aware that the car was filling up with escapees. He realised the Merc was an automatic. He was used to a gear-stick.

The teenager from the house was standing close by, mesmerised by the whole scene. *"C'mere, I want you a minute, Son."* McFarlane moved over to the driver's door of the Mercedes which was still open. *"I'm not a hundred per cent on these 'automatics' so I need your help. Small pedal on right is the accelerator. The larger one on the left is the brake. Right?"* The boy nodded in confirmation *"Okay,"* McFarlane moved to the stick. *'N' is neutral; 'D' I presume is drive and 'P' is what?* "Parking," answered the youth. *"That's all I need to know Son. Thanks for your help,"* said McFarlane without a hint of irony in his voice. He reached out and closed the door. Immediately, the car moved off leaving the young man staring after them in wonderment but relieved that they had gone. As the family vehicle turned left onto the road he moved back towards the house.

McDonnell had thrown the other set of keys to Marty McManus. McManus couldn't drive but he shouted to the others. *"Anybody want to drive the van?"* Marcus Murray was about to get into the packed Mercedes, but instead he took the keys and got into the van with McManus. He tried to start the van a couple of times but failed. He realised it was a diesel engine that takes a bit longer to warm up, he tried it again this time with less haste. The engine roared and they drove off. The young lad ran back into the house to check the phone but the lines had been ripped from the wall.

As they reached the Bog Road, Murray could see two prison guards running towards them from the right about twenty yards away and closing. He turned left and with a squeal of tyres took off watching the guards give up the chase in the mirror. McManus was shouting, *"Head for the city,"* meaning Belfast, as it was only ten minutes drive away and McManus was a city man. *"No way,"* Murray insisted. He had been working in Belfast years before when another escape had occurred and he remembered how militarised the city had been.

Eight of the republicans were now in the car. They were buzzing as the car picked up speed. The short delay when McFarlane was familiarising himself with the car had put them a bit more on edge. It had taken all of two minutes but in the atmosphere of a jail-break it seemed more like twenty minutes. Some humour was returning in the comfort of the speeding car. *"Now Bik are you sure you can handle an automatic? It isn't a gun!" "Trust you to get a Merc ye snobby bastard. Here if you're the OC of the car can I be OC of its wing?"* Others were more tense. *"Is there a map in the glove compartment?" "Does anybody know where we are?" What direction are we travelling in?" "The chopper is bound to be in the sky any minute." "Look out for roadsigns," "Can we risk hitting Belfast?"*

To McFarlane most of it was background chatter. Seamy McElwaine was in the passenger seat talking, at a lower pitch but more insistently, directly to McFarlane. He was concentrating on driving but was glancing across at McElwaine, listening. Almost from the start of the car journey McElwaine had argued to get rid of the car quickly. *"We need to ditch the car and hit the fields Bik." "We're only in the fucking car Seamy,"* Bik had retorted a bit annoyed. He knew and respected McElwaine who was a countryman from Co Monaghan across the border in the South. He knew by reputation that he was a solid, quiet and thoughtful Volunteer. *"I know a chara,"* said McElwaine calmly *"But it is still daylight. The Brits will be throwing up roadblocks all over the place. They'll put the choppers up too. Do a short few miles in the car to get a distance away from the jail and then ditch the car and take to the fields. We'll be safer and the Brits can't cover the whole countryside. But we'll need to hide the car as well to give ourselves a chance."*

Just as the car moved out of a fairly sharp bend in the road, they spotted two women who were out power-walking just ahead. McFarlane wound the window down and pulled over,. *"Hello there, how's it going?"* He said to catch their attention. *"I'm looking for the Moira roundabout?"* He knew the Moira roundabout was on the main M1 motorway about five miles further west than the jail. He didn't want to use the M1 but they needed some notion of where they were, relative to the jail. The women wanted to be helpful but didn't want to interrupt their exercise either. *"You're almost at the dual carriage-way between Lisburn and Banbridge. If you go towards Lisburn you'll see the sign for Moira,"* he was informed. *"Thank you ladies,"* replied McFarlane politely as he drove off watching them in his side mirror. They had walked off without looking back. *"Good,"* murmured McFarlane to himself. They wouldn't be going there anyway.

McFarlane turned off the minor road onto the dual carriageway heading towards Banbridge which would take them further away from Long Kesh. He was thinking that there was sense in what McElwaine was saying but he still wanted to get a good distance between them and the prison. At 60mph they could make a good ten miles in ten minutes! Just then two British Army jeeps passed at speed going in the opposite direction to them. *"You're right Seamy!"* said McFarlane *"Let's get off this road anyway. I don't think the Brits took any notice of us there but just in case."*

He took the next minor road off to the left which was small enough not to have any town or village road signs at its entrance. After a short distance the road surface got progressively worse which slowed them down. *"Keep your eyes peeled for a house or barn to hide the car lads,"* McElwaine said. He would've been happy enough with a small wood or covered-in laneway to hide the car but then he spotted a set of gates leading to what appeared to be a small grey cottage. More interestingly, there was some sort of outbuilding or a garage to the right hand side of the house.

5pm
Sunday September 25th
Dromore, County Down

McElwaine touched McFarlane's arm to get his attention and pointed. McFarlane stopped the car and checked his rear-view mirror. There was no other vehicle in sight. The road in front was also deserted and as far as he could see the nearest house was a good distance away at the top of the next hill. He had stopped the car a few yards past the entrance.

McFarlane handed his pistol to McElwaine. *"Let's try this house lads. Take it as quietly and quickly as you can. I'll bring the car in. Right everybody out except Oda."* He needed McNally to watch for cars coming while he reversed back past the entrance and then drove in. Seamus McElwaine and Paul Brennan circled around to the back of the house. The door was closed but not locked. There was a man and woman in the kitchen. They turned to see the two men, but the gun in McElwaines hand took their full attention. Brennan spoke first, *"we're not going to hurt you. Don't panic. We are Republican prisoners who have just escaped from Long Kesh jail."* The couple still hadn't spoken, then the woman seemed to recover,

"What do you want with us? We have children here."

Outside McFarlane parked at the side of the house and both he and McNally rushed into the house to find that their comrades were holding an understandably bewildered and frightened family.

There was a mother and father, two sons of 11 and 12 years of age and a baby. McFarlane and McNally went straight through the kitchen to find what they were looking for: a door led into the attached garage come workshop. They set about making space by pushing a workbench, a fridge and other bits and pieces to the back wall. They then opened the up-and-over door. McFarlane did a quick check up and down the narrow road and then quickly drove the Mercedes in. McNally closed the garage door. It was perfect; to all intents and purposes they had disappeared at least for the moment.

By an odd coincidence the family bore the same name as McFarlane. They were confused and frightened. Brendan McFarlane moved to re-assure them first, telling them that they meant them no harm; that they would only be there a short while. They were escapees and simply wanted to move on. He wanted to remove the notion of danger so that the man or woman would not themselves try anything fool-hardy.

Marty McManus and Marcus Murray The Van

When McManus and Murray had driven away from Dixon's farm in the blue van, they had come on to the Belfast to Newry dual carriageway. They headed in the direction of Newry. They wanted to make distance but also knew they had to get rid of the van. They had been driving at least ten minutes, maybe more, and knew they were pushing their luck.

Murray pulled off the carriageway onto a smaller road which was not signposted. However, after less than five minutes it led back on to the dual carriageway again. Before they could find another minor road they spotted an RUC vehicle checkpoint. They couldn't turn so stopped to bluff their way.

Murray noticed that the cop approaching him casually unclipped the holster on his side arm, though he did not remove it. *"Your licence please sir,"* he said. Murray made a show of searching his pockets, *"Sorry left it at home,"* he offered. *"Where are you coming from?"* *"Belfast, down on a welding job,"* Murray continued knowing that there was welding gear in the back of the van. *"Open the back doors for me please,"* the cop asked. As Murray opened the door to get out he noticed that a second RUC man had gone to the passenger side. The third was staying

218

slightly back but with a submachine gun at the ready. *"What's your name?"* The cop asked. *"Billy Dodds,"* Murray replied trying for what he thought was a protestant name. *"What's your mate's name?"* *"Sam Lyons,"* Murray tried.

On the passenger side of the van McManus was asked his name. *"Gerry Miskelly,"* he said as the first name that came into his head. *"Have you a licence"* *"I don't drive"* *"What about I.D.?"* McManus did a pocket search and came up empty. He had noticed one of the cops looking down at his own hand as he approached the van and had suspected he already had the licence plate number of the van written on his palm.

"You've no form of identity lads so you'll have to come to the station. There was an incident a bit earlier down the road," said the cop who had questioned Murray.

At Banbridge station they were put in separate rooms but the doors were left open. A Special Branch man was present. *"What's your name,"* he asked Murray. Murray who was standing with his hands in his pockets just laughed They were then both locked in cells and transported to Castlereagh later that night.

On the way to the Castlereagh Interrogation Centre in Belfast they passed a large number of military checkpoints. On arrival Murray and McManus were questioned straight away. They refused to speak. Just before midnight Senior Prison Officer George Smilie entered their cells, *"That's Murray. That's McManus."* Was all he said before leaving again. They were kept in Castlereagh until Friday when they were transferred to the jail.

McFarlane and the McFarlanes

During the conversation that McFarlane had with the householders it seemed to him that the man was most affected. The woman was calming down much more quickly. After a short period of conversation they realised that the family were profoundly Christian. McFarlane took McDonnell and McElwaine to the side where they had a quick yarn about how to deal with the family. The escapees would be leaving in a few hours and needed guaranteed time to make substantial headway on foot and undetected. They discussed the limited options. Take one of the family with them or leave someone guarding them or tie them up and phone someone like a clergyman later to release them. They all immediately rejected the third option of tying the family up. Neither of the other two options seemed very enticing either. They needed a guaranteed space of at least 24 hours before anyone was informed.

McFarlane took the woman to the side. *"Look Mrs McFarlane. I have a dilemma. We have got this far and we aren't going to jeopardise our chances. When we leave, you could raise the alarm. Let me first say that none of your family will be harmed in any way. I give you my word as a Republican. It may not mean a lot to you but when I give my word it won't be broken."* The woman was listening intently but without expression. Inside, her stomach was in knots wondering what was coming next.

"So listen, I have only two options. One is to leave one of the lads here to guard you and send transport for him in a couple of days and the other unfortunately is to take one of your sons with us and release him after a few hours." The woman barely let him finish before she started pleading with him not to take her son. The mother's anguish was deep though she held herself together. McFarlane felt sorry for her but he continued, *"Look, I understand, but the third option was to tie the family up and phone the local clergy once we got away. We rejected that idea because you have a young family."* He could see her anguish deepen *"We still have a dilemma so I want you to find us a solution with these two men,"* he finished pointing to McElwaine and McDonnell. She went off with them to another room.

The conversation between the woman and the two prisoners didn't take that long. The fact was that none of the options were good but an alternative idea had to come from her. She needed ownership and commitment to it. The woman suggested the Bible as an alternative plan. She pleaded that they would swear on the Bible that they would not tell anyone for a period of 72 hours if the Republicans didn't take any of the family with them. The escapees pushed them on their oath but were glad in fact that they were agreeing 72 hours. They certainly didn't want to have to do the long and difficult trek ahead with an unwilling passenger. Neither was anyone going to volunteer to stay at the house.

After they had sworn on the Bible the woman turned to Bik McFarlane directly and asked him to give her his word that they would not take her son with them. McFarlane gave his word as a Republican. To him, his word was indeed his bond but he still looked at what he thought was her obvious relief with some wonder. That she could accept the word of people who had turned her life inside out in a matter of minutes showed that she was assessing the situation calmly, under the most difficult of circumstances.

The truth of course was that neither could be certain of the other: both were taking a calculated risk to protect family or comrades. Both had to trust each other's words for the sake of these two groups of very different people thrown together by fate.

In less than an hour, after breaching the perimeter walls of the Long Kesh Prison Camp, the escapees knew that at least eight of the 38 political prisoners had got away and seemingly disappeared off the face of the earth. The house was close to Dromore town. It was maybe only ten miles from the jail but for now it was a great start. For the moment, they were as relaxed as anyone could be on the run. Men were posted at the windows just in case.

They learned that the husband was an accountant and that he was expecting someone to call at 6.00pm for papers he had prepared at. It was decided that he was still too jittery to deal with the situation. He still had some work to do so was encouraged to finish the accounts. He asked the escapees had they any cigarettes as he had none. As he worked he smoked his way through all of the roll-ups that Tony McAllister had brought with him. McAllister became ever grumpier though silent, while his non-smoking comrades became ever more amused at his agitation.

Decision Time for South Armagh Brigade

"They should be here by now, the place will be crawling soon,"* said Magee sitting in the doorway of the Box Lorry. They were keeping an eye on their hostage and whispering now. They knew they should've been back at base by now but decided to give it to 4.30pm just in-case the escapees arrived. *"Start the engine and keep it ticking over"* said Moley. Burns turned the ignition key. After stuttering for a few moments it

Volunteers of the South Armagh brigade of the IRA with some of the weapons that were in the lorry waiting to collect the escapees

kicked into rhythm. Burns revved it a bit then removed his foot slowly from the accelerator. The diesel engine turned over heavily but steadily. Magee and Lynch stepped inside with their Armalites cradled to wait and listen to the radio which by this stage was going haywire. The well-oiled British war machine was apparently in absolute turmoil.

Moley started the Audi easily and let it warm up. He was listening to the radio as well. After a while he left it to go down to the road again where it was much quieter between the occasional noise of Sunday traffic. He wanted to stay as long as possible but he knew they were well past their safety point. He wanted to get the political prisoners away safely but he also didn't want to get this squad of experienced men imprisoned, or their weapons caught.

Operation Vesper was building and Moley knew it. There would be concentric circles of checkpoints set up at varying distances from the jail. The chopper would be up and covering wide areas. A lorry and a car at a derelict farm would be investigated.

He checked his watch. It was 4.45pm. They had been there for over two hours and had held a hostage for almost the same time. When would his family get suspicious and be out looking for him. As he pondered a decision his ears picked up the whisper of a chopper in the distance. He looked up but couldn't pinpoint it. Lynch had casually pointed out that they would, *"Get the problem going home now,"* meaning it was no longer a clean run as all police stations and British Army barracks would be on the alert.

Moley returned to the lorry. *"We'll give it to 5 O'Clock. If the lorry made it out it should have been here with us already."* 5pm came and went without any change. *"We'll have to go lads. No stopping at any checkpoints okay?"* *"No problem,"* was the return chorus as expected. He beckoned the lorry out onto the road. A bit dejected but still very much alert he got into the driver's seat of the Audi and took off after his comrades, overtaking the lorry within moments so he could scout the route.

Burns saw Moley's Audi coming up to overtake. He didn't have to slow down. Burns had rechecked the Kalashnikov rifle again just after restarting the engine. Despite the disappointment of heading homeward without the escaped comrades the adrenalin rush was in full flow again. Although there was a steel plate fitted to his driver's door the rest of the cab of the lorry was not armoured. He did take a certain degree of comfort from the heavy police flak-jacket which he wore under his windbreaker. It was the real thing, liberated from the RUC, which contained Kevlar, ceramics and steel. He also knew it was more of a psychological comfort than anything. Still it would stop rifle fire if they got into trouble - as he knew from personal experience having fired at British soldiers and the RUC.

He had his foot to the floor on the accelerator. Better to make distance from the security cordon than worrying about looking suspicious at this stage. The solid rubber tyres they had fitted slowed the vehicle down but meant the tyres couldn't be shot out. The route was mostly side roads right back to South Armagh and Base. He was changing gears a lot and was comforted in seeing Moley's scouts at every crossroads they came to.

Most of them didn't know even then what the operation was but as the lorry passed, a scout car would pull out behind it to fill the road and drive at a slower pace so as to prevent any other vehicle overtaking or following the lorry. This generally allowed the lorry a clear run at least for that section of a road. As they approached Poyntzpass, a sleepy village still in Unionist territory Burns shouted, *"One heading our way lads. Green Ford Granada – looks heavy on the axle."* In the back, Lynch leapt to the Browning .50 as Magee pulled the shutter up at the rear. Only then did Lynch prepare to swing the heavy .50 calibre machine-gun into position along its custom-built rail. Magee held his hand up to stay his actions. He couldn't see the car. Just then Burns shouted above the rattle of the engine. *"He turned off the road lads."*

Magee moved quickly to close the shutter again but it stuck half of the way down. He wrestled it with Lynch's help but it took a long five minutes to get it fully shut again. They were both strangely disappointed that there hadn't been an enemy to engage.

After they travelled a few miles the lorry slowed to a halt. Burns called for Lynch. Although the front cab was sealed off from the back of the lorry they had rigged a small pipe for communications if necessary. Lynch went to it. With the engine idling it was much easier to hear. *"Walk yer man into the field and tell him to keep walking."* *"OK."* Lynch and Magee pulled their balaclavas down over their faces again. Magee spoke as he lifted their hostage to his feet and removed the mail-bag from over his head. Lynch opened the side door and covered him with one of the rifles. *"Right, out you go. Climb the gate."* Magee climbed the field gate after him and pushed him ahead. He had drawn his short arm but kept it discreetly by his side. *"Keep walking,"* he said as they headed into a growth of high nettles and brambles. *"Don't look back or I'll shoot you. Walk to the other end of the field. You're a Brit so count yourself lucky. If I had my way you'd be coming the whole way back with me!"*

The man said nothing and ploughed on through nettles relieved to get out of the lorry but waiting to hear a shot. He thought his captor had stopped following him but he could hear the lorry was still idling. He quickened his pace a little without panic. He daren't turn round but relief was building with every step. He did not hear the lorry move off but when he got to the hedge at the other side of the field he jumped through a gap and ran left along the ditch as fast as he could. He realised he was on his own. Only then did he chance looking at the road. The red lorry was nowhere to be seen. He relaxed, for what seemed a long time but was really only moments. Once he composed himself he scanned the area for dwellings and then set off to raise the alarm. This was a day he would not forget.

The rest of the journey home was uneventful. They pulled into the farm at the border which was their Base for the operation. There were a few cars parked in the yard. Burns headed straight for the huge shed where the doors were slid apart. There were more cars inside and an expectant group of drivers who Moley had organised and who only now knew they were there because of the prison escape.

Burns cut the engine and jumped to the concrete floor as the drivers moved towards him. *"How many?"* one of them asked. Burns couldn't help himself. *"Get in a line lads,"* he beamed, as he moved to the door in the side of the lorry and slapped it loudly twice with the palm of his hand. The door opened and Magee got out followed by Lynch. The line of eyes widened with expectation but no-one followed. *"Go on youse eejitts,"* laughed Burns with a glee he didn't feel. *"It's only your long lost mates. Are youse not glad to see us!"*

"What happened? The escape took place – we heard it on the radio!" "I know, but nobody got as far as us. We stayed a couple of hours beyond the agreed time but had to leave in the end."

Dromore
The Comfort of Darkness

By the time 6.00pm came McNally was hiding in a small shed close to the front gates of the McFarlane household just in case he might have to arrest the family's visitor, if the man noticed anything untoward and tried to raise the alarm. The man drove in at 6.30pm. McFarlane had instructed the man of the house to finish the work but not to contemplate leaving a message in the accounts that might alert his friend to their predicament.

When Mrs McFarlane was given the accounts they had been thoroughly checked for any sign of secret messages, or at least checked as far as possible. She was nervous but nowhere near as obviously nervous and frightened as she had been when the Republicans had first entered her home. The unwelcome visitors were clearly determined and desperate but courteous and well mannered. She was ushered to the front door to await the man and open the door a few moments after he knocked.

She apologised immediately that her husband was not home but she didn't invite him in. McElwaine and McFarlane were hidden inside the house near the entrance porch. The visitor was in an excitable state. Barely hearing the woman's apology he explained that he had been stopped at a number of Army roadblocks on his journey to the house. Had she heard about the mass escape of armed Republicans from the jail?

The escapees listened intently as the woman engaged him as briefly as she could, without appearing bad-mannered, in a conversation about hearing it on the radio and how terrible it was. She brought the conversation skilfully to a close without giving anything away. Her only interest at that moment was her family. Listening closely to their conversation, the escapees, despite the tension, felt a growing respect for this woman whose family life they had so recently turned upside down. McNally watched as the man got into his car and drove off without incident.

The house had already been searched for any personal weapons. It was now searched again for items they would need once they left. A couple of haversacks were found. Heavy clothing like anoraks and sweaters were confiscated. Water was essential so whatever bottles could be found, were filled at the sink. They also took a small bedside clock and portable radio.

They decided to eat, as all were hungry, and pack whatever food they could. They explained all of this to the man and woman of the house asking them what was essential to be left, in terms of food for the family. When everything had been gathered McFarlane wrote an IOU list and signed it at the bottom. The supplies were then divided up amongst the escapees to carry. To their surprise and relief they had also found a road-map and compass.

There was still a few hours wait ahead of them. While some of them were posting guard at windows, others were in the sitting room watching TV or listening to the news reports on the radio.

The man and woman were still very nervous but they seemed to have accepted that their family would not come to any harm. The two boys appeared to have relaxed fairly quickly. It seemed a bit of an adventure to them. Some of the prisoners were talking football with them. After a while they asked their mother could they watch TV in the sitting room with the men. She reluctantly agreed and they shifted over to give the boys room on the sofa.

Seamus McElwaine was the only one of the political prisoners at the house with rural craft. He knew the countryside well. He knew the border area best around Co. Fermanagh and Monaghan, of course, because that is where he was reared and where he was on active service for the IRA before being imprisoned. But more importantly for this team, he knew the way of the countryside. McFarlane ushered him over to the road map which he had opened.

They looked at it. McElwaine instinctively traced a route through Co. Armagh and Tyrone to Fermanagh. He was sure of using his own contacts once he got there. It was, however, a long trek – twice as long at least as the nearest border crossings in Co. Down or Armagh.

The South Armagh Brigade had been the IRA team who were to collect them on the original escape plan and bring them to safety. It was logical therefore to head to the South Armagh area for help now. They opted for South Armagh as the destination. It was, however, still about 30 miles away and they would have to travel at night, on foot and in the fields. The going would be hard and slow. *"How long do you think Seamus?"* *"Some of it depends on luck, It will be slow but maybe three days and nights if we hide during the daylight hours."*

"Let's call it two days for the team morale," McFarlane said smiling. *"What time should we leave?"* They discussed this for a while and decided on 10.30pm when the ordinary daily traffic at least would be vastly diminished. Since the roads would be less busy, crossing them unseen would be much easier.

Gary Roberts

G ary Roberts had been one of the first prisoners into the back
of the food lorry once the order was given to get on board.
He had already heard two shots so he knew the situation had
suddenly become more dangerous. He had only been told of the
escape and his part in it the previous evening by Rab Kerr. He
hadn't slept a wink all night with a strong cocktail of excitement,
dread and disbelief inside him.

He was part of taking over D-Wing but had been told nothing else.
So he had been standing in the circle area after having done his
part successfully still wondering where they went from there.
Peter Hamilton was moving about hyper, as was his nature giving
a running commentary on events. Roberts grabbed him by the
arm as he was whizzing past. *"Skeet. How are we getting out?"*
Hamilton looked at his comrade, *"The Happy Wagon, Big Balls."*
He answered with devilment in his eyes and abruptly moved on.
Calling the food lorry, 'The Happy Wagon' went right back to the
blanket protest days when the prisoners were only given half their
daily rations of food as part punishment for protesting.

When the lorry filled, Bobby Storey, in full guard's uniform
addressed everyone. *"No talking, no coughing, absolute silence
for the journey. Bígí ciúin."* He repeated in Irish for emphasis.
"It hasn't gone exactly as expected but we are in full control of

231

H7 and we're heading to the main gate. So, I repeat: absolute silence." He reached up to pull the shutter down but turned to the group of potential escapees again: *"By the way. Great job up to now. Well done everyone!"* As the shutter was pulled noisily down enveloping them in darkness his few words had lifted their morale again. *"Half way there,"* Gary thought hopefully.

The journey was made shorter by Pádraig McKearney sitting beside him whispering in the dark. He was clearly enjoying himself cracking jokes and quipping away. While he was barely audible Roberts, who normally enjoyed his craic preferred the 'absolute' silence Storey had asked for. At one point the lorry stopped and a number of prisoners wearing warders' uniforms got out of the lorry.

The next stop, shortly after that, was like an eternity. Roberts could feel the tension rising in the back of the lorry. There were occasional raised voices and his heart was sinking when suddenly the shutter shot up. Storey spoke as the tail gate below the shutter was dropped. *"Right, the balloons up lads, It's over."* He said it so loud and matter-of-factly that it stunned his audience. They saw Storey raise his hands and point his gun away from the lorry and shouting, *"Get back or I will shoot!"*

By this stage most of those sitting in the lorry had scrambled to their feet to at least see what was going on and where they were. Storey turned his head momentarily without moving his weapon from a firing stance. *"Run men the gate is open!"* He shouted.

No second call to action was necessary as prisoners scrambled over and down the sides of the lorry. As Roberts had been first in he now found he was last out. The pace – at least in the lorry – seemed snail-like. When he got out through the gate he moved towards the green of the fields straight ahead. After momentarily studying the barbed wire entanglements he climbed up one of the narrow metal stanchions and jumped quickly for fear it would break. Many others were doing the same and Joe Simpson landed almost on top of him. Roberts felt his shoe and sock being trailed off and reached down to grab the shoe. He noticed a guard repeatedly raising his baton to hit something or someone. As he hesitated Brendan McFarlane was in his face – in fact he nearly hit him on the head with the gun. *"Run, run,"* was all McFarlane shouted. Roberts picked up his shoe and moved up the hill following other escapees.

As he neared the crest he heard a shot. He dived to the ground as another louder crack went off. He knew it as a pistol followed by a rifle. He saw Hamilton running close to him *"Get down Skeet. Did you hear those shots?"* *"Fuck them!"* Retorted Hamilton without breaking pace *"Get up and run!"* Roberts took the moment he needed to put on his shoe and followed. Roberts followed the straggly line of other escapees down the next field and over a gate. Most of them had turned left on the road that the gate opened on to.

Remembering his rural comrades in jail always talking of avoiding roads and keeping to the fields, he crossed the tarmac and pushed through the hedges. He could see the distinctive swagger of Hamilton half a field away and there was no mistaking Storey's height in front of Hamilton. He followed them but couldn't close the gap so he decided to change direction slightly, thinking that one person would be harder to spot than numbers of people.

Roberts crossed another road and could see a small gathering of people close to houses some distance away. He moved to the hedge for cover as he saw a motorbike on the road and then some cars. He came across a wide river, which he guessed was the Lagan, and heard a distant helicopter on the wind. He couldn't cross because he couldn't swim and the river appeared dangerous. However, the sound of the helicopter moved him into the river to hide under its bank. It was ice-cold but he didn't care.

Within moments, it seemed, he heard a shot off to his right but relatively close. This was the third sound of shooting since the escape began. He imagined the British and RUC were taking no prisoners after the guard had been shot inside the jail. He moved out from under the river-bank and scanned what he could see of the field and the sky. Seeing nothing, he pulled himself out on to the bank and headed off away from the sound of the gunshot.

Fairly soon he came across a small stream or drain. It was deep, cutting into the field to a depth of about 12ft and it was overgrown. He stayed in the ditch and followed it for about 200 yards or so. Looking to the top of the ditch above him he saw a curious cow looking down, then another and then another – like a group of spectators. He tried to shoo them away but to no avail. *"Touts! Informers!"* he whispered loudly to them and then sniggered to himself before moving on.

He was disoriented now believing he was perhaps caught between the jail and the river Lagan but he had cover and it would soon be dark. All the time he could hear the stutter of the British Army chopper on the wind, seemingly close and then distant. He was starting to worry about hypothermia as he was cold and soaked, but he forged ahead till he spotted a tree a small distance into a field. He thought it was a Weeping Willow with its branches hanging to the ground. He got under its shelter to wait until dusk, suddenly aware of how white and bright his running shoes were. He jogged on the spot to keep warm and took off his denim jacket to give it a chance to dry.

While it was still light he saw three men with two dogs in the adjoining field. He could make out shotguns crooked on their arms. They were following the ditch at a leisurely pace. He resisted the urge to make a bolt for it and instead walked away keeping the tree between himself and the men with dogs and guns. It was on the edge of dark now. He soon crested a hill and saw the ordered rows of lights which could only be the jail. He put them to his back and walked directly away. He came across a road where two jeeps were racing up and down. He could hear the English accents of soldiers standing up in the jeeps slagging each other.

He timed their movements for a while and then ran quickly across the tarmac jumping through a gap in the hedge. He dropped 10ft but got up unhurt and moved on. He passed an old graveyard and some houses and found himself at the M1 motorway. It was empty of cars so he thought it had been blocked off by the British authorities. He moved a field away from the motorway but walked parallel to it until he came up against the Lagan again. He had no choice then but to follow the river to find a crossing point. Every now and then he would stop and listen for any sounds. A heavy mist had fallen.

Suddenly a figure appeared out of the mist. He and the figure stopped in shock at seeing each other for a moment. Roberts heard a distinct metallic click. It was a safety lock being released just as a second figure appeared with a rifle at shoulder height. A Scottish voice demanded, *"Are you one of the prisoners?"* It was the first figure, *"What prisoners?"* Roberts tried puzzlement in his voice, *"I'm out looking for my sheep."* *"Of course he's a fucking prisoner!"* Insisted the second soldier who was right beside him now. *"Look at the state of him."* *"What's your name?"* Asked the first soldier. *"Paul Brennan,"* lied Roberts fluently before feeling embarrassed by his comment. He had picked the name of another escapee as it was the first name that had come to his mind.

The game was up. At this stage he was surrounded by a patrol of at least eight British soldiers. They frisked him and then walked him to a nearby road. Roberts was worried but musing that they had shown professionalism and no great antagonism towards him. *"They've got one. They've got one,"* was the next shout he heard as RUC cops started appearing on the road moving quickly towards him. He could feel a sudden change in atmosphere as the first cop approached. The cop then came up to him and started screaming questions in his face with no time between each question to actually get an answer. Another RUC man started interrogating him. Yet another was shouting at the British soldiers. This one appeared to be in charge. He spoke directly to Roberts then *"What's your name and where are your mates?"* Roberts made no reply. At that moment Volunteer Peter Cleary came to his mind: He was a volunteer in the IRA who had been shot dead alone in a field in Co. Armagh shortly after Roberts' arrest in 1976.

Roberts was frightened but he wasn't running. He closed his eyes for a moment in the dark to compose himself. *"We've already reported his capture,"* said the Scotsman. Roberts, didn't know if the Scottish soldier had been telling the truth but he was very grateful either way as he was worried about the intent of the RUC men.

Roberts was frogmarched to an unmarked car and shoved to the floor in the back. A heavy-set RUC man sat on the seat with his feet on top of him After that he could hear a radio discussion as to whether they were taking him to the notorious Castlereagh Interrogation Centre or back to the jail. Roberts hoped for the police interrogation centre. He had suffered severe interrogation by the RUC Special Branch but, thought, returning to the jail would be worse - at least this soon after the escape.

He was returned to the jail. There was still utter confusion over six hours after the escapees had exploded through the perimeter. The first guard Roberts saw was known as the 'Red Rat' because of his particular brutality during the protest years. He asked the cops who they had. *"Roberts"* was the reply. *"No,"* answered the obviously drunk guard, *"That's McRoberts,"* He said as he tried to reach into him. Roberts wasn't a very Irish Nationalist name so the 'Red Rat' had always insisted on 'fenianising' it by adding 'Mc' to it.

The car was waved through to the jail reception. The RUC man in the back spoke to Roberts prone on the floor during the journey into the jail. *"Did you know that two prison officers are dead. Hey boy, see that van in front of us. It's packed with their mates and they can't wait to get at you!"*

At that the car stopped and as the cop got out one side, Roberts was trailed out the other by his hair. Blows rained down on him as he was thrown into the reception area. As he was fired into a booth he felt some relief in seeing P.O. (Principal Officer) that he recognised as he was one of the few guards who had resisted beating prisoners on protest. When he was taken to be finger-printed and photographed Roberts got a glimpse of his face in a mirror. His eyes were slits in a badly beaten face.

When the booth door opened again he knew it was to take him to 'The Boards' or segregation block. He was handcuffed with his hands behind his back, which was not a good sign. A semi-circle of warders stood between him and the transport van waiting to take him to the segregation block. It was the blanket protest all over again – in spades. Roberts took a deep breath and charged headlong into the gauntlet with a determined pride.

After a torrent of abuse and blows he felt himself being lifted bodily and thrown into the van and onto the floor.

It was a relief when he landed heavily on the cell floor. The segregation block was called 'the boards' because it was basically a bare cell without any furnishings whatsoever, barring a long concrete plinth with wooden boards screwed to it. A small concrete table about 18" square in the corner and a concrete seat against the back wall were the only furnishings. A prisoner was entitled to a mattress, pillow and blankets but on this night they had been removed. The last act before the cell door was locked was for a guard, nicknamed 'Busted Sofa', to thrust Roberts face hard against the corner, breaking his tooth. He collapsed unconscious and when he awoke, perhaps only moments later, the handcuffs were removed and the cell door had been shut.

Early the next morning, Roberts heard Bobby Storey shouting to Peter Hamilton *"Skeet, who was that poor bastard brought in late last night?"* *"It's me Bobby, Gary Roberts."* Then to Hamilton who was in a closer cell, he spoke to him in Irish. Roberts had become fluent in Irish while on the blanket protest but knew Hamilton wasn't so he tried simple words known by almost all prisoners. *"Skeet, An dtuigeann tú 'Coimeádóir'?"* *(Do you understand the word "screw")* *"Beirt"?* *(Two of them)* *"fuair bas"* *(died)*. Hamilton who was small in stature but known to be afraid of no-one understood well. *"I don't give a fuck! You didn't do it and they still beat the crap clean outta ya. It's just revenge and if I get outta this cell I've some revenge in me to get out of my system."* Roberts cut the Irish lesson at that point.

Later in the morning when the guards who had been on duty were replaced, the prisoners were let out in twos to go to the toilet and get washed. Roberts was out with Storey who had actually been charged with him in 1976, but Storey had beaten the charge. *"Jesus Gary, you wanna see the state of your face,"* Storey said when they met. *"And yourself Big Lad,"* Roberts half laughed pointing at Storey's back because you'd have thought someone peeled every inch of skin off it.

10pm
Sunday, September 25th
Long Walk to Freedom

At 10pm the McFarlane family wanted to go into one bedroom together. The escapees agreed as they knew it was nearing their departure time and they wanted to have a yarn and make some last minute preparations. McElwaine was to lead and McDonnell was to take up the rear. All light coloured clothing was darkened down or covered. Faces were blackened. Instructions were simple:- They were to move a few paces apart from each other in single file and at any sight or sound of traffic they were to jump off the road and into the ditch beside them. They had worked out that they needed to follow the road for approximately 3 miles to a cut off point heading South. At that point they would take to the relative safety of the fields. There would be no casual chat and any necessary information would be passed from man to man in a whisper.

With blackened faces they left the house quietly just after 10.30pm. They wanted the family to think they were still in the house for as long as possible. Paul Brennan had closed the door of the bedroom when the family was settled. He had told them that there would be two Volunteers staying behind for a few hours to give the others a head start. It wasn't true but was worth the try to keep them from leaving the bedroom. Brennan's last act before leaving the house with the others was to cut the telephone wires.

The footfall on the gravel outside, however, broke the silence with an amplified crunch which made them wince a little. All except McElwaine who led off swiftly through the gate, the crunch quietened to a muffled thud on the tarmac road.

No-one was happy being on the road but it did allow them to move at a fast walking pace. The drone of the Brit helicopter was, in a way, comforting in its obvious distance. It was too far away to see its searchlight which was undoubtedly being used. If it had come in their direction they would have had to bury themselves deep into the ditches and hedgerows.

A thick mist then settled and deepened the silence and brought visibility down to less than 50 yards at times. It had defeated the droning chopper and equally lifted the spirits of the hill walkers for that very reason. McElwaine at the front quickened the pace a little more. On three occasions while they were on the road cars had passed, forcing a scattering of bodies into brambled hedgerows. Some were better than others, or luckier, climbing out scratched and bleeding but blithely unaware of any such small injuries. Spirits were high despite the thick fog.

After a while they came to the junction of the minor road and the main road. McElwaine spotted the road sign with directions to Belfast and Newry. The dual carriage-way stretched into the distance both ways. The road was empty. *"Cross quickly but watch out for headlights,"* he whispered to McFarlane who passed it down the line. They all jogged across quietly to a field gate on the other side and climbed over at the hinges end, to minimise the tinny rattle.

They entered the field with the last man using his sleeve to quickly wipe away any obvious muck left by their boots on the rungs of the metal gate. McFarlane checked the small clock. It was almost midnight. There was another good four or five hours walking in them before daylight.

As they walked, the mist lifted revealing the type of speckled sky that can only be seen in country areas where there's no light pollution. Paul Brennan spotted the Starry Plough constellation and its accompanying North Star. He suggested checking the small compass for a true reading. They were delighted to see the reading tallied well.

After 5am they started searching for a hideaway to get through the day. The weather had been mild so they didn't need to chance any barns or buildings. They wanted heavy foliage to hide in, well away from any roads and preferably with a good view of the countryside around them.

They found what seemed the perfect undergrowth, between two fields and big enough to hold them all. It had been, perhaps the most eventful and memorable day of their lives. The forced march in the darkness had been long and arduous. They made themselves as comfortable and secure as possible and as day broke at least half of them were sleeping huddled together for warmth.

McElwaine and McFarlane were still too alert and excited despite their exhaustion. They wanted to get the early news on the radio. They whispered when one of them felt like saying anything. While both felt a great exhilaration, McElwaine felt most comfortable looking over the rolling hills and farm land. The scenery felt like a huge comfort blanket and he was well used to lying out in it at night when he had been on active service for the IRA in the border areas.

They listened to the local news at 7am on Radio Ulster and then swapped about throughout the day to Radio Éireann to get the Southern Ireland perspective and other British and Irish news reports. It appeared like every State force was out searching for them. The British Army, The Royal Ulster Constabulary, The Ulster Defence Regiment, The RUC Reserve, The Irish State Army and Garda Síochána. Even pro-British farmers were out. After hearing it all on the first news bulletin, McFarlane winked at McElwaine and whispered, *"Well at least we know the Irish Republican Army will be out looking us as well after we didn't turn up at the rendezvous!"* It also appeared from news reports that ten comrades had been caught.

6am
Monday, September 26th
Paul Kane and
Brendy Mead

P aul Kane and Brendy Mead awoke at dawn to the sound of a farmer checking his sheep and talking away to himself – or the sheep. A mist had fallen with the dawn. Sometime later, but still very early, a woman tending cattle passed them close-by but made no greeting. They set off again hoping to spot some friendly sign of a nationalist or republican area. Eventually they spotted a slogan on a wall: *"Up The IRA."* They were near the village of Leitrim on the outskirts of Castlewellan –a mainly Irish nationalist town in Co. Down. They lay watching a house sitting on its own, wondering for a while could they take it over and then make contact with local Republicans. There was no sign of people and there was no traffic on the narrow side road beside the house. So they decided to move down towards it. They wanted to cross the road to get a better view of the front door. The mist had thickened substantially. As they walked across the road towards the house an unmarked RUC patrol car appeared out of the mist. It was on to them too quickly to run.

On seeing the dishevelled pair, one of whom was wearing a prison officer's uniform, the car skidded to a halt and the two RUC men

243

bounced out. The passenger raised his sterling sub machine gun to a firing position and shouted to Mead and Kane to get on the ground. Mead and Kane tried to bluff it by asking, *"What's the problem. We're doing a bit of hunting,"* But the cops were having none of it. They had been up most of the night and the only thing on anybody's mind that day was the jailbreak. The driver was out of the vehicle now with a pistol in hand and both were moving towards the escapees. *"Put that weapon down,"* he shouted at Mead indicating the pitch fork. *"Get on your stomachs. Put your hands on your head."* They were excited by their good luck and couldn't wait to report in.

In the meantime a woman had come out of the house that the escapees had been checking out. She stood now leaning on her gate watching the drama unfold. One of the RUC men looked back at the car, some yards away. They didn't want to leave the dangerous republicans they were holding at gunpoint but they had to report in. *"Listen Ma'am,"* one shouted excitedly to the woman, *"Phone 999. Give your location and tell them to send help. Tell them we have arrested two of the terrorists from the Maze Prison!"*

When he finished the woman looked first at Mead and Kane lying prone on the road and then directly at the RUC man. *"Phone them yourself!"* She retorted, and walked back into the house. *"Fuuuuuck!"* was all that Kane could muster, thinking that if they had gone to the house earlier they most likely would've been welcomed in and taken care of.

Noon
Monday 26th,
Gilford, County Down

The day was quiet up to about lunchtime when Mc Ilwaine spotted two men and a dog skirting the large field in front of them. They were worried about the dog sensing them but it didn't come near. They were close enough however to see that one of the men was carrying a shotgun. They may have been hunting. Glances were exchanged between the escapees and McFarlane quietly checked his pistol, just in case. The two men however never looked in their direction and moved through a gap in the hedge into another field. The republicans settled down again. A couple of the lads who had been sleeping woke up so they were given the radio with the instructions not to waste the batteries but listen to the news on the hour. It still wasn't clear how many of their comrades had evaded capture. McFarlane and McElwaine then lay down to try to get some sleep as there was a long night of walking ahead of them.

In truth no one slept for long periods but the resting-up itself was important. At 8pm they set off in a southerly direction again after eating whatever they had left. They left no wrappers or rubbish as evidence of their presence. They reckoned that they had about nine hours of darkness ahead and hopes were high of making substantial distance if the terrain they were facing remained as firm and open as the night before.

It wasn't to be that simple though. After a couple of hours walking, Tony McAllister went over on his ankle and sprained it badly. They had to rest for a while as the ankle swelled up. It was demoralising for everybody but McAllister also had ulcer trouble and no tablets to ease the problem. At this stage, all they had were bottles of water which they had replenished at a cattle trough.

Despite his pain, McAllister, fairly quickly got himself on his feet and assured his comrades that he could take the pain. Jim Clarke and Terry Kirby both stood over 6ft tall and immediately offered to help their comrade. McAllister put up token resistance but in truth he needed the help and was delighted with the comradeship. It was inevitable however that they all adapted to the pace of the slowest walker. A further obstacle to their progress appeared at about 1am as they crested a ridge to see the lights of a town in front of them.

Gilford was a small town, still in County Down. They found themselves wedged between a main road on one side which was lit up like a football stadium in floodlights. On the otherside was a fast flowing river which was quite wide and of an indeterminate depth. It was the river Bann. They couldn't risk the crossing in the dark, especially since not everyone could swim. They decided to find somewhere safe to hold up and have a look at their surroundings in the dawn light.

They quickly came across a demesne or large estate and moved through the gateway to explore the grounds. There was a sloping lawn with a greenhouse at the top. They found a small orchard and filled the haversacks with crab-apples. But the river was still an obstacle to bypassing the town. There had been a cluster of thick bushes and evergreen trees a short distance from the gateway so they made their way back there and quickly fashioned a hide in the darkness. There were loads of fallen leaves further back and they used them to soften the surface to lie on.

Everyone was annoyed that they had lost four or five hours walking time, none more so that McAllister. They had hoped to be much closer to the border by now. McAllister's ankle was throbbing with pain and although he was prepared to walk on he was quietly relieved to rest it in the hope that the swelling would decrease. They took turns on guard, draping all the coats over those who lay down to give them extra heat to make it easier to sleep. *"Ah well, C'est la vie lads,"* whispered McNally philosophically as he closed his eyes. There was no point worrying about it all. *"Second night of freedom,"* Brennan whispered back. *"Oíche mhaith a Chairde." (Good night friends)* Everyone was glad it hadn't, as yet, rained.

Tuesday Morning
September 27th
Gilford, County Down

Tuesday morning came dry and quiet. The news bulletins were the main focus again. It looked like some more escapees had been recaptured but that there was still a substantial number at large. At about 11am a car drove through the open gate up to the greenhouse where a country squire type and a woman disembarked with two dogs. There was an involuntary moan from the bushes at the sight of dogs and their sensitive noses, but they all moved around the greenhouse out of sight.

Everyone was awake and peering intently out from behind foliage, but when the man and woman didn't re-appear they all relaxed a bit thinking that they might be just in to work in the greenhouse. The escapees had decided not to explore the river for a crossing point until the edge of darkness. Then there would be enough light to see but a darkness to blend into if they had to get away quickly.

A couple of hours later the woman reappeared on her own and took off in the car. Then at about 3pm the man came into sight at the top of the sloping lawn with the two dogs and walked towards where the republicans were hiding. The young dogs were frolicking about his legs but both stopped suddenly and started barking loudly in the direction of the hide. The man shouted at them and changed direction down a path which brought him away and out of sight. Everyone relaxed again. *"I wish it was fecking dark again!"* whispered McElwaine who didn't like to swear. *"I don't like dogs about. Do you think we should move on?"* This started a whispered discussion on the pros and cons especially since, at this stage, everyone was, to a great

The River Bann which the escapees came to, north of Gilford

extent relying on McElwaine's country 'know how'. In the end everyone thought it was too much of a chance to take, to move in daylight. Darkness would come soon enough.

Half an hour later a car stopped at the open gateway. McFarlane thought it might be the woman returning and focussed in on the driver's door. He felt a tingle running down the back of his neck when he spotted the unmistakeable dark green of an RUC uniform. Three armed policemen disembarked from the vehicle. By now everyone was aware of the situation and were shuffling in the dead leaves for a better look.

McFarlane whispered for everyone to be quiet. As all other movement stopped he was acutely aware that he had no shoes on and quickly slipped his feet into them. Someone whispered faintly into his ear, *"Lets get out of here."* McFarlane lifted his hand to cut him off. They didn't dare move, at least, not just then. Eight men moving at once would be very hard to do with complete silence. One of the cops moved onto the lawn while the other two walked off down the path.

Lifting the small pistol up McFarlane sighted quickly. It had a silencer but the calibre was very small and the RUC men were armed with heavier calibre automatic weapons. More importantly they were wearing body armour that would stop rifle fire never mind .25 or .22 calibre bullets. Its only use would be if one of them came close enough to grab. Then they could use the weapon as a threat and possibly disarm the others. Plan 'B' which was probably plan 'A' in everybody else's mind was scattering in all directions if they were spotted.

The cop on the lawn seemed relaxed and unconcerned. He wasn't holding his weapon at the ready although he was looking up and down the lawn and then directly at the line of trees and bushes that concealed the escapees. It looked like the man had phoned the local barracks on the basis of the dogs barking. The belief that kids were raiding the orchard, however, may have been the reason for phoning. The local RUC men may have been checking out the grounds for the local landowner precisely because he was a landowner.

After what seemed an age, the two other policemen returned to the car and the third followed them. As the car moved out of sight the relief was palpable and audible as the republicans started to move and talk in hushed tones. Some were putting shoes back on. Tony McAllister hadn't dared take his off because of the sprain for fear of not being able to put his boots back on again. *"Right, we're getting out of here now lads. That was too close a call!"* Seamus McElwaine was adamant. McFarlane nodded his agreement as he led off. They all crawled to the top of a steeply sloping field. One by one they followed McElwaine as he rolled under a wire fence and onto a muddy pathway. They crossed it and moved into more trees and undergrowth where they could hear the rush of the river.

At one point, as they moved parallel to the river, they could see a couple of fishermen casting away, oblivious to their presence. They had made a good distance from their previous encampment and most of the journey had been under cover. They were going down a narrow mud-path now, with loads of heavy brambles and berries bordering it. McElwaine moved off to the side and whispered for the others to move into the undergrowth but to leave as little signs of their entry as possible. He had spotted a good point to cross the river where the water was not so frothy with underlying rocks. The lads collected berries for a bit of a feast while they waited for sunset.

Their feast was short lived as two youths with fishing rods almost fell over Gerry McDonnell and Jim Clarke who were the designated berry collectors. The lads seemed a bit startled and moved off the path and hurried away from the river. They didn't think the boys had seen the others but McFarlane looked at McElwaine who spoke, *"We can't take the chance. This is as good a place as I've seen to cross over."*

McFarlane looked in the direction the young lads had taken and satisfied himself that the trees and undergrowth gave the cover, *"What are we waiting for a chara?"* he shrugged. But they were all very aware of the daylight as they moved towards the water. It was 3.45pm – quite a while to go before dark. McElwaine couldn't swim but there was no hesitation as he stepped into the icy water which rose towards his chest as he reached mid-stream. They all followed him in single file and were across in moments. Clarke and Kirby held on to McAllister and moved as a team. The icy water eased McAllisters still throbbing ankle. Brennan and McNally at 5ft 5" in height got ever more worried as the water level moved towards their necks but luckily it levelled off there.

251

They helped each other scramble up the steep bank on the other side into more bushes. They were a couple of hundred yards away from a bridge as they made their way on up the sloping field into trees. As they settled down they could see a busy road at a T-junction, not far away. Most were wishing they were in the cars they saw stopping, instead of freezing cold in their wet clothes.

They were well sheltered so they removed shoes and socks to try and dry them out before they set off after dark. Some even removed trousers to wring out the excess water before putting them back on. McAllister was a bit worried about the walk ahead but still eager to get on with it. It had been an eventful day and they were all hoping for a full and uneventful night walk.

5pm
Sunday, September 25th
Jim Smyth, Joe Corey,
Tony Kelly and
Paddy McIntyre

A s Jim Smyth drove through the village of Moira, Joe Corey in the front passenger-seat, recognised a guard from H7 out walking his dog. He warned the others in the car not to turn their heads and draw unwanted attention. They headed towards the small town of Castlewellan as they knew some prisoners who hailed from there. He knew they had to ditch the car quickly but also knew they had to reach a Nationalist town. All four discussed the options as they travelled.

As they drove into Castlewellan they saw 'Up the IRA' painted on a wall. They turned into a laneway at the back of some houses to get off the main street. Two young girls were approaching so Paddy McIntyre asked, *"Do you know anyone in Sinn Féin, girls?"* *"Yes,"* one answered. *"Where do you live?"* *"In there,"* she pointed to a door in the alleyway itself. Two teenage boys were in the kitchen and tried to run but were caught and settled down. One took Tony Kelly and Smyth to a restaurant and bar and introduced them to a local Republican. They explained the situation but the man just laughed at them, *"Get the fuck out..."* He hadn't finished the sentence when they heard a huge cheer from the bar. An old woman came out of the kitchen screaming with joy. The man moved through the door to see what was happening. It was a newsflash announcing a mass escape from the jail.

"Right lads," the man was no longer disbelieving, *"let's get you outta here to somewhere safe."* He drove them to another part of the town but was refused help. They heard a man saying, *"No disrespect to the lads but everybody is watching you."* From the car they scanned the street to discover quite a few people were watching what was going on. Their hearts sank thinking time was running short for them to be in safe hiding or across the border which they knew wasn't too far away. He eventually drove them to a cottage in the hills about ten minutes outside Castlewellan. The driver told them to wait till he came back. He didn't tell the farmer anything so they sat for sometime with the four of them staring quietly at the man of the house.

His daughter arrived shortly afterwards shouting excitedly as she came through the door, *"Daddy, did you hear the news about the escape from Long Kesh?"* The farmer was delighted to be an accidental part of a huge event. More importantly for the escapees, there were no nosey neighbours. His daughter put on the pan after shaking hands with them all and prepared a welcome Ulster Fry. As they started to eat they heard the farmer on the phone saying, *"Do you want to meet the lads who escaped?"* Tony Kelly near choked on his bacon as the four looked at each other. The man explained with an almost disarming smile, *"It's just the family."* It was not a good omen but there was nowhere else to go until their driver returned.

About six or seven members of the family arrived, adults and children and a party of sorts started. After an hour and a half the original driver came back. *"Two have to go and two have to stay for now,"* he said. Smyth was up on his feet, *"I'll go"* and Tony Kelly sounded like his echo with, *"I'll go!"* straight after Smyth spoke. The party had increased their nervousness. They were brought to Mayobridge a few miles away and then they were driven by a young man in his twenties to a terraced house in Derrybeg Estate in Newry. A young couple made them feel at home and later another man arrived to talk to them about further arrangements.

About an hour after Jim Smyth and Tony Kelly left, another car came and collected Paddy McIntyre and Joe Corey. They were driven a few miles away close to Leitrim Village. There were two houses close to each other just off the road. McIntyre and Corey stayed in one house with an older man whose son and daughter-in-law lived in the other.

The next morning, Monday, they heard that two escapees had been recaptured a short distance away early that morning. They thought it might be Tony Kelly and Jim Smyth but found out later it was Mead and Kane. In any case they couldn't be moved as the area was now difficult to move in with State Forces out in strength. They spent the day listening to the news and reading newspapers.

Tuesday Morning
27th September
Paddy McIntyre and
Joe Corey

The next morning, Tuesday, Paddy McIntyre and Joe Corey were told that the search teams seemed to be moving away from the area so they were hopeful of moving across the border that night. During the afternoon McIntyre remarked to Corey that the road was very quiet. It wasn't a busy road but would have had cars passing intermittently.

Just then the daughter-in-law came in and said that someone wanted to talk to them on the phone next door. They knew there was no phone in the house they were in. *"Who is it?"* Corey inquired. The woman answered simply, *"I think it's the police."*

McIntyre turned to Corey. *"I'll take the call. You should hide, they mightn't know there are two of us."* Corey started to argue but his friend cut him off. *"You're doing life with more to lose. It's worth a try Joey."* He turned and walked out the back door. The first thing he saw was a long line of British Army and Police. All were armed and it looked like anyone with a rifle was pointing it at him. They were only about 30 yards away so he took a deep breath and walked as casually as he could to the next door house.

A high ranking member of the RUC introduced himself on the phone. *"The house is surrounded. You have absolutely no chance of getting away. There are civilians involved here so we don't want anyone to get hurt. Have you any weapons?"* *"What is your name? And how many others are with you?"* The cop inquired. McIntyre ignored the questions, *"I want a Sinn Fein representative here if I am to come out."* *"There is no way I am bringing a Shinner here for that,"* said the cop with finality.

"It was worth a try," McIntyre thought to himself. *"Okay,"* he spoke into the phone, *"I need the local priest as a guarantee of safety."* *"Leave it with me,"* said the cop. McIntyre then walked back across to talk to Corey. As he walked back he looked to the road which was awash with Crown Forces and military and police vehicles. It was obvious they knew he was not alone and equally obvious that they would thoroughly search both houses.

The local priest arrived soon afterwards and identified himself. He relayed what was expected of them. Corey and McIntyre came out with their hands above their heads. Only then did they realise the full extent of the arrest operation. The road was covered in vehicles and personnel as far as they could see in both directions.

Four top cops in braid were in attendance and it was being videoed. They were told to get down on the ground where they were searched for weapons. They were then transported to Newcastle Barracks and later that night to Castlereagh Interrogation Centre in Belfast. They were kept there until Friday but at this stage the Interrogators knew none of the escapees were giving any useful information.

Tuesday Night
September 27th
The Walk Continues

McFarlane and the others were still wet but got off to a good start after nightfall. A couple of the escapees had been coughing and sneezing. They were all cold, hungry and tired. While they had been in hiding for quite long periods none of them had slept well over the last few days and it was telling on them.

After passing a farmhouse they discussed taking it over to dry out and get food. McElwaine and McDonnell left the others some distance away and went towards the house to check it out. As they got close they satisfied themselves that there were no dogs and crept up to the windows to look and listen. There were visitors so they decided they'd have to wait until they left. The two of them hid behind a gate on the other side of the road facing the house.

After about a half an hour of waiting and whispered discussions, they changed their minds about the house takeover. It could be a repeat of the first one but they had travelled a good distance since then. That could be jeopardised if they couldn't keep this family silent as well. They could give their position and direction of travel away as well as the fact that they were still on foot. It wasn't worth the risk.

6am
Wednesday, September 28th

A ll eight escapees set off again with renewed determination,
although they were tired and the going was slow. It was
Wednesday and they found a hiding place at the top of a hill full
of wild bushes which gave plenty of cover. It was around 6am.
Despite a deep hunger they made themselves as comfortable as
they could. A rota to keep watch was agreed and the rest tried to
get some sleep. The day passed without incident. Their vista was
broken only once when a farmer appeared in a field some distance
away with hay to feed some cattle.

As darkness fell, with faith in their compass and relief at the
continuing mild weather, they set off in single file in a southerly
direction. They had taken to walking minor roads after midnight.
The going was faster and easier on legs and ankles. After a few
hours they came across a railway track. It had to be the Belfast
to Dublin line as it was the only railway in the area. It wouldn't
be as safe as the fields but the railway was the shortest and
straightest route South. They checked the compass again and
headed off along the tracks.

The single file had got a bit straggly with some of the escapees
finding it harder than others, so the pace slowed somewhat.

259

Coming up to 4am Seamus McElwaine in the lead could see the glow of a large town. It had to be Newry, a town sitting right on the border with the South of Ireland. He passed the word knowing that it would lift everyone's morale and spur them on.

Pace increased again and soon afterwards they walked across a bridge over the main road with the bright lights of Newry nestling to their left. They knew they were entering the normally highly militarised border area. It would be even more dangerous in the aftermath of the jail break. They spotted a minor road off to the right and McElwaine slid down the steep embankment on his hunkers to read the road sign: 'Camlough three miles' it read.

Camlough was a village in republican South Armagh. This was good news and bad news. They were entering into the very active South Armagh Brigade area of the IRA. The bad news was that it could mean more British Army Patrols and undercover squads.

They headed west now taking the narrowest of winding hilly roads and crossing fields to avoid houses. But it seemed every house here had dogs as there always seemed to be one barking somewhere. Now was the time to approach a house, but which one? They were entering friendly territory but that didn't mean every house was friendly.

It wouldn't be long to dawn. While the others took a rest, McElwaine went off to investigate some farmhouses. He used a simple yardstick: the poorer the farm the more likely it was to be Irish nationalist. He came from farming stock himself. There was too much machinery at the first two, he observed, and too many vehicles. He was under pressure for time but the third farm house looked promising. The house was not modern and was quite small, though there was a barn and milking parlour.

He re-joined the others and explained his choice. They all moved quietly into the milking parlour and drank their fill of milk hungrily – friend or foe they needed sustenance in case they had to spend another night walking.. They then retired to the hay-barn where all of them had the best sleep since the previous Saturday night in the natural heat and insulation of the hay into which they burrowed deeply.

8am
Thursday, September 29th
Camlough, County Armagh

L ater that morning after dawn, a man left in the only car in the farmyard. Not long afterwards another man, somewhat younger, left on foot into the fields. At about 8am, when the man hadn't returned McFarlane and McElwaine moved to the back door of the house and went inside. McElwaine spoke to the woman they found in the kitchen, *"You wouldn't have a cup of tea for an escaped Republican Prisoner, would you?"* The woman looked round to see the two strangers. She was obviously startled but her face broke into a smile. *"Sure why wouldn't I,"* she said and reached for the kettle.

"Actually there's another six of us in the barn," smiled McFarlane, in what he hoped was a disarming way, *"Do you mind if they join us?"* *"You are having me on Son!"* The woman said in disbelief. *"I'm afraid not,"* McFarlane laughed. *"There's a whole family of bedraggled escapees in your barn and they would like you to play Mammy – just for breakfast we hope!"*

McFarlane then asked the woman who else was in the house.

"My daughter's sleeping upstairs and my son will be back shortly from the fields," she informed him. A few moments later a young

woman came down the stairs. The kitchen was packed with men so her mother explained.

"You may find this hard to believe," she told them *"but I was dreaming last night that the escapees came to our house."*

"Well dreams do come true – so thank you for dreaming about us," McAllister said, smiling after Clarke and Kirby plopped him on the kitchen chair. They ate voraciously everything the woman and daughter placed on the table.

As they tucked into mugs of tea and freshly baked bread in the warmth of a farmhouse in the hills of South Armagh they felt they were home –almost. This was a welcome take-over and they were mothered and fussed over. They took turns to have long overdue baths. When the son came in from the fields all was explained to him. Gerry McDonnell knew an old republican activist in the area. He named him and the young man knew him and where he lived. McDonnell then wrote a personal note to the Volunteer saying things that would let him know the note was genuine. He included a list of all the Volunteers in the farmhouse. The note was kept deliberately short and sealed in cling film with the instruction that the young man should carry it in his mouth; that he should give it to no-one but the named person and that if he was stopped at any British Army or RUC checkpoint, he should immediately swallow it.

Within the hour the local veteran activist arrived. The IRA had been out looking for them so it was great to see them all he told them. A number of cars would arrive after dark to take them to safety. And so it was. Most were sitting watching Top of the Pops on TV and enjoying a great meal when a number of cars pulled up outside. Brendan Moley and Brendan Burns were ecstatic to get eight of the escapees in one place. They were full of banter and had an air of confidence which was contagious. It was about 8pm, on the edge of darkness.

The escapees bade their farewells to the family who had treated them so well, with lots of handshakes and hugs. Within minutes, they were on their way. No headlights were used, despite the breakneck speed the cars were going until they came to main roads. The occasional crackle of CB radios in the cars was a comforting sound. All felt they were in good hands.

Others were taking the burden of the journey off them. It was sinking in. They had indeed "smashed the H-Blocks." they had turned one of the best known slogans in Ireland into a reality by bursting out of the most secure prison in Europe – well at least it used to be! They were tasting freedom.

6pm
Wednesday September 28th

Seán McCool walked into the bar in the Ballymascanlon Hotel and immediately spotted the NC OC sitting in a corner reading the paper. He scanned the room which was almost empty. Nothing looked out of place so he went over, shook hands and sat down facing him. The waiter came over and asked what he wanted and he ordered a coffee. The NC OC was already drinking tea. McCool opened the conversation, *"I have some good news for you."*

"That's good I could do with some good news. There are still nearly 20 escapees unaccounted for," the older man replied in a dead pan voice.

"Well...." McCool was enjoying his moment. *"I have some of them,"* he smiled broadly.

The other man sat up in his chair, *"How many?"*

"Just eight," he smiled again.

He could see the relief in his comrade's face. *"Are you serious? How long have you had them?"*

"Since the day of the escape"

"Why are you only telling me now?" He was trying to hide both his annoyance and his excitement aware that he was in a public place.

McCool explained, *"Well first of all I have them in a safe place. They are in Lurgan, I wanted to see if there were going to be raids. There have been none. I thought the main priority was that we had them and I didn't want to leave town until things died down a bit."*

"Well, what do you mean they are safe?"

"Well I have them all together. They are hidden in an old unused arms-dump under a house. Incidentally the arms-dump has been used for many years but was never discovered. An absolute minimum of me, the householders and one other person knows where they are."

The conversation continued on for a half an hour during which the Lurgan OC arranged for the safe transportation of his comrades across the border.

Saturday 8th October 1983
Lurgan

I t was Saturday 8th October. Kelly awoke to the realisation that he was still free and that it was his son Gerard's 10th birthday. He was, however, staring into a solid blackness and the knowledge that he and his comrades were still lying under the floorboards of a house in the town of Lurgan, in the North of Ireland. None of them had expected that they would still be there almost two weeks later, when one by one they had first crawled through the narrow trapdoor, under the stairs.

He knew that he would be talking to a member of the IRA's Northern Command that day. The others knew as well of course, so there was an air of expectation, as well as everyone pushing Kelly to make sure they were moved as soon as possible. Miraculously, there had been no raids or searches by the British army in Lurgan, despite the fact that quite a number of people had seen them in the Shankill area on the first day.

That night the trap-door was opened and the welcome face of McCool, the Lurgan OC looked down at him. Kelly felt very unsteady on his feet and mildly dizzy from the long spell under the house. The NC rep was introduced to him though not by name. *"Good to see you,"* Kelly said as he shook his hand.

"You too, how's it going?" He enquired.

"Well I feel a bit like a 'blanket-man' down there," he smiled. He was bearded and pale, as were all the escapees, as might be expected. *"As you know, we're under the floorboards nearly two weeks now and there's a growing impatience to move on and get back to the struggle."*

"Well at least youse aren't in jail," he responded a bit too reproachfully for Kelly.

He glanced sideways at the OC feeling an urge to retort, but resisted it as best he could. *"True, Comrade and I am not here to whinge. But we've been lying under floorboards for two weeks without enough room to sit up. We're smelly and attracting dogs to the air-vents. We're delighted to have escaped with the help of and in partnership with our comrades in the Army outside but also eager to move on, to re-join the struggle and to have some contact with our families!"*

"Well I'm not too sure about contacting families, Gerry. The good news is we'll be moving you out in pairs from tomorrow night. Two people each evening on the edge of dark," he said with the hint of a smile. *"Don't expect to see your families anytime soon though. This has been a huge blow to the Brits but each time one of you is recaptured they will make a big deal of that so they're searching every nook and cranny for damage limitation, apart from Lurgan, it seems. In a way the best thing the IRA could do now is to find somewhere far away and just hide all of you there for a few years!"*

The initial tension had dissipated but Kelly was listening intently as was the Lurgan OC. *"I fully understand that,"* he replied after a moment. *"But we escaped to return to the struggle. It was one of the issues dealt with while choosing who would be on the escape and I don't know anyone who wants to simply go away and hide."* He smiled again to hide his slight annoyance even though he understood his point. *"I am confident that the leadership will find good uses for us all."*

Kelly and Finucane were to go on the Monday evening. They showered and shaved and put on their freshly washed and laundered clothes courtesy of their hosts. Kelly had written a short poem for the child that they were expecting. He presented it along with a gold chain as a token of thanks to the very brave couple who had risked so much and had taken such good care of them, keeping them safe in a maelstrom of pressure from the British authorities and the media.

The girl who had brought them to the safe house returned and retraced the steps back to the housing estate and into a different house. McCool, had a small team gathered. *"Right lads, you'll be in the car with this man,"* he pointed to a man in his fifties. *"These two will be in scout cars – one in front of you and one behind. They will be in radio contact with each other at all times."* He indicated two young guys in their early twenties. *"I am not going as I'm a red light,"* he smiled, referring to the fact that he was too well known to the British. *"However none of these lads are known by the Brits. Good Luck."* He finished by shaking hands with Kelly and Finucane. As they waited the few minutes for the street to be checked out for any British army activity, the man of the house offered them a drink. *"Do you want a vodka, rum, brandy or beer lads?"*

"No thanks," Kelly answered as both he and Finucane shook their heads. *"I want to be clear-headed for this particular trip!"*

It was getting dark as they left the house. Finucane got into the front passenger's seat beside the driver and Kelly settled himself in the seat behind Finucane. They pulled off following the scout car. Within minutes they were in the countryside. The OC hadn't told them where they were going and they hadn't asked since they wouldn't have known the rendezvous anyway and didn't want an embarrassing refusal to answer such a question.

It was a moonlit night and they had a relatively clear view for the most part. They were hyper-sensitive to everything around them. The older man driving sensed it and made casual conversation unconnected to the night's task. About ten minutes out of Lurgan they turned a corner and found themselves at the top of a hill. There was a long empty section of road ahead which dipped steeply and then rose again. Finucane pointed towards a light coloured car in the middle of the road on the far hill. It was static. The scout car was about 100 metres ahead. *"Stop for a minute till we see what's happening,"* Kelly said to the driver, who pulled in. They watched closely as the lights of the scout car got closer and stopped. Looking hard, Kelly saw the silhouette of a large vehicle alongside the car. It was too far away to properly make out in the dusk, but could be a roadblock.

If it was a roadblock they didn't want to alert them by staying where they were with their headlights on so Kelly asked the driver to pull in to a side road close by.

They were at some old farm buildings so were covered once they pulled in and turned off the lights. They were discussing what to do when a man was spotted walking in their direction carrying something over his arm. He passed alongside the car looking at the three occupants with curiosity. It was only as he got closer that they realised he was carrying a shotgun in the crook of his arm. It was, however open at the breech for safety. As he moved past they realised he was out hunting – but not for them.

They decided to pull out onto the road again, ready to turn left or right. Looking towards the road to their right, the white car was nowhere to be seen or indeed any other car, so they returned to their journey. The lorry was a cattle-trailer sitting quiet and empty on one side of the road. There was no sign of the scout cars.

"Do you know where we're going okay?" Fincuane asked casually as he had noticed there was no C.B. or handheld radio in the car, although both scout cars had been equipped.

"Surely," answered the local man driving *"Don't you lads be worried, I'll get you there safely."* The answer niggled at Kelly a bit as there was no information in the answer. He reasoned that it was need-to-know information and they didn't need to know. So he let it pass.

Shortly afterwards the driver asked them to look out for a sign for Gilford or Tandragee. Kelly's antennae went up. *"Where are we going a chara?"* He asked more directly but again the answer was more in the way of assurance rather than detail of destination.

After another ten minutes Kelly spotted two dark vehicles on the road to his right running almost parallel to them. *"Are they jeeps?"* he asked to no-one in particular as they appeared to be travelling in tandem. Very quickly his eyes traced the road and realised it joined the one they were travelling on about a hundred yards ahead. It was like a slip road. They watched in some horror as one moved smoothly in front of them and then the other came in behind them. They were indeed British army Landrovers! All three vehicles were travelling at about 60 miles per hour.

Kelly leaned forward and spoke to the driver, *"Don't do anything sudden, a chara, but just drop your speed slightly so that the jeep ahead starts pulling away. I want to see if the other one overtakes us, okay?"*

"Not a problem lads, I don't think they'll stop us." The driver answered trying to reassure his passengers. Kelly couldn't help himself as the adrenalin levels in both passengers had just rocketed.

"Hopefully not Big Lad, but if they try to stop us we aren't

271

stopping. I'll be fucked if I'm gonna get caught now! okay?"
Finucane added *"It's dark – we can take to the fields if we have to, but I'm not throwing the hands up tonight."*

"I get the message loud and clear lads." The driver looked calm and sounded it. He had already slowed the pace slightly and the front jeep was widening the gap. He glanced in his mirror a few times. Kelly wanted to check behind him but didn't dare. Finucane was keeping an eye in the passenger wing mirror when the back jeep moved out of view. A moment later the rear jeep accelerated past on the driver's side.

Both jeeps widened the gap but a couple of minutes later they drove off to the left onto another minor road. *"Close or what!"* Finucane said to Kelly.

"Way too close Dermy," he agreed in the middle of his sigh of relief. *"Listen Big Lad,"* Kelly spoke *"Do you know exactly where you're bringing us?"*

He pronounced the words deliberately, *"Don't worry Lad – we'll be fine"*

"Just tell us where we're going!" Kelly interrupted sharply and then regretted his abruptness.

"I'm not sure." The driver admitted.

Finucane and Kelly look at each other in the dark. *"The scouts lost us."*

Kelly leaned forward. *"Do you know how to get back to Lurgan?"* He tried to keep sarcasm out of his voice but failed.

"I do," answered the driver calmly without a hint of retaliation.

"Then take us back to base now!" Kelly said a bit dramatically though he was unaware of it.

They got safely back to the house they had left. It was obvious that their arrival caused confusion and relief to the group gathered. Along with the OC were the two young scouts and the man and woman of the house. *"I'll have that vodka now,"* Kelly said to the man with some feeling. When he got it the OC led him and Finucane upstairs.

"The lads thought you were caught. They were shattered. What happened?" They explained the detail to the OC but all were now relieved that they were safe. The intense atmosphere diminished rapidly and they prepared for the following night as they had missed the contact and time of the arranged rendezvous. Kelly knew that he had been over cautious in calling the cattle lorry incident but McCool had the good grace not to point it out.

The following night the OC took a fully active part. McCool did not return home but stayed in a 'billet' until then. He wanted to make sure there were no hitches. This time all the remaining escapees went instead of just two. They took the narrow back roads which McCool knew intimately. They deliberately travelled through the more pro-British areas where there was less chance of roadblocks. On arrival at the carpark of the lake-side beauty spot near Camlough, they all got out of the cars. The OC ushered them over the wall and down the field along the ditch some distance. The vehicles that had dropped them off drove away.

After five minutes – though it felt like an hour to the escapees, who had no idea whether this was North or South of the border - -two large Ford Granada cars pulled into the carpark. The South Armagh Brigade had been observing their arrival and making sure they had not been followed.

Brendan Moley got out of the first car and spoke to McCool who then walked the short distance to get the escapees. McCool shook hands with them all and then disappeared over the wall again to wait on his own driver returning to bring him back to Lurgan.

Members of the South Armagh Brigade moved them rapidly across country, hugging the border to Leitrim where they were picked up by Volunteers in that Brigade area. They were taken the back lane into a side room of a pub in Balinamore.

Kelly and Finucane hadn't a clue where exactly they were although the OC was an ex-prisoner and a Tyrone man. They were fed and then a well dressed older man was introduced to them as John Joe McGirl. He was a veteran republican who they had all heard of and who had been elected as a TD in the area in the 1950s. They were delighted to meet him but Kelly was already worrying about them being in a hot spot watched by the Southern Special Branch.

Within the hour cars arrived to disperse the escapees to various safe houses, John Joe McGirl drove Kelly and Finucane to a house in the surrounding hills. They were greeted by two sisters in their twenties in the kitchen. *"Great to meet you both,"* one whispered. *"I'm afraid we have visitors so we need to be quiet."* They brought them into the hallway where they could hear voices coming from the front sitting room. When they got into one of the bedrooms, the women explained that they were due to go to a local function so they had to excuse themselves. That explained why they were so well dressed. The table in the room had tea and a variety of food for them to eat. *"Good food and good company – and I am not talking about you Dermy!"* Kelly said after they left. *"Now, I feel we've made it!"* Finucane was already eating so he missed the obvious twinkle in Kelly's eye.

Epilogue

T he mass escape from Long Kesh Prison Camp / HMP Maze was international news. British Prime Minister Thatcher described the crisis as 'The gravest in our prison history'. The pro-British Unionists and Loyalists called for the sacking of British Secretary of State, James Prior, as well as Prisons' Minister, Nicholas Scott.

In fact, secret documents have been released by the British Government under the '30 year rule' which show that Thatcher wrote her thoughts across the top of a classified document which landed on her desk five days after the escape occurred. Thatcher wrote, it was *'even worse than we thought'*. A strongly-worded telegram was also sent off by the British Foreign and Commonwealth Office to its missions and dependent territories saying: *'You should take every opportunity to limit the propaganda benefit the IRA will reap from the Breakout.... The Government regard the Breakout most seriously... PIRA and their sympathisers overseas will be doing all in their power to reap as much propaganda benefit from the escape as possible.'*

Sir James Hennessy, the Chief Inspector of Prisons, arrived from England on September 26th, the day after the escape. He published an 84-page report on his investigation into the escape which contained 118 conclusions and recommendations.

He noted, *"It should not surprise anyone that an escape – even from a prison such as the Maze should have been planned and attempted. What is surprising, perhaps, is that it should have succeeded, and in such large measure. Here was a prison designed to contain terrorists, and intended to be the most secure prison in Northern Ireland, with its perimeter breached by no less than 35 prisoners.*

Viewed in this light the escape was not merely audacious and daring, it must be judged the most serious escape in the recent history of the United Kingdom Prison Services."

It was perhaps, the epitome of 'closing the stable door after the horses have bolted!' Not surprisingly most of the Hennessy recommendations were quickly implemented. These included some physical reconstruction. Areas such as the Block's Control Rooms, the Tally Lodge and Main Gate complex, and the visiting and goods reception area, were rebuilt or radically changed to increase security.

A much tougher regime was re-introduced which involved controlled movement of prisoners, closed visits and further restrictions on rights and privileges. A system of 'Red Books' was introduced which categorised some prisoners as 'maximum security'. It meant that any 'Red Book' Republican was moved to a different Wing or Block at least every three weeks and at times more often.

However, the POWs were strategizing and planning also. It was mostly leadership figures within the jail who were being moved about, so they used the system to reorganise.

By moving around all the Republican wings on a regular basis, the leadership brought about standard practices and systems for advancing political education and discussion. They also used it to collate intelligence for further possible escapes. They were able to access individual guards, to know the hard cases and the liberals. Hennessey had tacitly acknowledged three categories of guards: those motivated by career prospects, those motivated by hatred of Irish Republicans and those motivated primarily by high earnings.

"No prison," said Hennessey, *"is ever more secure than the weakest member of its staff."* The POWs had already come to that conclusion in the build up to the '83 Escape. Within about 6 months of the escape the Republican Camp Staff had completely reorganised its modus operandi. While they maintained a small but strong military infrastructure, their emphasis was on building a strong community of prisoners.

The code name for the September '83 Escape was 'S.P'. or 'Set Piece', which was taken from IRA military set piece operations outside jail – that is planned operations as opposed to spontaneous operations. The new plan was simply 'S.P.2'. They were planning a bigger and better escape. They had recognised that Hennessey's focus was to primarily deal with the gaps or weaknesses shown up in September '83. So they decided to go in an entirely different direction.

'S.P.2' was to be a night-time escape which would involve the taking over of the central Emergency Control Room (E.C.R) situated in the Administration Block beside the Hospital at the heart of the jail. It was borrowing from the '83 Escape in that, by capturing the H/ Control Room they had controlled all communications in and out of the Block.

277

By capturing the Central Emergency Control Room they would have control of the whole jail because all communication and alarm systems went via the central E.C.R. All authority after 'Lock-Up' at night time resided in the E.C.R.

But, as they say, "that was the plan…and someday, I may divulge what actually happened!

April 1988

In April 1988, almost five years after the escape, 18 of the POWs were sentenced for their part in the escape. Although the RUC and the Public Prosecution Service charged each escapee with 75 individual charges, the Lord Chief Justice took a different view.

In his judgement Lord Lowry described the escape as 'ingeniously planned – cleverly executed' and as being, not a 'clandestine flight, but a walk-out, or more accurately, a drive-out in broad daylight'.

He slammed the evidence given by the guards as contradictory, inaccurate, and as being motivated in many cases by a wish to conceal failures on the part of individual guards. He described the guards' perception of what had happened on the day of the escape as a 'humiliating experience they would prefer to forget.'

None of the H7 Rearguard were ever identified or charged. In later court actions taken, many of the recaptured escapees received compensation for the injuries received in the aftermath of September 25th 1983. Indeed, many more of the non-escapees left in H7 that day, who had been viciously beaten by the guards and bitten by their dogs, also received compensation.

No guards were ever charged in connection with any of the assaults. Warder John Adams returned to work. Campbell Courtney also returned to work and was later head of security in a private firm which managed the H-Blocks after they were decommissioned. Gerry Kelly, as a Member of the Legislative Assembly (MLA) became a Junior Minister in the Office of the First and Deputy First Ministers in 2007. At that point one of his responsibilities was the whole Maze Long Kesh site which contain the H-Blocks. He had moved from tenant to landlord!

"It always seems impossible until it's done."

Kevin Barry Artt

Kevin Barry Artt from Belfast was the last of the escapees to be told of the plan, less than two hours before it took place. He was just beginning a life sentence following the Christopher Black 'paid perjurer' trial. (All those convicted on Black's evidence had their convictions and sentences quashed at a later appeal). He was also an ex-Internee.

After escaping, Artt travelled to the USA where he lived in San Fransisco, later moving to San Diego in 1986. He worked as a successful car salesman under the name of Kevin Keohane. He was arrested in June 1992 by the FBI on passport violation charges. The British failed to have him extradited and he lives in America to this day.

Paul Brennan

Paul Brennan from Ballymurphy in Belfast was an ex-internee. After escaping he travelled to the USA in 1984 and settled in Berkeley, California. He met Joanna and married her in 1989. Paul worked as a carpenter and lived under the names Richard Earl Martin and then Pól Morgan. He was arrested in January 1993 and charged with passport violation offences and obtaining a sporting weapon using false identification. While the British failed to have him extradited he was eventually deported to Ireland in 2009. He now lives in Donegal.

Jimmy Burns

Jimmy Burns was interned in early 1972 and released later that year. He was re-arrested in 1973 and escaped in December that year through the visitors complex of the Cages area of Long Kesh. He was shot and arrested in July 1976 and given a life sentence. He was part of the team of escapees dressed as guards who took over the Tally Lodge and Main Gate area during the 1983 escape. Unfortunately, he was caught in a taxi at an RUC checkpoint at 4.28pm, shortly after escaping through the front gate. He was released in 1993 after serving seventeen years of a life sentence. He lives and works in his native Belfast.

Seamus (Spanner) Campbell

Seamus Campbell from Coalisland in County Tyrone had been serving a 14 year sentence when he escaped. He had four years left to complete but saw it as his duty to escape. He went on the run and kept a low profile staying mostly in remote areas of rural Ireland at first. He continued as an active Republican and later moved about more freely with good cover from false identities. He is one of only three escapees never to have be found by the various authorities.

On the 4th of December 1983, Pádraig McKearney and himself arrived at a safe house near the border to spend the night. It was on the news that two IRA Volunteers had been shot dead in Coalisland. His brother Brian and his comrade Colm McGirr had been executed by the SAS. It was a very difficult time for his family but being on the run added to the trauma as the British would be staking out his brother's funeral in the hope of recapturing Seamus. However, he continued to avoid the State Forces and lives openly now in County Galway as a free man. He runs a successful business.

Jim Clarke

Jim Clarke is a native of Donegal but was arrested in Derry in 1978 and sentenced to 18 years. He was one of the team of escapees who walked to South Armagh. He was rearrested on December 3rd 1984 after a car chase in Pettigo, close to the Fermanagh border.

This was the day after a British Army ambush which had resulted in the deaths of Volunteers Antoine MacGiolla Bhrighde and fellow escapee Kieran Fleming, as well as an SAS soldier.

He was sentenced to 18 months for possession of a rifle found in the car. While in Portlaoise Prison he again tried to escape with eleven other men – this time unsuccessfully. He received another 3-year sentence for that. Jim Clarke, along with Dermy Finucane, finally won their battle against extradition in the Irish Supreme Court. He was set free on the 13th of March 1990 returning to a rapturous welcome in his native Donegal where he lives and works today.

Seamus Clarke

Seamus Clarke from North Belfast, escaped with the team who drove to Lurgan and spent two weeks under the floor boards of a house. He had been arrested in 1975 and was serving a life sentence when he broke out of the H-Blocks. He remained on the run until 1987 when he was arrested in Dublin and sentenced to 7 years imprisonment in Portlaoise Jail. After being released in March 1993 he settled in Dublin.

Joe Corey

Joe Corey hailed from County Derry. He and Paddy McIntyre managed to get as far as the town of Castlewellan in County Down. They were both arrested on the Tuesday after the escape, hiding in what they thought, was a safe house. Joe had been serving a life sentence and was finally released in 1992 after serving 14 years. He lives and works in County Derry.

Dennis Cummings

Dennis Cummings was a quiet County Tyrone man who was arrested in 1977 and given a life sentence plus 18 years. When asked by Bik McFarlane if he was interested in escaping he answered, *"would a cat like sweet milk?"* He was one of the three Volunteers who held the Tally Lodge, full of arrested guards, to buy time for the other escapees to get away. He was therefore one of the first to be recaptured and served 16 years of his sentence, being released in 1993. He lives and works in County Tyrone.

Jimmy Donnelly

Jimmy Donnelly from Ardoyne in Belfast was another escapee convicted on the discredited evidence of Christopher Black. He was serving a 15-year sentence but had only been in the Blocks a matter of weeks. He was in the car that crashed the front-gate of the Prison Camp. He was knocked unconscious momentarily, which left him as the last of the six to exit the car. So he was recaptured. The 'Black case' collapsed on appeal in 1986 and Donnelly got bail awaiting the upcoming escape trial. He jumped bail remaining at liberty until being arrested in Belfast in 1989. He was sentenced to 5 years on charges connected to the escape but was released in 1990 because of time already served on remand. He lives in Ardoyne in North Belfast.

Dermot Finucane

Dermy Finucane was arrested on the day that Hunger Striker Micky Devine died in August 1981. He was given an 18-year sentence. After escaping he was re-arrested in November 1987 in Grannard, County Longford, during an operation in which 50,000 houses were searched by the Irish Army and Garda.

These were raids in the aftermath of the IRA weapons ship Eksund being captured.

Finucane was held for the following two and a half years without bail in Portlaoise on extradition warrants. This was not relaxed even when his brother Pat, a high profile Belfast solicitor, was shot dead in his home by Loyalists. On the 13th of March 1990 the Supreme Court in Dublin refused to uphold his extradition and he was released. He lives in County Meath and works throughout Ireland and abroad.

Kieran (Hush Hush) Fleming

Kieran Fleming was 16 years old when he was arrested in Derry and sentenced to the Secretary of State's Pleasure (SOSP is equivalent to a life sentence). A quiet big fella who became fluent in Irish, he was to be part of the Tally Lodge team. But on the Thursday before the escapee in a clash at football, ironically with another escapee, Brendy Mead, his arm was fractured.

When the Doctor came to see him on Friday morning, for fear of being kept in Hospital over the weekend, Fleming told him his arm felt much better. The Doctor gripped him by the hand and twisted it. Fleming, white-faced with excruciating pain, grinned back at him in response. He got on the escape but was replaced in the Tally Lodge team. On the 2nd of December 1984 after a gun battle with the British Army in which his comrade Antoine MacGiolla Bhrighde and an SAS soldier were killed, the rest of the IRA Active Service Unit were forced to move back across the border on foot. Despite the fact that Kieran Fleming could not swim, he tried to cross the River Bannagh which was in flood at the time. His body was not recovered until December 21st. A few weeks before he died Kieran Fleming had been shot and wounded in a previous gun battle. After losing his weapon he swore it would not happen again and made his own lanyard so that his rifle would be attached to his arm no matter what might happen.

Mourners at his funeral in Derry were savagely attacked by the RUC using baton charges and plastic bullets.

Gerard (Rinty) Fryers

Gerard Fryers from Turflodge in Belfast was sentenced to 20 years in 1980 and was one of the group who arrived in Lurgan in the turbo charged car. He returned to the Struggle in the border area. After the Finucane / Clarke High Court judgement he gradually moved out of hiding and his secret life, into the open. He lives and works in County Monaghan. He is one of only three escapees never captured by the various authorities.

Billy Gorman

Billy Gorman from the New Lodge area of Belfast was sentenced to SOSP / Life in 1979. He had been wrongfully charged and convicted of a killing when he had been 14 years old. He got entangled in the barbed wire of the

British Ministry of Defence outer perimeter of the Camp and was recaptured on the day of the escape.

He served 14 years of a life sentence and was released in 1993. He appealed his case twice but it wasn't until the court of appeal hearing in 1999 that his conviction, and that of his fellow accused, were overturned. The judges accepted it was a miscarriage of justice. He still lives in his native Belfast.

Peter (Skeet) Hamilton

Peter Hamilton was small in height but big in stature with his comrades – especially those from his own district of Ardoyne. He was given a life sentence after his arrest in 1975. He had spent time in the cages of Long Kesh but ended up in the H-Blocks in 1982 after trying to escape with Gerry Kelly, Francis McIlvenna and Ned Maguire.

He was one of the four caught within an hour hiding in the nearby River Lagan under its banks. He was afraid of nothing and game for everything. He was also known for his wit. When another, young escapee said to him just before the breakout "I'm going to be sticking close to you Skeet," knowing that he had tried to escape on a number of occasions before, Hamilton laughed. "Don't follow me – I'm the worst escaper in the world!" he responded. After taking a savage beating when caught and thrown into the punishment block he called out to see who else was there. Jimmy Donnelly who was 22 years old and also from Ardoyne identified himself. Despite having been caught himself and being in pain from his injuries, Hamilton retorted *"How did you get caught ye stupid bastard! I'm gonna knock your bollix in as soon as I see you."*

He was finally released in April 1993 and returned to the Struggle immediately. A few months later he had to go on the run and moved to Dundalk in Co.Louth where he settled. In 2011 he was diagnosed with cancer and his health rapidly deteriorated though his humour and craic didn't. He died on the day that Gerry Adams was elected as TD for Louth in February 2011. Without telling anyone Peter Hamilton presented himself at the local polling station before opening time and was one of the first to vote for Gerry Adams. His last political act was indicative of his lifelong commitment to Irish Republicanism.

Paul Kane

Paul Kane had been arrested in Co. Down on the Monday after the escape along with Brendy Mead. He was released on bail in 1986 after the 'Black' convictions were quashed at the Appeal Court.

He jumped bail and went on the run but was arrested along with Finucane in Grannard, Co. Longford in November 1987. The extradition warrants served by the British were defective, so he was released. However, the Gardai pursued him closely and re-arrested him on a bogus charge the same day so he could be held until the new warrants were served.

He was extradited to the North of Ireland in April 1989 but released later that year after the period spent on remand was deducted. He settled again in the Ardoyne district where he grew up and still lives today.

Gerry Kelly

Gerry Kelly was born in Belfast in 1953. He was arrested in Dublin in August of 1971 and jailed for two years. He escaped from Mountjoy Jail in January 1972 and returned to Belfast where he went 'on the run'.

He was arrested again in March 1973 with nine others in London and was given two life sentences and 20 years imprisonment. After a prolonged hunger strike for Political Status he was transferred to the Cages of Long Kesh in April 1975.

Having tried to escape from Wormwood Scrubs in England, he tried again from Lagan Valley Hospital in 1977 while receiving medical treatment. In early 1982 he tried to escape from the Cages of Long Kesh with Francis Mc Ilvenna, Ned Maguire and Peter Hamilton. The British stripped them all of Political status and transferred them to the H-Blocks.

After the mass escape of September '83. Kelly returned to Republican activity in the Armagh border area but then in 1984, travelled to Continental Europe with his comrade Brendan (Bik) McFarlane. They were arrested in Amsterdam in January 1986.

The Dutch would only allow Kelly to be extradited on seven charges connected to the '83 escape (the British had levelled 75 charges against each individual escapee), with the proviso that his original London charges be quashed. The British agreed and when Kelly was returned to the Crumlin Road Jail it was as a remand prisoner.

In 1988 Kelly received a 5-year sentence and was released in June

1989 having served 17 months on remand. Upon release he joined Sinn Féin. In 1993 he was part of the secret talks with British Government Representatives and in 1994 he was chosen as part of the original Sinn Féin negotiating team in the talks which eventually led to the Good Friday Agreement in 1998. Part of that Agreement was the negotiated release of all remaining political prisoners from the H-Blocks. He was first elected in the Forum Elections of 1996 and then as a member of the new Legislative Assembly (MLA). He has been elected MLA for North Belfast every election since. He remained in the negotiating team through various talks which included the St. Andrews Agreement 2007 and the Hillsborough Agreement in 2010. Between 2007 and 2011 he was a Junior Minister in the Office of the First and Deputy First Minister. Since 2011 he has been Policing spokesperson for Sinn Féin and their lead on the Policing Board. He is married to Margaret and lives in Belfast.

Tony (Spazzer) Kelly

Tony Kelly was the youngest member of the escapees. He was sentenced to SOSP/Life in 1980. He had a determination and commitment which belied his slight build.

Tony Kelly didn't get to see his family for the first time after the escape until February 1984. He met them in a safe house in Sligo, only to be told by his mother that his brother John had died the week before. He was devastated by his death but also by not having been able to see him before he died or even attend his funeral. This was compounded later that year with the killing of his close friend and fellow Derryman Kieran Fleming whom he shared a safe-house with in Donegal, alongside Jim Clarke.

He found himself near to death in 1985 when on St. Patrick's Day the Gardai raided a house from which he fled half dressed. It was snowing and he hid in a ditch until nightfall while they searched for him. He moved across fields and after falling into freezing water he dug into a ditch again for shelter during the day. It snowed all day while the search continued and when night came it was only the thought of Kieran Fleming drowning that forced him to get up and move. He was literally frozen stiff. He found a phone box but it took him an hour to manage a call. When his friend found him he had frostbite and hypothermia. It took him a month to recover.

In July 1985 he was arrested in Killybegs in Donegal and charged with possession but got bail and went on the run again. He was re-arrested in Dublin on 26th November 1987 with fellow escapee Seamus Clarke. He got a 7-year sentence in Portlaoise. He was released on April 1st 1993 and settled in Donegal with his wife Marie who he had met while on the run.

Rab Kerr

Rab Kerr was originally from the New Lodge district of Belfast. He was serving a life sentence at the time of his escape. Leading the Tally Lodge team he, along with Cummings and O'Connor, held off the guards under the worst possible pressure. The minutes gained allowed for every other POW to breach the main gate.

He knew at that point that his capture was inevitable and would lead to a savage beating. He held his ground but was then overwhelmed. His last act was to flick on the safety catch of his short-arm and toss it away as he hit the ground.

Rab Kerr was released in 1995 and now lives on the outskirts of Belfast. He has written several books and a number of historical pamphlets.

Terry Kirby

Terry Kirby hailed from Andersonstown in West Belfast. He was serving a life sentence and was one of the team who trekked for days from the McFarlane home near Dromore, Co. Down to the farm in Camlough in Co. Armagh.

In jail he used to be slegged for being a hypochondriac because of his many ailments. But his comrades all report that he was one of the strongest and least complaining of the walkers. When Tony McAllister badly sprained his ankle, Kirby was the first to offer assistance to help him move on.

After he got away, Kirby made his way to the USA but did not surface for over a decade. However, he now lives and works as a freeman in San Francisco.

Brendy Mead

Brendy Mead from the St. James area of West Belfast was serving a life sentence. He held the pedestrian entrance gate in the main wall through which all the guards entered and exited on foot. He was arguably the fittest Republican in the Blocks and it held to him as he and Paul Kane made headway. They took to the fields immediately, after a short car journey.

He had ditched the guard's uniform he was wearing, as soon as they took to the fields. Unfortunately they were caught near Castlewellan, Co. Down the following day. They were brought to Newcastle Barracks and then the short distance to Ballykinlar British Army Camp from where they were transported to Castlereagh Interrogation Centre. He remembers women spitting on them in Castlereagh. They weren't wearing any sort of uniform and he thought at the time that they must have been girlfriends or escorts. After his release he returned to live in West Belfast.

Tony (Tank) McAllister

Tony McAllister from Ballymurphy carried out the first arrest of the Breakout along with Bobby Storey in the guard's canteen. He was jailed for life in 1979. He is the only one of all the 38 escapees who never reappeared in the public eye again, although it is known that he left the country sometime after the Mass Escape. It is believed that sadly Tony passed away through natural causes under an assumed name. He had carved out a new life with a loving wife and children.

Jim (Jaz) McCann

Jim McCann was serving a 25-year sentence to which 5 years were added following the escape. He was caught by the British soldier on the Bog Road close to the jail. On returning to jail he continued his education. A year before his release in 1994 he was awarded an Open University First Class BA (Hons) degree in Humanities.

Since his release he has put his educational qualifications to good use in the Belfast community where he was raised and served as a republican activist.

When being searched immediately after his capture, he inquired why they were searching him. "To see if you are carrying any weapons," was the reply. McCann is reputed to have retorted. "Sure, if I had been in possession of a gun I would have shot you –you fool," in a posh accent. He has always denied being middle-class!

Gerry (Blute) McDonnell

Gerry McDonnell from the St. James area of West Belfast was first charged in May 1972 and remanded to Armagh Gaol. He was released in July but interned in Long Kesh in September 1972 for over three years. He was later remanded in Walton Prison in Liverpool, after being released. He had been serving a 16-year prison sentence which he received in

1978. After a number of years as a 'blanketman' he had ended his 'no work' protest shortly before the escape, as had Jackie McMullan and John Pickering – both of whom were serving life sentences. They had been housed in A-Wing of H7. McMullan and Pickering were unexpectedly moved out of the Block by the Governor, but McDonnell was lucky enough to be shifted within H7 to another wing. He carved the wooden replica of a handgun which was so necessary to the escape.

He was recaptured in Glasgow in Scotland in June 1985. He was sentenced to life imprisonment for conspiracy to cause explosions. He is now free and lives in Belfast.

Seamus McElwaine

Seamus McElwaine came from a staunch Republican family who hailed from Knockatallon in County Monaghan, south of the border.

He was with the team who walked to South Armagh and all agree that his rural craft was crucial to them completing that journey safely.

He had been serving a life sentence when he escaped and returned to the struggle without hesitation along the border he knew so well. He had been a member of Na Fianna Éireann when he was 14 years old and had hidden his age to join the ranks of the IRA at just 16 years of age. By the time he was 19 he was the OC (Officer Commanding) of the IRA in County Fermanagh.

Seamus McElwaine and his comrade Seán Lynch were ambushed in the early hours of April 26th 1986. Both were injured by an initial burst of gunfire. The denim-clad British undercover soldiers searched for them in the dark and captured Seamus McElwaine but Seán Lynch managed to hide himself in a ditch.

For up to half an hour the soldiers interrogated the wounded McElwaine but he would not answer any of their questions. They then fired three shots, two of which struck Seamus in the head killing him.

Brendan (Bik) McFarlane

Brendan McFarlane was arrested with Seamus Clarke and Peter Hamilton in 1975. All three received life sentences. Originally they had political status in the Cages of Long Kesh but this was removed from McFarlane when he tried to escape along with Larry Marley and Pat McGeown in March 1978.

He was a close friend of Hunger Striker Bobby Sands and was appointed OC of the H-Blocks during the prolonged Hunger Strike of 1981. McFarlane was one of the eight who walked to South Armagh.

He was active along the Border before being asked to go to Continental Europe along with Gerry Kelly. While on the run there, he met his future wife in Paris. He was arrested in Hollland along with Gerry Kelly in January 1986 and was extradited in December of the same year. Unlike Kelly, the Dutch court did not quash his original life sentence. However, they would only allow him extradition on five of the original 75 charges connected to the escape that the British were demanding. He received another 5-year sentence.

When he was released he returned to live in the Ardoyne area where he was raised. He is a well-known musician and singer, as well as a Gaeilgeoir.

Seán (Chinkey) McGlinchey

Seán McGlinchey was another life sentence prisoner from a strong and well-known Republican family in County Derry.

He was part of the Tally Lodge team and was recaptured shortly after escaping. He was hiding in the nearby River Lagan.

After serving 16 years of his sentence, he was released in December 1990. He was instrumental in re-organising and strengthening Sinn Féin in his home area. He was later elected as a Sinn Féin Councillor – a position he holds to this day. He was also elected as the first Sinn Féin Mayor of Limavady Council.

Paddy McIntyre

Paddy McIntyre is a native of Co. Donegal and lifelong friend of Jim Clarke. He was recaptured along with Joe Corey in a dramatic stakeout of a house in Co. Down two days after escaping.

He was given pre-release parole in 1986 but did not return to the jail as the escape charges were still hanging over him.

He was re-arrested in Killybegs in Co. Donegal under the Offences Against the State Act in January 1987. When his case was heard on 7th May, Judge Gannon ordered his release as he had been held illegally. Despite the ruling, the Garda and Prison staff refused to release McIntyre forcing the judge to repeat that he had ordered his unconditional release. Paddy McIntyre sped away on a motor-bike.

Although charges laid against him in the extradition warrants collapsed in the escape trial of his co-accused in Belfast, he was forced to stay on the run. In May 1988 he spoke publicly but from a secret location: "I find myself in the position that even though I am a citizen of this State, and am not wanted for anything in this State, I have to go on the run."

He now lives and works freely in County Donegal.

Pádraig McKearney

When Pádraig McKearney got 14 years on possession charges after his arrest in 1980, it was his third jail term. From a strong Republican family hailing from Moy he was first imprisoned at the age of 17. He was one of the escapees who reached Lurgan.

Without hesitation, he returned to active service and was involved in a string of military attacks on the enemy in Counties Tyrone and Armagh.

On the 8th of May 1987, an Active Service Unit of the IRA set out to attack Loughgall Barracks. They were ambushed as they reached it in a van. The British SAS attacked the van from a number of vantage points. The eight Volunteers were shot and then executed leaving no survivors. A civilian was also shot dead by the British in the same incident. It was the biggest loss of Volunteers in a single engagement since the Tan War.

Pádraig was laid to rest on May 13th which was also the anniversary of his brother Seán who died on Active Service in 1974, along with his comrade Volunteer Eugene Martin.

Marty McManus

Marty McManus from Ballymurphy in Belfast was serving a 15-year sentence after being arrested in 1978. He got another 5 years added after the escape trial. He was caught with Marcus Murray on the A1 dual carriageway at Banbridge. During the escape he recalls stopping to have a short rest and cigarette. The delay made him miss the Hillman car but left him boarding the van in Dixon's farm. A minute was the difference between freedom and capture. He was released in September 1989 and lives in a rural setting in Co. Down.

Dermot (Oda) McNally

Dermot McNally was from Lurgan but was not in the team who reached Lurgan. Instead he bypassed his hometown and walked with seven others to Camlough in County Armagh. He had been serving a life sentence in the H-Blocks.

He returned to the Struggle and went on the run. He talks about the people who fed, sheltered and clothed the escapees. Like other escapees he describes these people as heroes. They were kept and cared for by Fianna Fáil supporters, Fine Gael and Labour supporters; even people who did not necessarily support the IRA helped escapees to stay free.

He did not go out during the day and walked the hills and fields by night. After a number of months, when he had solid but false identification papers, he and others were encouraged to get used to moving about more freely.

When the Clarke / Finucane judgement came he moved further out into the open. He was still cautious though. He actually got charged under a false name for salmon poaching. In the middle of the case a Garda rose to his feet and said "I challenge you that you are not the person you are claiming to be." McNally denied it but after that he moved to another place to live and signed on the 'dole' under his own name. He now lives and works freely in Sligo on the West Coast of Ireland.

Harry Murray

Harry Murray was brought up in a staunchly pro-British 'Loyalist' area of North Belfast and has the tattoos to prove it. However, he became an Irish Republican while living in the Irish Nationalist area of Andersonstown.

He was given a life sentence after his arrest and trial in 1979.

Courageous to a fault, Murray, who was part of the Tally Lodge team, turned back to assist his comrade Billy Gorman but to no avail. After a confrontation with an armed guard Murray shot the guard in the leg and was in turn shot by the British soldier from the watchtower.

He boasted the longest sentence from the escape trial in 1988. He lives and works now in Andersonstown – his adopted home.

Marcus Murray

Marcus Murray was a proud Fermanagh man. He was serving one of the shorter sentences of the escapees. But a 10 year sentence is big enough and Marcus Murray saw it as his duty to escape. He was recaptured at Banbridge in a Mercedes van with Marty McManus. They were brought to Newcastle Barracks and then spent seven days in Castlereagh Interrogation Centre. They were shifted back to the jail with five others and Marcus Murray saw another POW in front of him being beaten.

He made up his mind to get stuck in. He got a bad beating but felt better for fighting back. One of the prison doctors arrived and asked to see his injuries. Murray thought he was just messing and verbally insulted him. However, years later when his case for compensation came to court the doctor's marked body chart from that day won the case.

He was released in 1991 and now lives and works in Sligo.

Eddie O'Connor

Eddie O'Connor was one of the first three escapees to be arrested as he held the Tally Lodge with Kerr and Cummings for crucial minutes. Like them, he was serving a life sentence. Slightly built, he was beaten black and blue, losing consciousness on a number of occasions. He hailed from Keady in Co. Armagh and in common with all the escapees is still very proud to have been part of such an operation. He remembers a nun, who was a member of the 'Board of Visitors', coming in to see him some days after his capture. As soon as she saw him she said, "Take this man to hospital," which they duly did. When they gave him a tetanus injection, the needle broke and they had to use tweezers to remove it, but a visit to the hospital was still a welcome break.

Today he lives and works in Keady.

Gary Roberts

Gary Roberts from Belfast was serving SOSP/Life. He was caught late on the night of the escape by Scottish soldiers. He became fluent in Irish while in jail and pursued educational qualifications post the escape. He was released in 1989 after serving 14 years.

An ardent Gaeilgeoir, he was instrumental, alongside other ex-POWs in spreading the language to a much wider population. A new generation of native speakers and Irish medium schools has been created. Gary Roberts taught his beloved 'teanga' (language) rising to the position of school principal. He lives in Belfast.

Robert (Goose) Russell

Robert Russell was serving 20 years for something he didn't do. He was in H-Block 3 with Larry Marley and was part of the team gathering intelligence for the escape. He made it to Lurgan on the day and returned to the Struggle.

He was re-arrested in Dublin on 26th May 1984 and sent to Portlaoise Prison where he again tried to escape in 1985 but was not so lucky this time. He was extradited to the North in 1988 after serving a 3-year sentence for attempting to escape.

Russell had lodged a second appeal of his case before escaping in 1983 and won the case – the conviction was overturned. Ironically he had already served all but three weeks of his full sentence, including the 5-year sentence he received for the escape itself.

He was finally released in 1992 and lives in Ballymurphy, where he grew up.

Joe Simpson

Joe Simpson was one of the four escapees caught in the River Lagan. He was released in 1993 after serving 13 years of his sentence. He has been an active republican all his adult life and continues with his community activism to this day. He lives in Andersonstown.

Jim Smyth

Jim Smyth was serving a 20-year sentence when he successfully escaped. He later travelled to America and lived and worked in San Francisco under an assumed identity. He was arrested by the FBI on 3rd June 1992 – the same day as fellow escapee Kevin Barry Artt.

Jim Smyth was imprisoned and bailed on a number of occasions as he fought the extradition case. At one point his lawyers asked to be provided with unpublished British documents on the Stalker/Sampson inquiry. The judge agreed but the British refused to release them.

Smyth was eventually deported and he now lives and works in Cork City in the South of Ireland.

Bobby Storey

Bobby Storey became active within Republicanism in Belfast in 1972. He was interned on his 17th Birthday in April of 1973. After release in April 1975, he was remanded to prison a further six times between 1976 and 1981 on various charges connected to the conflict.

This included being arrested and charged in London in connection with attempting to hijack a helicopter for a jail-break. He was held in various jails including Crumlin Road, Brixton, Bristol and the H-Blocks of Long Kesh.

On August 20th 1981, the day that Hunger Striker Mickey Devine died, he was arrested in Belfast with two other comrades including Dermy Finucane and was sentenced to 18 years in jail. He received another 7 years consecutive to that for charges connected to the '83 escape. He was released in 1994 but was subsequently re-arrested and charged in November 1996. He was acquitted in June 1998.

Bobby Storey is currently the Chairperson of Sinn Féin in Belfast and is a long-term advocate of the Peace Process in Ireland today.

PRISONERS WHO ESCAPED

Name	Sentence(s)
Kevin Barry Artt (Belfast)	Life
Pól Brennan (Belfast)	16 Years
Jimmy J Burns (Belfast)	Life
Seamus (Spanner) Campbell (Co.Tyrone)	14 Years
Jim P Clarke (Co.Donegal)	18 Years
Seamus J (Cleaky) Clarke (Belfast)	Life
Joe H Corey (South Derry)	Life
Dennis Cummings (Co.Tyrone)	Life
Jimmy G Donnelly (Belfast)	15 Years
Dermy Finucane (Belfast)	18 Years
Kieran G (Hush Hush) Fleming (Derry)	British Secretary of State's Pleasure / Life
Gerard J (Rinty) Fryers (Belfast)	20 Years
Billy G Gorman (Belfast)	British Secretary of State's Pleasure / Life
Peter C (Skeet) Hamilton(Belfast)	Life
Paul A Kane (Belfast)	18 Years
Tony (Spazzer) Kelly (Derry)	British Secretary of State's Pleasure / Life
Gerry Kelly (Belfast)	Life
Rab Kerr (Belfast)	Life
Terry Kirby (Belfast)	Life
Tony (Tank) McAllister (Belfast)	Life
Jim P (Jaz) McCann (Belfast)	25 Years
Gerry P (Blute) McDonnell (Belfast)	16 Years
Seamus T McIlwaine (Co. Monaghan)	Life
Brendan J (Bik) McFarlane (Belfast)	Life
Seán (Chinkey) McGlinchey (South Derry)	Life

Paddy J McIntyre (Co. Donegal)	15 Years
Pádriag O McKearney (Co. Tyrone)	14 Years
Marty G McManus (Belfast)	15 Years
Dermot J (Oda) McNally (Co. Armagh)	Life
Brendy JP Mead (Belfast)	Life
Harry H Murray (Belfast)	Life
Marcus L Murray (Co. Fermangh)	20 Years
Eddie J O'Connor (Co. Armagh)	Life
Gary J Roberts (Belfast)	British Secretary of State's Pleasure / Life
Robert P (Goose) Russell (Belfast)	20 Years
Joe Simpson (Belfast)	20 Years
Jimmy J (Snout) Smyth (Belfast)	20 Years
Bobby Storey (Belfast)	18 Years

Volunteers who assisted in the success of the escape who have since died

Cormac McArt
24th September 1952 - 30th October 2008

Cormac McArt was born in the Short Strand area of Belfast on the 24th September 1952. His mother and father, however, came from Omagh in Co Tyrone. Cormac was a committed Republican Activist from his teenage years and was interned in Long Kesh at the age of eighteen. He returned to active service on his release, only to be arrested and sentenced to 13 years imprisonment. Whilst in prison he  joined the blanket protest and was committed to breaking the prison regime. After his release in 1987 he immediately reported back for active duty and remained a committed Activist. Cormac was a father of five children. He died at the age of 56 from cancer on 30th October 2008.

Larry Marley
24th July 1945 - 2nd April 1987

Larry Marley was an active Volunteer from the early 1970s onwards. He was first imprisoned in the Cages of Long Kesh in 1972, and in March 1975 he was one of ten Republicans who escaped from Newry Courthouse while appearing on charges related to another escape.

He was recaptured in Belfast in 1976 and charged with possession of weapons during his time on the run, and sentenced to another ten years in jail. He was released in 1985 after serving nine years. On Thursday night, 2nd April 1987, UVF gunmen sprayed shots through the front door of the Marley home in Ardoyne, fatally wounding Larry. Within hours of the tragic murder the Marley family began to experience what was to become a week of ghoulish intimidation by the RUC. Hundreds of RUC poured into the area, clearly intent on disrupting the funeral. The first attempt to bury Larry Marley took place on Monday morning. Scores of RUC Landrovers and a large force in full riot gear attacked the funeral, forcing the Marley family to abandon attempts to bury him.

Tuesday morning saw the RUC double its presence outside the Marley home. The funeral had to be postponed again. Shortly before 10.30am on Wednesday morning, the Marley family carried the Tricolour draped coffin from their Ardoyne home. Despite continued attacks by the RUC and after several hours of determined resistance by thousands of mourners, Larry Marley was finally laid to rest.

Finbarr McKenna

30th October 1953 - 2nd May 1987

Finbarr McKenna joined the Republican Movement in the midst of violent loyalist pogroms in the Kashmir Road in 1969. Following the introduction of internment in 1971, Finbarr faced continuous Crown Force harrassment. He was arrested on his 18th birthday and was interrogated in Palace Barracks where he was brutally tortured. On his release, he returned to active service. In 1974 he was arrested and detained on fabricated charges. During this period members of the RUC Special Branch took him to an isolated area, held a gun to his head and threatened to shoot him. At one stage an 'X' was scraped into his forehead, a warning that he was marked for assassination. It only made 'Finn' more determined and committed. In the years that followed, he was arrested and tortured many times and was imprisoned in Long Kesh between 1976 and 1986. He was only out of Long Kesh ten months when he was killed on active service on the 2nd of May 1987. He remained to the end unassuming but confident and unafraid. He was an inspiration to his comrades whom he always looked out for.

Brendan Burns
9th February 1958 - 29th February 1988

Brendan Burns was born and bred in South Armagh. He joined the IRA at 16 years of age and from the outset was impatient to become fully active. He enjoyed the craic and radiated a confidence and determination which belied his youth. By 1984 Brendan was on the run from the North. He was arrested by Gardai Special Branch on foot of an extradition warrant and spent two years in Portlaoise Prison. From then on Brendan was on the run North and South of the border but this did not deter him and on many occasions he had narrow escapes as the British Army hunted him. He was involved in military operations and his coolness under pressure typified the kind of man he was and this among other outstanding personal qualities, led him to be held in the highest esteem among the people of South Armagh. He was very well respected and liked by the local community and this was shown by the massive number of people who attended Brendan's funeral, despite the huge numbers of the British Army trying to intimidate mourners.

Brendan Moley
25th January 1958 - 29th February 1988

For many generations the Moley family have lived in the Dorsey area, near Cullyhanna in South Armagh with the first recorded families dating back to the 1600s. At the time of the present phase of the struggle, Brendan's parents, Michael and Mary were living there on a small farm with their nine children. Brendan, the fourth child and eldest son, was born on the 25th  January 1958. With a keen interest in Irish history and politics, from an early age he questioned the British presence and interference in Ireland and at the age of 16 he joined Na Fianna Éireann before quickly progressing into the ranks of Óglaigh na hÉireann, where he became a full-time active service Volunteer. He was arrested many times by the Crown Forces but was never deterred from his chosen course.

Brendan was a trusted and respected member of his community whose advice was sought by many. He was involved in some of the most dangerous and daring attacks carried out by the IRA in South Armagh and, typical of his character, he would never ask Volunteers to do anything that he wasn't prepared to do himself.

Brendan was killed on active service on 29th February 1988 and his death was a great loss to his family, friends and comrades in South Armagh.

Kevin McCracken
22nd June 1956 - 14th March 1988

Kevin McCracken grew up in Turf Lodge in Belfast, the eldest of five children. Kevin was so deeply affected by the suffering of the people, that he joined Fianna Éireann in 1972 when he was 15 years old. Three years later he had joined Óglaigh na hÉireann, and was soon at the forefront of IRA attacks in West Belfast for the following two years. Arrested in April 1977, he was sentenced to 13 years for IRA membership and possession of incendiaries.

During his time in Long Kesh he took part in the 'blanket and no-wash' protest for political status. On his release in November 1985, Kevin immediately reported back to Óglaigh na hÉireann and was actively involved in broadening the republican base in Turf Lodge.

Kevin was shot dead by a British soldier on Monday night, 14th March 1988. He was preparing to launch an attack on the Crown Forces that had saturated the area in an attempt to intimidate the family of Volunteer Seán Savage who lived nearby.

Seán Bateson
28th March 1956 - 7th June 1990

Seán Bateson came from a tight-knit community in the Bone area of North Belfast. Traumatised like most of his generation by the renewed onset from loyalist death squads in 1968/69, Sean quickly came to see that his people's only chance was to organise for resistance. He became an active member in Na Fianna Éireann and shortly after his 16th birthday he joined the IRA.

Later that year British soldiers arrived at the Bateson home in the early hours. Both Seán and his father John were taken to Long Kesh Internment Camp. Sean spent two years in Long Kesh and after his release in 1974, he resumed his involvement in the Army. During this period he survived an assassination attempt.

Seán Bateson was arrested in 1977 and taken to Castlereagh Interrogation Centre. He arrived there on May 3rd and was subjected to gruelling and brutal interrogation techniques. Seán became another victim –of the many –processed on the infamous conveyor belt of Castlereagh/Diplock/H-Block. He was sentenced to life imprisonment and given a recommendation that he serve a minimum of 30 years.

On Thursday 7th June 1990, Volunteer Seán Bateson died from a heart attack in Long Kesh, aged just 34. He had served 15 and half years and had spent all his adult life serving the cause of Irish freedom.

Pat McGeown
3rd September 1956 - 1st October 1996

Pat – or Pat Beag, as his friends and comrades knew him grew up around Beechmount and Cavendish Street. Like most youths in his area he experienced intense harrassment and was first arrested at 14 years of age. In 1973, whilst travelling to a training camp, he was arrested and interned. Released after eighteen months he married his girlfriend Pauline and began a family.

Arrested once again in 1975, he was physically assaulted for several days before being charged with, and later sentenced to, 15-years. He was transferred to the H-Blocks after attempting to escape from the Long Kesh cages and he immediately joined the 'blanket protest'. In 1981 Pat replaced Joe McDonnell on Hunger Strike after his death. On the 46th day of his Hunger Strike he lapsed into a coma but was revived after being taken to Musgrave Park Hospital. On recovering he was returned to the H-Blocks. He was adjutant in the H-Blocks at the time of the 1983 escape. He was released in 1985 and returned to The Struggle. Pat by now was suffering from heart disease as a result of his Hunger Strike but he threw himself into the political struggle helping to develop Sinn Féin's Peace Strategy. He became Chair of Belfast Sinn Féin and was then elected as Councillor for the Mid-Falls area of Belfast. Pat was a soldier, a revolutionary and a thinker but died at the early age of 40 on the 1st October 1996.

Chronology of Escapes

1590	December	-	1 escape from Dublin Castle
1592	29th December	-	3 escape from Dublin Castle
1798	3rd January	-	1 killed following attempt to escape from prison Hulk in Belfast Lough
1798	2nd July	-	1 escape from Belfast Jail House
1801	29th December	-	14 killed during the Hercules mutiny
1803	December	-	2 escape from Kilmainham Jail Dublin
1854	2nd August	-	2 escape from Tasmania
1861	25th August	-	1 escape from Van Dieman's Land
1865	24th November	-	1 escape from Richmond Jail Dublin
1867	19th September	-	2 escaped in Manchester, England
1867	13th December	-	Attempted escape from Clerkenwell London, 15 killed in explosion
1869	17th February	-	1 escape from Freemantle, Western Australia
1876	17th April	-	6 prisoners escape from Freemantle, Western Australia
1918	11th November	-	1 escape from Cork Jail
1919	22nd January	-	4 escape from Usk Gaol, Wales
1919	3rd February	-	3 escape from Lincoln Jail, England
1919	16th March	-	1 escape from Mountjoy Jail, Dublin
1919	29th March	-	12 escape from Mountjoy Jail, Dublin
1919	6th April	-	1 killed while escaping from Limerick Union Hospital

317

1919	25th October	-	6 escape from Strangeways Jail, England
1920	June	-	1 escape from Sligo Jail
1920	30th October	-	4 women escape from Mountjoy Jail
1921	14th February	-	3 escape from Kilmainham Jail, Dublin
1921	15th February	-	1 escape from Derry Jail
1921	29th April	-	3 escape from Spike Island, Cork
1921	9th September	-	50 internees escape from Curragh Camp
1921	10th November	-	7 escape from Spike Island, Cork
1921	22nd November	-	43 escape from Kilkenny Prison
1921	November	-	7 escape from Mountjoy Jail, Dublin
1922	April	-	1 escape from Gormonstown Camp (T Barry)
1922	27th July	-	106 prisoners escape from Dundalk Prison
1922	11th October	-	23 escape from Courthouse in Kanturk
1922	18th October	-	141 escape from Newbridge Internment Camp, Curragh
1922	18th October	-	10 escape from Sligo Jail
1923	October	-	2 escape on route to Kilmainham Jail
1924	16th March	-	1 escape from the Curragh Camp (P O'Donnell)
1925	25th November	-	19 escape from Mountjoy Jail, Dublin
1926	26th February	-	1 escape from Dundrum Lunatic Asylum (T McKeough)

1927	9th May	-	4 escape from Belfast Jail
1941	5th June	-	5 escape from Belfast Jail
1942		-	Eddie Gill escapes from Peterhead
1943	15th January	-	4 escape from Belfast Jail
1943	20th March	-	21 escape from Derry Jail
1958	13th April	-	Attempt to escape from Mountjoy Jail
1958	24th September	-	2 escape from Curragh Internment Camp
1958	3rd December	-	16 escape from Curragh Internment Camp
1959	12th February	-	1 escape from Wakefield Prison Yorkshire (P Murphy)
1960	26th December	-	1 escape from Belfast Jail (Dee Donnelly)
1966	21st February	-	1 escape from Limerick Jail (R Behal)
1971	June	-	1 escape from Belfast Jail (J McCann)
1971	16th July	-	1 escape from RVH, Belfast (G Fitzgerald)
1971	9th November	-	9 escape from Belfast Jail
1971	2nd December	-	3 escape from Belfast Jail
1972	7th January	-	1 escape from Palace Barracks (F Dunlop)
1972	22nd January	-	1 escape from Mountjoy Jail (Gerry Kelly)
1972	7th February	-	1 escape from Long Kesh Dressed as a priest (F McGuigan)
1972	17th February	-	7 escape from Prison Ship, Maidstone, Belfast Lough

1972	18th April	-	2 escape from Musgrave Park Hospital Belfast (Frank Quigley and Jim Mulvenna)
1972	7th June	-	1 escape from Mater Hospital (Bobby Campbell)
1972		-	1 escape from the Lagan Valley Hospital (Jim Brown)
1972	29th October	-	7 escape from Curragh
1973	13th January	-	1 escape from Belfast Jail (D Keenan)
1973	22nd February	-	1 escape from Belfast Court House (Jim Bryson)
1973	11th March	-	1 escape from Long Kesh (Billy Kelly)
1973	7th April	-	2 escape from Long Kesh Compounds (re-captured 3 hours later)
1973	16th August	-	1 escape from Altnagelvin Hospital Derry (Eamon Campbell)
1973	4th September	-	1 escape from RVH, Belfast (Billy McAllister)
1973	9th September	-	1 escape from Long Kesh Compounds Dressed as priest (John F Green)
1973	31st October	-	3 escape from Mountjoy Jail, Dublin
1973	8th December	-	1 escape from Long Kesh Compounds (Brendan Hughes)
1973	12th December	-	1 escape from Belfast Jail (G Dowdall)
1973	13th December	-	1 escape from Long Kesh Compounds (J Burns)

The Escape

1974	11th March	-	1 escape from Mountjoy Jail (K Littlejohn)
1974	15th April	-	1 escape from Long Kesh Compounds (Ivor Bell)
1974	8th July	-	1 escape from Long Kesh Compounds (recaptured within 3 hours)
1974	11th August	-	1 escape from RVH, Belfast (Joe McKee)
1974	18th August	-	19 escape from Portlaoise Prison
1974	5th November	-	3 escape from Long Kesh. 1 killed.
1975	March	-	1 escape from Magilligan Camp (D Keenan)
1975	March	-	12 escape from Newry Court House
1975	17th March	-	1 killed during escape attempt at Portlaoise
1975	7th May	-	2 escape from Magilligan Camp (P O'Hagan and P McCann)
1975	19th May	-	5 escape from Belfast Magistrates Court
1975	20th July	-	1 escape from Long Kesh dressed as Priest (P Campbell)
1975	14th August	-	2 escape from Curragh Military Hospital
1976		-	1 escape from Magilligan Camp (M Monaghan)
1976	5th May	-	8 escape from Long Kesh Compound
1977	15th July	-	4 escape from Green Street Special Court (3 captured immediately - M O'Rourke gets away)
1980	16th December	-	1 escape from Brixton Prison (G Tuite)

1981	10th June	-	8 escape from Belfast Jail
1983	25th September	-	38 escape from H-Blocks of Long Kesh Prison Camp
1991	7th July	-	2 escape from Brixton Prison, England (P McAuley and N Quinlivan)
1995	1st November	-	1 escape from Belfast City Hospital (Caught on Lisburn Road) (Michael Bennett)
1997	10th December	-	1 escape from H-Blocks of Long Kesh dressed as a woman (Liam Averill)